BRIAN DE PALMA

INTERVIEWS

CONVERSATIONS WITH FILMMAKERS SERIES

PETER BRUNETTE, GENERAL EDITOR

Photo credit: Photofest

BRIAN
DE PALMA
INTERVIEWS

EDITED BY LAURENCE F. KNAPP

UNIVERSITY PRESS OF MISSISSIPPI / JACKSON

www.upress.state.ms.us

11   10   09   08   07   06   05   04   03   4   3   2   1
∞

Library of Congress Cataloging-in-Publication Data

De Palma, Brian.
    Brian De Palma : interviews / edited by Laurence F. Knapp.
        p.   cm. — (Conversations with filmmakers series)
    Filmography: p.
    Includes index.
    ISBN 1-57806-515-1 (cloth : alk. paper) — ISBN 1-57806-516-X (pbk. : alk. paper)
    1. De Palma, Brian—Interviews.   2. Motion picture producers and
    directors—United States—Interviews.   I. Knapp, Laurence F., 1965–
    II. Title.   III. Series.

PN1998.3.D4 A5 2003
791.43'0233'092—dc21   2002071396

British Library Cataloging-in-Publication Data available

CONTENTS

INTRODUCTION

BRIAN DE PALMA HAS ALWAYS been the odd man out, but that's a role he's been cultivating since the late 1960s. For De Palma, directing is taking control, but that control has eluded him since 1970, when Warner Bros. removed him from his first Hollywood feature, *Get to Know Your Rabbit*. De Palma wanted to be the next Jean-Luc Godard and revolutionize American cinema. Instead, he found himself ostracized and overwhelmed by the cultural and political fallout of the 1960s. He sought the refuge of Alfred Hitchcock and the low-budget horror film until the late 1970s, when his surreal approach to horror became a genre unto itself. Ironically, just as De Palma achieved the success that his fellow Movie Brats George Lucas, Martin Scorsese, and Steven Spielberg had enjoyed since the mid 1970s, he couldn't hide his resentment toward Hollywood. In his 1980 piece for *Esquire*, "A Day in the Life," De Palma made his bitterness a matter of public record: "The lesson to learn is that as successful and powerful as I am, I can still be outmaneuvered. In an industry filled with half-truths and inflated praise and all kinds of false signals, you have to have a very clear idea of how you are actually regarded. If you get sucked in, you can get wiped out. I've seen a lot of people leveled because they misread signals: they thought they were being offered a three-picture deal when they were actually being put out to pasture."[1]

De Palma describes directing to Peter Keough as a "schizophrenic profession" that requires a split personality to balance the extremes: "Directing is standing behind the camera and watching what other people do. You are a person with an active, provocative role and then you're a person that has to have a very quiet sensory presence. . . . You have to make things happen and then you have to sit back and see what you have created and in order to make it effective you've got to be detached." That schizophrenia informs De Palma's vision of himself, his style, and the many characters in his films whose identity and sanity are frequently in question. In 1973 De Palma cautions Richard Rubinstein that "megalomania is a very real problem for the successful director," but ten years later he proclaims to Lynn Hirschberg that "I want to be *infamous*. I want to be *controversial*. It's much more colorful." This contradiction is a product of De Palma's antipathy toward commercial filmmaking and a public that has no patience for searing reality or narrative experimentation. What else could explain the lurid images of *Dressed to Kill* or the ultraviolence of *Scarface* or *Body Double*? De Palma found himself bludgeoning his audience and critics, daring them to watch a chainsaw enter a man's skull.

Many auteurs benefit from a biographical legend that frames their many interviews—i.e., Fritz Lang's escape from Nazi Germany, Clint Eastwood's rustic upbringing, or Oliver Stone's tour of duty in Vietnam. The salient details from De Palma's past that his interviewers recycle—De Palma's tolerance for blood gleaned from watching his father, an orthopedic surgeon, at work; De Palma's early interest in psychics, electronics, and computer science; De Palma's nascent use of a movie camera and other surveillance equipment to record his father in the act of adultery; and De Palma's being shot and arrested by the NYPD in 1963—contribute to De Palma's image as a cold, cynical voyeur and sadist. These biographical details are merely anecdotal in the 1970s, but with the release of *Dressed to Kill* in 1980, De Palma is only happy to capitalize on them to promote himself as the "master of the macabre."

De Palma has described himself as a visual stylist since 1969, but his provocative use of sex and violence complicates his longstanding belief that the exploding body in *The Fury* or the murder of Angie Dickinson in *Dressed to Kill* amounts to no more than hyperkinetic visuals. De Palma reveals to Paul Mandell that "things that shock other people don't shock me." Resolutely anti-censorship, De Palma emphatically repeats the refrain that there is no correlation between real violence and movie violence. De Palma defends his exaggerated display of violence to Lynn Hirschberg as the only way to manipulate an audience: "Slashing someone with a razor is a very visceral image. What are you going to do? Hit them over the head with a sponge?"

He explains to Leslie Bennetts that he never stages empty moments of grisly spectacle to distract or disarm his audience. Everything is carefully set up and motivated to reach an emotional crescendo: "You have to scare people; it's part of the genre, but it's not the most important part. It's the anticipation, the waiting for something that's going to happen. The dread, that's where the artistry is involved."[2]

What De Palma didn't realize was that his technical skills—his flawless use of film stocks, split screens, slow motion, Steadicam tracking shots, and, later, in the mid to late 1990s, digital special effects—were too effective to be dismissed as mere technique. In 1978 De Palma was all too aware of how potent his style had become: "I really like seeing an audience respond in a visceral way. It gives you a real sense of satisfaction to know you're emotionally caught up with your audience. The thing is when you're effective at what you're doing, you are always accused of manipulating your audience" (Mandell interview). With *Dressed to Kill*, *Blow Out*, and *Scarface*, De Palma wasn't content to just entertain his audience. He wanted to force them to confront situations and impulses that tested the ideological boundaries of good taste. By 1984 De Palma, inflamed by his treatment by the critics and the MPAA ratings board, lashed out with *Body Double*. It was meant to be a wicked exercise in pornographic excess, but De Palma's notoriously over-the-top "crotch shot" of the power drill disemboweling Deborah Shelton was the last straw for feminists, who did not share De Palma's assertion that movie violence had no effect on the male psyche.

De Palma's unapologetic attitude toward the representation of women in his films reaches a queasy crescendo with his tense standoff with Marcia Pally in " 'Double' Trouble." De Palma claims to be fond of women but teases Pally with the roguish comment, "I don't particularly want to chop up women, but it seems to work." He remains unrepentant about his use of women in peril until 1987 when he finally admits to Bennetts that the changing status of women prevents him from revisiting the old cliché of the damsel in distress: "Women in peril are inherently more dramatic than men in peril, because they're more vulnerable. It's just a convention of the genre. But now if you put a woman in peril, you're into a political issue of violence against women, when you're just thinking about making an effective horror movie. I think it's unfair. If a man gets killed, does that make it any better or more morally redeemable?"[3] De Palma tried to revisit the thorny issue of violence against women in a moral context in *Casualties of War* but by then the charges of misogyny and sadism had stuck. From the mid 1980s onward, De Palma had to endure a standard interview template. Paula Span's "Brian De Palma, Through the Lens" is a prime example of this pattern. Span is threatened initially by De Palma's dark, brooding persona. She becomes nervous when De Palma insists on videotaping her before she is able to begin the interview. Objectified by what appears to be De Palma's sinister camera-eye, Span remains apprehensive, but eventually, much to her surprise and relief, she learns that De Palma is a gentle, soft-spoken man who has little control over his public image.

As Bruce Weber recounts in "Cool Heads, Hot Images," De Palma had to contend with a much bigger problem than his biographical legend—staying employed in a radically changing industry. Although De Palma proved that he could deliver a marketable high-concept film with *The Untouchables*, he had a difficult time adjusting to the destabilizing practices of studio previews and last-minute, studio-imposed happy endings. Weber takes us to a test screening of *Casualties of War*, in which De Palma remains resistant to anyone's opinion but his own. De Palma persevered, but *Casualties of War*, his most personal film since *Blow Out*, did not resonate with the American public. Eager for another hit, De Palma tried to play by Hollywood's rules with *The Bonfire of the Vanities*, allowing Warner Bros. to interfere with casting and the overall tone of the picture. Budgeted at nearly $50 million, *Bonfire* brought in a paltry $15.4 million. It nearly crippled De Palma's status as an A director. Two post-*Bonfire* interviews included here, "Out of the Ashes" and "De Palma Comes Back, Sort of," feature a shell-shocked, chastened De Palma who offers no excuses, blaming his own bad judgment for the film's failure: "With *Bonfire* we tried to please too many people and pleased none of them."

After testing the patience of audiences and critics with the audacious and self-assured *Raising Cain*, De Palma reluctantly decided that the viewing public could no longer tolerate bizarre subject matter or the narrative innovations brought to America's shores by the European art film. He shunned the press junkets for *Carlito's Way* and *Mission: Impossible*, resurfacing briefly to promote *Snake Eyes*. The once high and mighty master of the macabre may have retreated from public scrutiny, but he hasn't lost his need for control. Even in 1998 De Palma can't resist declaring to Wade Major that "The thing you can determine from me and my career is that I never gave a damn what anybody thought."

Throughout his interviews, De Palma is refreshingly candid about his allusions to other films and directors. Unlike many auteurs who hide their references or refer to them cryptically as homages, De Palma openly dissects the works of others as a source of inspiration for his own films. He tells David Bartholomew, "You can reinterpret good material in different ways, into your own framework. If you have a style of your own and individuality, you'll take good things from other people and make them better. Great artists have done it, and it sure doesn't scare me." De Palma quotes openly, and unapologetically, from other films: Jean-Luc Godard's *Masculin/Féminin* for *Greetings*, Robert Weine's *The Cabinet of Dr. Caligari* for *Phantom of the Paradise*, Michelangelo Antonioni's *Blow-Up* for *Blow Out* and *Femme Fatale*, Sergei Eisenstein's *The Battleship Potemkin* for *The Untouchables*, David Lean's *The Bridge on the River Kwai* for *Casualties of War*, Michael Powell's *Peeping Tom* for *Raising Cain*, and Stanley Kubrick's *2001: A Space Odyssey* for *Mission to Mars*.

Of course, De Palma is best known for borrowing liberally from Hitchcock, the "master of suspense." *Rear Window* is reworked in *Hi, Mom!*, *Sisters*, and *Body Double*; *Vertigo* in *Obsession* and *Body Double*; and *Psycho* in *Sisters*, *Dressed to Kill*, and *Raising Cain*. For De Palma, Hitchcock reigns as the consummate master of film grammar. Hitchcock's deft use of point-of-view, character psychology, omniscient camerawork, and structural narratives constitute a form of "suspense school" and "pure cinema" instrumental to anyone interested in precise storytelling. His films are also textbook examples of how to orchestrate and manipulate an audience. "Film is one of the only art forms where you can give the audience the same visual information the character has," he explains to Marcia Pally. "I learned it from Hitchcock. It's unique to cinema and it connects the audience directly to the experience—unlike the fourth wall approach, which belongs to the Xerox school of filmmaking." De Palma made *Sisters* in a Hitchcockian mode to work on his own shortcomings as a storyteller. With each successive "Hitchcock" film, De Palma has grown more confident and inserted more of his own preoccupations with gender, sexuality, and technology. He is eager to remind Jean Vallely in 1980 that his cinema is very different from Hitchcock's: "I am dealing in surrealistic, erotic imagery. Hitchcock never got into that too much." For those critics who dismiss De Palma as a postmodern, poor-man's Hitchcock, it should be noted that major directors such as François Truffaut (*The Bride Wore Black*), Roman Polanski (*Repulsion*, *Frantic*), Jonathon Demme

(*The Last Embrace, Silence of the Lambs*), Kathryn Bigelow (*Blue Steel*), Martin Scorsese (*Cape Fear*), Robert Zemeckis (*What Lies Beneath*), and David Fincher (*The Panic Room*) have quoted liberally from Hitchcock. De Palma's crime is that his Hitchcock films are variations on Hitchcock, not homages. De Palma may be a loyal student of Hitchcock, but he isn't afraid to interrogate Hitchcock and the perverse impulses that motivate his films. De Palma foregrounds that perversity, dazzling us with suspenseful set pieces, but tormenting us with gruesome, disquieting moments of psychosis and pathology.

What separates De Palma from Hitchcock is his rich background as an avant-garde, independent filmmaker and his early fascination with Godard. Hitchcock taught De Palma the value of story structure and narrative economy (not to mention the themes of voyeurism, paranoia, and Catholic guilt). Godard inspired De Palma's mantra "form equals content." De Palma's 1969 statement, "I'm a very strong believer in the fact that the camera always has to reflect the content. I'm very conscious of the attitude of the camera toward the material, always," still stands today.[4] As a visual stylist, De Palma relies on storyboards more than screenplays: "The content of my films is a secondary issue," he explains to Pally. "I don't start with an idea about content. I start with a VISUAL IMAGE." For De Palma the cardinal sin of cinema is coverage, shooting a dialogue scene straight, without any visual appreciation for the architecture of the scene. "I could take a script out and photograph it and I can be called a director," he tells Peter Keogh; "the story's all there, they walk in the door, they sit down, then they get in the car and there's a car chase. But to me, that's not directing, it's being asleep at the switch." By the late 1980s, as De Palma sought mainstream acceptance, he expressed greater interest in character development and content. In an interview with Bruce Weber, he concedes, "There are 8,000 quotes of me saying 'Form is content.' Well it's true. Form is content. But other stuff is content, too."

De Palma's style hasn't been easy for him to define, not because it has radically changed over the last thirty-five years, but because it is as schizophrenic as De Palma's view of his profession. He goes to great lengths to define himself as a surrealist who enjoys the camera's ability to lie. To "interpret reality in the most bizarre ways imaginable" (Appelbaum interview), his films are intentionally hyperbolic: "Movies have to be twenty-seven times bigger than real life, simply to communicate what the reality of the situation really is."⁵ Yet, while De Palma enjoys using style to captivate an audience, he also wants them to be aware of how space and time are manipulated in his films. He tells Richard Rubinstein that "First of all, I am interested in the medium of film itself, and I am constantly standing outside and making people aware that they are always watching a film. At the same time I'm evolving it. In *Hi Mom!*, for instance, there is a sequence where you are obviously watching a ridiculous documentary and you are told that you are aware of it, but it still sucks you in. There is a kind of Brechtian alienation idea here: you are aware of what you are watching at the same time that you are emotionally involved in it." De Palma wants to control his audience, but he also wants them to be conscious of the devices he is using to assert that control. This "split cinema"—part identification, part distanciation—is a product of De Palma's modernist sensibility and his efforts to synthesize commercial projects with his avant-garde work in the 1960s (*Murder à la Mod, Greetings, Dionysus in 69, Hi, Mom!*). De Palma feels that all forms of media are inherently coercive ("The media can make what is seemingly real false and what is seemingly false real" [Rubinstein interview]), so his schizophrenic style is designed to make you aware of how cinema can conceal and confound perception and the truth. This can be off-putting to those who believe that film style should be realistic and transparent.

Because De Palma asks an audience to identify with, then detach themselves from, his plots and protagonists, his attempts to make an audience aware of itself haven't always been successful. He faces the dilemma of appealing to a mass audience with a style that is guaranteed to alienate them. In every interview, De Palma insists that he has no illusions about Hollywood, but he frequently laments how difficult it is to test the boundaries of our viewing habits. Part storyteller, part agitator, De Palma vacillates between restraint and excess. "It's good to have people come and see your movies," he tells David Bartholomew; "that means you're tricking something in them. It doesn't mean you have to pander to them. At the same time, you have to make films that mean a lot to you, and hopefully they'll mean a lot to others." While De Palma enjoys determining how an audience responds to a scene, he shows even greater enthusiasm for a cinema of cruelty that offers little reassurance or closure: "Any movie that makes you a little uncomfortable is good news to me, because it means you're expressing things that you are not familiar with. But when you make a film that plays with form it throws a lot of people off" (Keough interview).

De Palma's solution has been to work within the boundaries of genre fil-mmaking. After creating his own genre with *Dressed to Kill* and *Body Double* (a genre that would take on a life of its own with such high-profile releases as Adrian Lyne's *Fatal Attraction* and Paul Verhoeven's *Basic Instinct*), De Palma relied on the gangster film (*Scarface, Wise Guys, The Untouchables, Carlito's Way*), the espionage/Bond film (*Mission: Impossible*), and the science fiction film (*Mission to Mars*) to stay fresh and marketable. De Palma sees it as an opportunity to visualize someone else's material and to escape his own demons. "You get tired of your own obsessions, the betrayals, the voyeurism, the twisted sexuality," he tells Wade Major. Still, De Palma in his interviews seems happiest when he's making a film that he's producing, directing, and writing (*Home Movies, Body Double, Raising Cain, Snake Eyes*).

A prominent part of any interview is De Palma's fatalistic worldview. In the interview with Bartholomew he admits to having a black sense of humor: "My view of the world is ironic, bitter, acid but basically funny, too. I'm a real gallows humorist. I see something funny in the most grim circum-stances." In his most personal, revealing works, usually the ones rejected by the public, De Palma holds fast to the comment, "Don't expect good faith; there's no such thing."[6] The standard De Palma protagonist is tragically flawed and hopelessly disempowered. The establishment crushes the individ-ual, leaving him or her in a near catatonic state of guilt and impotence. Much of De Palma's cynicism comes from the political and social failures of the 1960s: the assassinations, the conspiracies, and the ever-encroaching media, with its unyielding message of conformity and materialism. "When I made *Greetings*," he tells Jean Vallely, "I found myself on talk shows, talking about the revolution, and I realized I had become just another piece of soft-ware that they could sell, like aspirin or deodorant. It didn't make any differ-ence what I said. I was talking about the downfall of America. Who cares? In my experience what happened to the revolution is that it got turned into a product, and that is the process of everything in America. Everything is meshed into a product." Or, as Al Pacino succinctly puts it in *Scarface*: "Do you know what capitalism is? Get fucked." In De Palma's world, the poor soul who dares to speak out is either "executed or crucified or shot." For years, De Palma's worldview was tempered by his sense of humor, but by *Casualties of War* and *Carlito's Way*, De Palma committed himself to a cinema of tragedy and regret. *Mission to Mars*, a brazenly optimistic film, upset a number of critics who could not accept De Palma as an idealist. His dark

worldview, thirty-odd years in the making, proved to be too vivid and dura-
ble to ignore. Once again, De Palma was a victim of his own success *and*
excess.

Another recurring motif in these interviews is De Palma's feelings toward
his old friends and colleagues Lucas, Scorsese, and Spielberg. De Palma isn't
too proud to express both admiration and jealousy. The success of *Jaws* and
Star Wars impelled De Palma to accept *Carrie* and *The Fury*. He credits Scorsese's use of the Steadicam in *Raging Bull* for inspiring the Metropolitan
Museum of Art sequence in *Dressed to Kill*. Lynn Hirschberg's interview is
conducted in Spielberg's Los Angeles office, which is full of *Jaws* paraphernal-
ia. Spielberg makes an actual appearance in "Cool Heads, Hot Images." De
Palma grows apart from Spielberg in the 1990s, but he does rekindle his relationship with Lucas and Industrial Light and Magic to bring *Mission: Impossible* and *Mission to Mars* to life. Quentin Tarantino's 1994 confab with De
Palma, "Emotion Pictures," allows De Palma to distance himself from his
peers and to share Tarantino's enthusiasm for his work. Tarantino allows De
Palma to relax and bask in the knowledge that *Pulp Fiction* would not have
been possible without the influence of *Blow Out*. It's a touching moment
when De Palma isn't accused of ripping off Hitchcock, or, as some would
claim, himself in *Raising Cain*, but is instead credited with inspiring the next
generation of filmmakers.

De Palma's fascinating personality—his schizophrenic need to suspend
our disbelief then assault us with reality—is on full display in all of these
interviews.

In accordance with the policy of the University Press of Mississippi, the interviews are presented in their original form to preserve their historical value.
There is some overlap between the pieces, particularly in the 1970s, but this
repetition is important in how certain details or themes are used to construct
De Palma's persona and biographical legend. These patterns form the public
discourse that is De Palma.

This work would not have been possible without the kind stewardship of
Lester D. Friedman. Thanks also to Peter Brunette, Walter Biggins, Seetha
Srinivasan, and Anne Stascavage at the University Press of Mississippi, and
my many mentors over the last ten years: Mimi White, Chuck Kleinhans,
Scott Curtis, Walter Korte, Tag Gallagher, Gerald Peary, Ray Carney, George
Bluestone, and John Kelly. I would be remiss if I didn't thank Bill Fentum for
fact-checking the chronology and assisting me in finding several key inter-

views included in this volume. Credit should also be given to Geoff Beran and the many updates he has posted on his website, De Palma à la Mod.

In closing, I want to express my love and admiration for my wife Moyenda and our two precious sons, August and Christopher.

Notes

1. Brian De Palma, "A Day in the Life, *Esquire* (October 1980).

2. Leslie Bennetts, "*The Untouchables*: De Palma's Departure," *New York Times*, 6 July 1987.

3. Ibid.

4. Joseph Gelmis, *The Film Director as Superstar*, Doubleday: Garden City, NY, 1970.

5. Dale Pollock, "De Palma Takes a Shot at Defending *Scarface*," *Los Angeles Times*, 5 December 1983.

6. De Palma.

CHRONOLOGY

1940   Born September 11 in Newark, NJ.

1945   De Palma's family moves to Philadelphia, PA.

1958   Majors in physics and technology at Columbia University; becomes obsessed with filmmaking after seeing Alfred Hitchcock's *Vertigo*.

1962   De Palma's third student film, *Wotan's Wake*, wins the Rosenthal Foundation Award. Receives MCA writing fellowship at Sarah Lawrence College.

1964   Shoots *The Wedding Party*.

1968   Self-promotes *Murder à la Mod* in New York City in May. *Greetings* released on December 15.

1969   *The Wedding Party* released on April 9.

1970   *Dionysus in '69* released on March 22. *Hi, Mom!* released on April 27. Moves to Los Angeles, befriends George Lucas, Paul Schrader, Martin Scorsese, and Steven Spielberg. Warner Bros. pulls De Palma from *Get to Know Your Rabbit*.

1972   *Get to Know Your Rabbit* released in June.

1973   *Sisters* released on March 27.

1974   *Phantom of the Paradise* released on October 31.

1976   *Obsession* released on August 1. *Carrie* released on November 17.

1978   *The Fury* released on March 15.

1979   Marries film actress Nancy Allen.

1980   *Home Movies* released on May 16. *Dressed to Kill* released on July 25. Removed from *Prince of the City*; replaced by Sidney Lumet.

1981   *Blow Out* released on July 24.

1983   Spars publicly with the MPAA over an X rating for *Scarface*. *Scarface* released on December 9. Divorced from Nancy Allen.

1984   Shoots Bruce Springsteen "Dancing in the Dark" video. *Body Double* released on October 26.

1986   *Wise Guys* released on April 11.

1987   *The Untouchables* released on June 3 (De Palma's second highest grossing film to date with worldwide returns of $186.3 million).

1989   *Casualties of War* released on August 18.

1990   *The Bonfire of the Vanities* released on December 21.

1991   Marries film producer Gail Anne Hurd. Dell publishes Julie Salamon's *The Devil's Candy*, an inside account of the making of *The Bonfire of the Vanities* (with De Palma's blessing). Daughter, Lolita De Palma, born.

1992   *Raising Cain* released on August 7.

1993   *Carlito's Way* released on November 10. Divorced from Gail Anne Hurd.

1995   Marries Darnell Gregorio.

1996   *Mission: Impossible* released on May 22 (De Palma's highest grossing film to date with a worldwide gross of $467 million). Divorced from Darnell Gregorio. Daughter, Piper De Palma, born.

1998   *Snake Eyes* released on August 7.

2000   *Mission to Mars* released on March 10 (De Palma's third highest grossing film to date with worldwide returns of $111 million). Relocates to Paris, disavows blockbuster filmmaking.

2001   Shoots *Femme Fatale*. Subject of month-long tribute at the American Museum of the Moving Image in New York City.

2002   *Femme Fatale* released.

FILMOGRAPHY

Student and Short Films

ICARUS (1960)
660124, THE STORY OF AN IBM CARD (1961)
WOTAN'S WAKE (1962)
JENNIFER (1964)
MOD (1964)
BRIDGE THAT GAP (1965)
YOU SHOW ME A STRONG TOWN AND I'LL SHOW YOU A STRONG BANK
(1966)
THE RESPONSIVE EYE (1966)

Feature Films

1968
MURDER À LA MOD
Director: **Brian De Palma**
Producer: Ken Burrows
Screenplay: **Brian De Palma**
Directors of Photography: Bruce Torbert and Jack Harrell
Editor: **Brian De Palma**
Music: John Herbert McDowell
Cast: Margo Norton (Karen), Andra Akers (Tracy), Jared Martin
(Christopher), William Finley (Otto), Ken Burrows (Wiley), Lorenzo Catlett
(Policeman), Jennifer Salt (First Actress), Laura Rubin (Second Actress),
Melanie Mander (Mannequin), Laura Stevenson (Girl in the Shop)
80 minutes

GREETINGS
West End Films/Sigma III
Director: **Brian De Palma**
Producer: Charles Hirsch
Screenplay: **Brian De Palma** and Charles Hirsch
Director of Photography: Robert Fiore
Editor: **Brian De Palma**
Production Designer: Robert Fiore
Music: The Children of Paradise
Cast: Robert De Niro (Jon Rubin), Jonathan Warden (Paul Shaw), Gerrit
Graham (Lloyd Clay), Allen Garfield (Smut Peddler), Megan McCormick
(Marina), Richard Hamilton (Pop Artist), Bettina Kugel (Tina), Jack Cowley
(Fashion Photographer), Jane Lee Salmons (Model), Peter Maloney (Earl
Roberts), Ashley Oliver (Bronx Secretary), Cynthia Peltz (Divorcée), Rutanya
Alda (Linda), Mona Feit (Mystic Date), Carol Patton (The Blonde)
88 minutes

1969
THE WEDDING PARTY (filmed 1964)
AJAY Films
Directors: **Brian De Palma**, Wilford Leach, and Cynthia Munroe
Producers: **Brian De Palma**, Wilford Leach, and Cynthia Munroe
Screenplay: **Brian De Palma**, Wilford Leach, and Cynthia Munroe
Director of Photography: Peter Powell
Editor: **Brian De Palma**
Music: John Herbert McDowell
Cast: Charles Pfluger (Charlie), Jill Clayburgh (Josephine), Robert De Niro
(Cecil), William Finley (Alistair), Jennifer Salt (Phoebe), Valda Satterfield
(Mrs. Fish), Raymond McNally (Mr. Fish), John Braswell (Reverend Oldfield),
Judy Thomas (Celeste the Organist), Sue Anne Converse (Nanny), John
Quinn (Baker)
90 minutes

1970
HI, MOM!
West End Films/Sigma III
Director: **Brian De Palma**

Producer: Charles Hirsch
Story: **Brian De Palma** and Charles Hirsch
Screenplay: **Brian De Palma**
Director of Photography: Robert Elfstrom
Editor: Paul Hirsch
Production Designer: Peter Bocour
Music: Eric Kaz
Cast: Robert De Niro (Jon Rubin), Charles Durning (Superintendent), Allen Garfield (Joe Banner), Peter Maloney (Drugstore Manager), Abraham Goren (Pervert in Movie), Jennifer Salt (Judy Bishop), Gerrit Graham (Gerrit Wood), Lara Parker (Jeannie Mitchell), Nelson Peltz (Playboy), Floyd L. Peterson (John Winnicove)
87 minutes

DIONYSUS IN '69
Sigma III
Directors: **Brian De Palma**, Robert Fiore, and Bruce Rubin
Producers: **Brian De Palma**, Robert Fiore, and Bruce Rubin in association with the Performance Group
Directors of Photography: **Brian De Palma** and Robert Fiore
Editors: **Brian De Palma** and Bruce Rubin
Cast: William Finley (Dionysus), William Shepherd (Penthee), Joan McIntosh (Agave), Samuel Blazer (Coryphee), John Bousseau, Richard Dic, Vickie May, Patrick McDermott, Margaret Ryan, Ciel Smith (The Performance Group)
90 minutes

1972
GET TO KNOW YOUR RABBIT (filmed 1970)
Warner Bros.
Director: **Brian De Palma**
Producers: Steve Bernhardt and Paul Gaer
Screenplay: Jordan Crittenden
Director of Photography: John Alonzo
Editor: Peter Colbert
Production Designer: William Malley
Music: Jack Elliot and Allyn Ferguson

Cast: Tom Smothers (Donald Beeman), John Astin (Mr. Turnbull), Katherine Ross (The Terrific-Looking Girl), Orson Welles (Mr. Delasandro), Allen Garfield (Vic), Hope Summers (Ms. Beeman), M. Emmet Walsh (Mr. Wendel), Suzanne Zenor (Paula), Samantha Jones (Susan), Jack Collins (Mr. Reese), Helen Page Camp (Mrs. Wendel), Charles Lane (Mr. Beeman)
93 minutes

1973
SISTERS
American International Pictures
Director: **Brian De Palma**
Producer: Edward R. Pressman
Story: **Brian De Palma**
Screenplay: **Brian De Palma** and Louisa Rose
Director of Photography: Gregory Sandor
Editor: Paul Hirsch
Production Designer: Gary Weist
Music: Bernard Herrmann
Cast: Margot Kidder (Danielle Breton), Jennifer Salt (Grace Collier), William Finley (Dr. Emil Breton), Lisle Wilson (Philip Woode), Charles Durning (Joseph Larch), Mary Davenport (Mrs. Collier), Barnard Hughes (Arthur McLennen), Dolph Sweet (Detective Kelly)
93 minutes

1974
PHANTOM OF THE PARADISE
Twentieth Century-Fox
Director: **Brian De Palma**
Producer: Edward R. Pressman
Executive Producer: Gustave M. Berne
Screenplay: **Brian De Palma**
Director of Photography: Larry Pizer
Editor: Paul Hirsch
Production Designer: Jack Fisk
Music: Paul Williams
Cast: William Finley (Winslow Leach), Paul Williams (Swan), Jessica Harper (Phoenix), Gerrit Graham (Beef), George Memmoli (Harold Philbin), Harold

Oblong, Jeffrey Commanor, and Archie Hahn (The Juicy Fruits/The Beach
Bums/The Undead)
Academy Award Nominations: George Tipton and Paul Williams, Best
Original Song Score and/or Adaptation
91 minutes

1975
OBSESSION
Columbia
Director: **Brian De Palma**
Producers: George Litto and Harry N. Blum
Executive Producer: Robert S. Bremson
Story: **Brian De Palma** and Paul Schrader
Screenplay: Paul Schrader
Director of Photography: Vilmos Zsigmond
Editor: Paul Hirsch
Production Designer: Jack Senter
Music: Bernard Herrmann
Cast: Cliff Robertson (Michael Courtland), Geneviève Bujold (Elizabeth
Courtland/Amy Courtland/Sandra Portinari), John Lithgow (Robert La Salle),
Wanda Blackman (Amy Courtland as child), Sylvia Williams (Judy), Patrick
McNamara (Kidnapper), Stanley J. Reeves (Inspector Brie), Stocker Fontelieu
(Dr. Ellman), Nella Simoncini Barbieri (Mrs. Portinari)
Oscar Nomination: Bernard Herrmann, Best Music, Original Score
98 minutes

1976
CARRIE
United Artists
Director: **Brian De Palma**
Producer: Paul Monash
Screenplay: Lawrence D. Cohen (based on the novel by Stephen King)
Director of Photography: Mario Tosi
Editor: Paul Hirsch
Production Designers: Jack Fisk and William Kenny
Music: Pino Donaggio
Cast: Sissy Spacek (Carrie White), Piper Laurie (Margaret White), Amy Irving

(Sue Snell), William Katt (Tommy Ross), John Travolta (Billy Nolan), Nancy Allen (Chris Hargenson), Betty Buckley (Miss Collins), P. J. Soles (Norma Watson), Priscilla Pointer (Mrs. Snell), Sydney Lassick (Mr. Fromm), Stefan Gierasch (Mr. Morton), Michael Talbott (Freddy), Doug Cox (The Beak), Edie McClurg (Helen)
Academy Award Nominations: Sissy Spacek, Best Actress; Piper Laurie, Best Actress in a Supporting Role
98 minutes

1978
THE FURY
Twentieth Century-Fox
Director: **Brian De Palma**
Producer: Frank Yablans
Executive Producer: Ronald Preissman
Screenplay: John Farris (based on his novel)
Director of Photography: Richard H. Kline
Editor: Paul Hirsch
Production Designer: Bill Malley
Music: John Williams
Cast: Kirk Douglas (Peter Sandza), John Cassavetes (Childress), Amy Irving (Gillian Bellaver), Carrie Snodgress (Hester), Andrew Stevens (Robin Sandza), Charles Durning (Dr. Jim McKeever), Fiona Lewis (Susan Charles), Carol Rossen (Dr. Ellen Linstrom), Joyce Easton (Mrs. Bellaver), William Finley (Raymond Dunwoode), Rutanya Alda (Kristen), Jane Lambert (Vivian Nuckells), Dennis Franz (Bob)
118 minutes

1979
HOME MOVIES
SLC/United Artists
Director: **Brian De Palma** (& the Sarah Lawrence College Film Workshop)
Producers: **Brian De Palma**, Jack Temchin, and Gil Adler
Story: **Brian De Palma**
Screenplay: Robert Harders, Gloria Norris, Kim Ambler, Dana Edelman, Stephen LeMay, and Charles Loventhal
Director of Photography: James L. Carter

Editor: Corky O'Hara
Production Designer: Tom Surgal
Music: Pino Donaggio
Cast: Kirk Douglas (Dr. Tuttle, the Maestro), Nancy Allen (Kristina), Keith Gordon (Denis Byrd), Gerrit Graham (James Byrd), Vincent Gardenia (Dr. Byrd), Mary Davenport (Mrs. Byrd), Captain Haggerty (Officer Quinn), Loretta Tupper (Grandma), Theresa Saldana (Judy)
90 minutes

1980
DRESSED TO KILL
Filmways
Director: **Brian De Palma**
Producer: George Litto
Executive Producer: Samuel Z. Arkoff
Screenplay: **Brian De Palma**
Director of Photography: Ralf Bode
Editor: Jerry Greenberg
Production Designer: Gary Weist
Music: Pino Donaggio
Cast: Michael Caine (Dr. Robert Elliott), Angie Dickinson (Kate Miller), Nancy Allen (Liz Blake), Keith Gordon (Peter Miller), Dennis Franz (Detective Marino), David Margulies (Dr. Levy), Ken Baker (Warren Lockman), Brandon Maggart (Cleveland Sam), Susanna Clemm (Betty Luce)
105 minutes

1981
BLOW OUT
Filmways
Director: **Brian De Palma**
Producer: George Litto
Screenplay: **Brian De Palma**
Director of Photography: Vilmos Zsigmond
Editor: Paul Hirsch
Production Designer: Paul Sylbert
Music: Pino Donaggio
Cast: John Travolta (Jack Terri), Nancy Allen (Sally Bedina), John Lithgow

(Burke), Dennis Franz (Manny Karp), Peter Boyden (Sam), Curt May (Frank Donahue), John Aquino (Detective Mackey), John McMartin (Lawrence Henry), Deborah Everton (Hooker), Ernest McClure (Jim), Dave Roberts (Anchor Man), Maurice Copeland (Jack Manners)
108 minutes

1983
SCARFACE
Universal
Director: **Brian De Palma**
Producer: Martin Bregman
Executive Producer: Louis A. Stroller
Screenplay: Oliver Stone
Director of Photography: John A. Alonzo
Editors: Jerry Greenberg and David Ray
Production Designer: Ed Richardson
Music: Giorgio Moroder
Cast: Al Pacino (Tony Montana), Steven Bauer (Manny), Michelle Pfeiffer (Elvira), Mary Elizabeth Mastrantonio (Gina), Robert Loggia (Frank Lopez), Paul Shenar (Alejandro Sosa), Arnaldo Santana (Ernie), F. Murray Abraham (Omar), Miriam Colón (Mama Montana), Pepe Serna (Angel), Dennis Holahan (Banker), Harris Yulin (Bernstein), Richard Delmonte (Fernando), Richard Belzer (MC)
170 minutes

1984
BODY DOUBLE
Columbia
Director: **Brian De Palma**
Producer: **Brian De Palma**
Executive Producer: Howard Gottfried
Story: **Brian De Palma**
Screenplay: **Brian De Palma** and Robert Lavrech
Director of Photography: Stephen H. Burum
Editors: Gerald Greenberg and Bill Pankow
Production Designer: Ida Random
Music: Pino Donaggio

Cast: Craig Wasson (Jake), Melanie Griffith (Holly), Gregg Henry (Sam Bouchard), Deborah Shelton (Gloria), Guy Boyd (Jim McLean), Dennis Franz (Rubin), David Haskell (Drama Teacher), Rebecca Stanley (Kimberly), Al Israel (Corso), Douglas Warhit (Video Salesman), B. J. Jones (Douglas), Russ Marin (Frank), Lane Davies (Billy)
114 minutes

1986
WISE GUYS
Metro Goldwyn Mayer/United Artists
Director: **Brian De Palma**
Producer: Aaron Russo
Executive Producer: Irwin Russo
Screenplay: George Gallo and Norman Steinberg
Director of Photography: Fred Schuler
Editor: Jerry Greenberg
Production Designer: Edward Pisoni
Music: Ira Newborn
Cast: Danny De Vito (Harry Valentini), Joe Piscopo (Moe Dickstein), Harvey Keitel (Bobby DiLea), Ray Sharkey (Marco), Dan Hedaya (Anthony Castelo), Captain Lou Albano (Frank "The Fixer" Acavano), Julie Bovasso (Lil Dickstein), Patti LuPone (Wanda Valentini), Antonia Rey (Aunt Sadie), Mimi Cecchini (Grandma Valentini)
91 minutes

1987
THE UNTOUCHABLES
Paramount
Director: **Brian De Palma**
Producer: Art Linson
Screenplay: David Mamet
Director of Photography: Stephen H. Burum
Editors: Jerry Greenberg and Bill Pankow
Production Designer: William A. Elliot
Music: Ennio Morricone
Cast: Kevin Costner (Eliot Ness), Sean Connery (Jim Malone), Charles Martin Smith (Oscar Wallace), Andy Garcia (George Stone), Robert De Niro (Al

Capone), Richard Bradford (Mike), Jack Kehoe (Payne), Brad Sullivan
(George), Billy Drago (Frank Nitti), Patricia Clarkson (Ness's Wife)
Academy Award: Sean Connery, Best Actor in a Supporting Role
Academy Award Nominations: Ennio Morricone, Best Music, Original Score;
William A. Elliot and Patrizia Von Brandenstein, Best Achievement in Art
Direction; Hal Gausman, Best Achievement in Set Decoration; Marilyn
Vance, Best Costume Design
119 minutes

1989
CASUALTIES OF WAR
Columbia
Director: **Brian De Palma**
Producer: Art Linson
Screenplay: David Rabe (based upon the book by Daniel Lang)
Director of Photography: Stephen H. Burum
Editor: Bill Pankow
Production Designer: Wolf Kroeger
Music: Ennio Morricone
Cast: Michael J. Fox (Eriksson), Sean Penn (Meserve), Thuy Thu Le (Oahn),
Don Harvey (Clark), John C. Reilly (Hatcher), John Leguizamo (Diaz), Eric
King (Brown), Jack Gwaltney (Rowan), Ving Rhames (Lt. Reilly), Dan Martin
(Hawthorne), Dale Dye (Capt. Hill)
120 minutes

1990
THE BONFIRE OF THE VANITIES
Warner Bros.
Director: **Brian De Palma**
Producer: **Brian De Palma**
Executive Producers: Peter Guber and Jon Peters
Screenplay: Michael Cristofer (based on the novel by Tom Wolfe)
Director of Photography: Vilmos Zsigmond
Editors: David Ray and Bill Pankow
Production Designer: Richard Sylbert
Music: David Grusin
Cast: Tom Hanks (Sherman McCoy), Bruce Willis (Peter Fallow), Melanie

Griffith (Maria Ruskin), Morgan Freeman (Judge Leonard White), Beth Broderick (Caroline Heftshank), Kim Cattrall (Judy McCoy), Alan King (Arthur Ruskin), Rita Wilson (P.R. Lady), Andre Gregory (Aubrey Buffing)
126 minutes

1992
RAISING CAIN
Universal/Pacific Western
Director: **Brian De Palma**
Producer: Gale Anne Hurd
Screenplay: **Brian De Palma**
Director of Photography: Stephen H. Burum
Editors: Paul Hirsch, Bonnie Koehler, and Robert Dalva
Production Designer: Doug Kraner
Music: Pino Donaggio
Cast: John Lithgow (Carter/Cain/Dr. Nix/Josh/Margo), Lolita Davidovich (Jenny), Steven Bauer (Jack), Frances Sternhagen (Dr. Waldhelm), Gregg Henry (Lt. Terri), Tom Bower (Sgt. Cally), Mel Harris (Sarah), Teri Austin (Karen), Gabrielle Carteris (Nan), Barton Heyman (Mack), Amanda Pombo (Amy), Kathleen Callan (Emma)
91 minutes

1993
CARLITO'S WAY
Universal/Epic Productions
Director: **Brian De Palma**
Producers: Martin Bregman, Willi Baer, and Michael S. Bregman
Executive Producers: Louis A. Stroller and Ortwin Freyermuth
Screenplay: David Koepp (based on the novels *Carlito's Way* and *After Hours* by Edwin Torres)
Director of Photography: Stephen H. Burum
Editors: Bill Pankow and Kristina Boden
Production Designer: Richard Sylbert
Music: Patrick Doyle
Music Supervisor: Jellybean Benitez
Cast: Al Pacino (Carlito Brigante), Sean Penn (David Kleinfeld), Penelope Anne Miller (Gail), John Leguizamo (Benny Blanco), Ingrid Rogers (Steffie),

Luis Guzmán (Pachanga), James Rebhorn (Norwalk), Joseph Siravo (Vinnie Taglialucca), Frank Minucci (Tony Taglialucca), Viggo Mortensen (Lalin), Jorge Porcel (Saso), Adrian Pasona (Frankie), Al Israel (Rolando)
145 minutes

1996
MISSION: IMPOSSIBLE
Paramount
Director: **Brian De Palma**
Producers: Tom Cruise and Paula Wagner
Executive Producer: Paul Hitchcock
Story: David Koepp and Steven Zaillian
Screenplay: David Koepp and Robert Towne
Director of Photography: Stephen H. Burum
Editor: Paul Hirsch
Production Designer: Norman Reynolds
Music: Danny Elfman
Visual Effects Supervisor: John Knoll
Cast: Tom Cruise (Ethan Hunt), Jon Voight (Jim Phelps), Emmanuelle Beart (Claire), Henry Czerny (Kittridge), Jean Reno (Krieger), Ving Rhames (Luther), Kristin Scott-Thomas (Sarah Davies), Vanessa Redgrave (Max), Emilio Estevez (Jack), Ingeborga Dapkunaite (Hannah)
110 minutes

1998
SNAKE EYES
Paramount/DeBart
Director: **Brian De Palma**
Producer: **Brian De Palma**
Executive Producer: Louis A. Stroller
Story: **Brian De Palma** and David Koepp
Screenplay: David Koepp
Director of Photography: Stephen H. Burum
Editor: Bill Pankow
Production Designer: Anne Pritchard
Music: Ryuichi Sakamoto
Cast: Nicolas Cage (Richard Santoro), Gary Sinise (Commander Kevin

Dunne), John Heard (Gilbert Powell), Carla Gugino (Julia Costello), Stan Shaw (Lincoln Tyler), Kevin Dunn (Lou Logan), Michael Rispoli (Jimmy George), Joel Fabiani (Charles Kirkland), Luis Guzmán (Cyrus), Tamara Tunie (Anthea)
98 minutes

2000
MISSION TO MARS
Touchstone
Director: **Brian De Palma**
Producer: Tom Jacobson
Executive Producer: Sam Mercer
Story: Lowell Cannon, Jim Thomas, and John Thomas
Screenplay: Jim Thomas, John Thomas, and Graham Yost
Director of Photography: Stephen H. Burum
Editor: Paul Hirsch
Production Designer: Ed Verreaux
Music: Ennio Morricone
Visual Effects Supervisors: Hoyt Yeatman and John Knoll
Cast: Gary Sinise (Jim McConnell), Tim Robbins (Woody Blake), Don Cheadle (Luke Graham), Connie Nielsen (Terri Fisher), Jerry O'Connell (Phil Ohlmyer), Armin Mueller-Stahl (Ray Beck), Peter Outerbridge (Sergei Kirov), Kavan Smith (Nicholas Willis), Jill Teed (Renee Coté), Elise Neal (Debra Graham), Kim Delaney (Maggie McConnell)
113 minutes

2002
FEMME FATALE
Warner Bros./Quinta
Director: **Brian De Palma**
Producers: Tarak Ben Amar and Marina Gefter
Executive Producer: Mark Lombardo
Screenplay: **Brian De Palma**
Director of Photography: Thierry Arbogast
Editor: Bill Pankow
Production Designer: Anne Pritchard
Music: Ryuichi Sakamoto

Cast: Antonio Banderas (Nicolas Bardo), Rebecca Romijn-Stamos (Laure/ Lily), Peter Coyote (Bruce Hewitt Watts), Eriq Ebouaney (Black Tie), Edouard Montoute (Racine), Thierry Frémont (Serra), Gregg Henry (Shiff), Sandrine Bonnaire (Herself), Gilles Jacob (Himself), Rie (Herself), Régis Wargnier (Himself)

BRIAN DE PALMA

INTERVIEWS

The Making of *Sisters:* An Interview with Director Brian De Palma

RICHARD RUBINSTEIN/1973

RICHARD RUBINSTEIN: *How did you get the idea for* Sisters?

BRIAN DE PALMA: In 1966 I saw an article in *Life* magazine about a pair of Russian Siamese twins named Masha and Dasha. At the end of the article there was a picture of the two girls sitting on a couch and the caption said that apart from the fact that they were joined at the hip both girls were physiologically normal, but as they were getting older they were developing psychological problems. One of the twins had a very surly, disturbing look on her face and the other looked perfectly healthy and smiling. And this strong visual image started the whole idea off in my mind.

I am also a great admirer of Hitchcock and *Psycho,* and there are a great many structural elements here that are in all Hitchcock's movies: introducing a character and then having him killed off early in the film; switching points of view: taking the person who sees the murder and then involving him in solving the crime.

But the exposition—the history of the twins growing up in the Institute and their separation—is via a sort of dream imagery which I think makes it much more interesting. The idea derives from Polanski. I have always liked the dream sequence in *Rosemary's Baby* where the devil makes love to her. It was a good idea because you never really know whether or not it happened, and the imagery is terrific. It also avoids the scene in *Psycho* where the psychiatrist sits down and explains everything. An expository scene can be a kind of boring scene, but you need it because the audience doesn't know

---

From *Filmmakers Newsletter*, September 1973: 25–30. Reprinted by permission of the author.

what's happening and you've got to explain it to them. By placing it in a dream I think you get a sort of visceral feeling for what went on rather than specific information.

RR: *I see Bernard Herrmann did the music. How did you get him?*
BD: The idea for using Bernard Herrmann came from the editor, Paul Hirsch. When he was assembling the material he put a lot of Herrmann's music on it. We used the violins from the *Psycho* murder scene; *Marnie* over some of the love stuff on the boat; the whole *Vertigo* dream score over our dream sequence. And suddenly all this stuff we'd been looking at silently took on a very ominous dimension; it became scary and disturbing.

I didn't know what had happened to Herrmann. (Lots of people think he is dead. After all, his first score was *Citizen Kane,* and that's a long time ago.) But we found out through another director's uncle's brother's dentist's cousin that he was indeed alive and residing in London. We sent him the script and he liked it, and then we flew him over here to look at the movie.

We found out that he's a very temperamental conductor. He's in his late 60's or 70's and he's gruff and kind of scary. Our first meeting was pretty terrifying. He had just gotten off the plane and was still suffering from jet lag and we took him to see the movie. There wasn't a sound out of him as to whether or not he liked it; he only seemed interested in when lunch was. But after he saw the movie he said it reminded him of when he first saw *Psycho.* And that really made me feel good.

Apparently when *Psycho* was first screened for Herrmann, Hitchcock was very depressed about it because he thought he'd made a tawdry television picture: he had shot it with a television crew in about 6 or 8 weeks with his own money and he thought it looked as if it had been thrown together and that they should just slap it on television and forget about it. But when Herrman saw it he said, "Wait a minute. I think I can do something here." And he said the same thing about *Sisters.* I don't think my picture is anywhere near as great as *Psycho* (and I do think *Psycho* is a great movie), but it encouraged me to see that he was indeed interested in it.

But it was really something working with him! I wanted to start the movie with just white credits over the first scene as Danielle/Dominique is getting undressed. That was the first cue I discussed with Herrman, and he said, "That's *TERRIBLE!!*" (And he talks in a very gruff, deliberate way.) So I said, "What's wrong with it?" And he said, "Nothing happens in this movie for forty minutes!" And I said, "Yes, that's the idea. There is a slow beginning—you know, like *Psycho*, where the murder doesn't happen until about 40 minutes into the picture." And he shouted at me, "*YOU* are not Hitchcock; for Hitchcock they will WAIT!" And that is of course very true. Because it's a Hitchcock movie you KNOW something is going to happen.

R R : *Does Hitchcock know about the movie?*
B D : There have been so many different Hitchcock imitators that I would guess he doesn't pay much attention to them anymore. Actually though, I have found that people who like and are knowledgeable about Hitchcock also like *Sisters*—they know the references I am making to his films and they seem to appreciate it all the more for that. Which is good, because you could so easily be attacked as a tawdry Hitchcock rip-off.

There are only a few directors who are masters of this genre—Hitchcock and Polanski, for instance—and they are all by themselves. It is an extremely difficult genre to work with because it is so unreal and you can get into big trouble with people not following your vision and getting lost in understanding what you are doing.

The reason that I like the genre is because you can work in a sort of pure cinema form. That is why Hitchcock likes it too. It's all images, and your story-telling is entirely through images and not people talking to each other.

R R : *Last year at Cannes Hitchcock made the comment that there is too much talk in movies.*
B D : He's absolutely right. Films with endless jabber make me sleepy. How you deal with a genre in America after you have seen a lot of European movies is to make it slower. Then it seems like an Antonioni. So instead of, say, just making a bank-robber movie, you're making a comment on American society because everybody moves so slowly. Directors who do this seem to me to be embarrassed by the genre they are working in—they really don't want to be known for making detective pictures. They feel they are important directors and they can't be accused of making, say, a Raymond Chandler movie.

If you are making genre movies you cannot refuse to shoot the obligatory scenes: how do we get from A to B to C to D. But some directors feel that they are just boring parts because they are plot and who wants to hear about that—let's get on with the stylistic business. It's great to be a stylist, and I really like that, but on the other hand you cannot refuse to pay attention to the conventions you are working with. Make a new form and be Fellini, but then don't try to be Don Siegel.

I strongly believe there are reasons for genre forms and there are reasons that make them work. And if you ignore all the tenets of the form you are going to have something else which isn't going to be that genre. But if you are going to avoid telling stories, then you had better come up with another way to make a movie last 90 minutes because it becomes difficult any other way. Granted there are some genius directors who can get away with it, but by and large it makes me angry to see a good, major director subordinate the content of an expository scene to style so that you can't tell what's going on and who's doing what to whom.

RR: *Usually in this genre the expository scene, which is requisite for the understanding of the plot, is done in a much more straight-forward, unambiguous form than your dream sequence.*

BD: Granted. When you try to get complicated solutions to normal, simplistic problems you sometimes run into trouble. Of course there is an easy way to do that scene: I could just have the doctor sit there and talk to the girl and explain everything. You know, a nice close-up while he says, "Remember when you were a little girl back at the Institute . . ." Everything in focus and nice and clear and loud. You would have gotten all the information and known exactly what was going on—just like with the psychiatrist in *Psycho*.

But I tried to find a different way to do it. And I think that while image-wise it is fascinating, exposition-wise it is probably only 50% effective. If I had had more money I would have shot it a little differently because I can see some of the things that are unclear and that I should have made clearer. But then I am no Hitchcock—I don't have the resources or the time or the skill to do that yet.

RR: *What was the budget?*

BD: About a half a million and $250,000 in deferred. I got it financed independently. It took me a long time, and it was very difficult and I don't recommend it to anybody. We started with $200,000 and the producer just kept going out and raising more money until we ended up with a half million cash. But that was as far as he could go.

RR: *And you feel that the budget constrained you and that you could have or would have done things differently with more money?*

BD: With another $100,000 I could have re-shot a few things that I didn't like and it would have been better. But most directors feel that. I would also have liked to increase its size a little bit: it's always three characters in closed spaces. But to open it up more and add more people takes money.

One of the scenes which I would have completely re-shot had I had the money (and it's no longer in the picture because I couldn't re-shoot it) is one that I had thought about for years and years where the body is in the couch and it's bleeding through the bottom of the couch. The whole search scene is a Max Ophuls-type tracking shot about 6 minutes long, and while they are searching through the apartment the camera keeps coming back to the couch and the spot is getting bigger and bigger and bigger. I shot it, but because the camera could only get down so low and still go up high enough to shoot the rest of the scene we couldn't get down to the bottom of the couch and when we saw the rushes it looked ridiculous because it looked like the guy was bleeding up through the arm of the couch. So I had to throw out the whole tracking shot, and I was forced to use close-ups and television-type coverage—which bothered me a lot because it was a great conception for that kind of material. (In fact, the whole set had been constructed so that I could track through the entire length and back and around, just like Hitchcock did in *Rope*). But those are the kinds of things that make an immense amount of difference in this form.

Whenever I approach a scene I try to do it with a very strong visual concept: where the camera is placed is, to me, as important as the material itself. When I see a scene that someone else has done with, for instance, two people walking across a park shot through a panning long lens, I can just see dialogue written on the paper. All that is happening is that the director is covering—and to me, covering is the lowest form of direction. You hand a guy a script and he says, "Well, I'll take a master shot as the car pulls up and then a medium shot . . ." Well, that's television; that's not directing. It's sloppy and it's terrible and it doesn't say much for our art as directors.

On the other hand, I do try to stay within the limitations of what I have to work with. I don't write a scene where, for instance, someone is walking through Grand Central Station and then say, "Now how are we going to do that? Well, we can only afford five extras and we only have six lights so we can only light the one ticket counter near the OTB." A good director doesn't even conceive of things like that because they are impossible to shoot.

Also with *Sisters,* if I had had more money I would have gotten a big star, like Sidney Poitier or someone you can't even imagine getting killed, and I would have had him bumped off early in the picture. Or if I had had a star in the Grace Collier role—someone like Marlo Thomas whom you would immediately identify with—and she sees the murder, you would have had hundreds of thousands of people hanging in there for Marlo.

That's what Hitchcock did all the time: he got big stars that people could identify with. And it makes a difference in this genre. But when you don't have that, well, what have you got? You've got to carry it off with good actors—which is fine, but for this kind of form you really need that kind of star thrust. Screen stardom is a very real thing. Some people on film carry a kind of strength and power that merely good actors don't, and there is no getting around it. You watch good screen personalities and you are fascinated by everything they do. Sometimes they can even carry the worst turkeys.

On the other hand, we have reached a whole new level of reality vis-a-vis acting because of television. You can't have people pretending they are Gene McCarthy when you can watch the real Gene McCarthy. It also affects the style of acting a lot. You can't have the kind of naturalism that you had in the thirties (like the Kazan school): it looks too stylized and too overdramatic, and you just don't buy it anymore.

R R : *Since this movie is so tightly scripted and structured I would doubt that you allowed your actors much in the way of improvisation. It would seem that, like Hitchcock, you used them more as props to be moved about as you wanted them.*
B D : In this movie, yes. But you can get into a lot of trouble like that: once you start wheeling them around like props you don't believe it anymore because they are so unreal. And that is one of Hitchcock's big problems. Hitchcock needs really good actors, but I hear that he has gotten so big he doesn't think he needs anybody anymore. Megalomania is a very real problem for the successful director—you think it's me, me, me and I don't need anybody. And consequently your work suffers for it.

I think Hitchcock's break-up with Herrmann, for instance, has affected his work. He threw out Herrman's score for *Torn Curtain* and used someone else's and they got into a big fight and don't speak anymore. And that makes Hitchcock weaker. When your ego gets so big that you get into fights it's not conducive to good work. And that can happen with writers and actors and directors and cameramen. But a director especially needs to use the best people he can because it ultimately only makes him better.

Actually I tend to work very well with actors because I depend on them a lot. An actor brings reality to your fantasy and grounds it so that it doesn't get too far away.

R R : *To return to the subject of genre, what about comedy as an aspect of this particular form? The detective, for instance, is a comic figure and you made him so intentionally.*

B D : The suspense genre usually has comic relief sheerly to reduce the audience tension by giving them a chance to laugh and relax. Then you start again with the tension. And Hitchcock also talks about how you emotionally involve an audience. You can't sustain tension for too long; you have to drop it out occasionally, and comedy helps to do that. On the other hand, it is a very hard line to walk, and you have to be careful not to go too far over to the other side and make fun of the genre. It is also very difficult because you can fall into a kind of macabre humor and then you are really getting into questionable areas.

R R : *I think some of your uses of split screen ranks with the best I've ever seen. For instance, when the police get off the elevator and barely miss Emil but you see how they miss him via split screen instead of cutting. Or certain real-time aspects like Danielle and Emil cleaning up after the murder and Grace waiting for and then delayed by the police, which gives the others time to clean up after the murder—but you are watching both simultaneously.*

B D : First of all, I am interested in the medium of film itself, and I am constantly standing outside and making people aware that they are always watching a film. At the same time I am evolving it. In *Hi, Mom!*, for instance, there is a sequence where you are obviously watching a ridiculous documentary and you are told that and you are aware of it, but it still sucks you in. There is a kind of Brechtian alienation idea here: you are aware of what you are watching at the same time that you are emotionally involved in it.

Actually I think the prototype for split-screen is *Woodstock*, which has got every sophisticated documentary split-screen technique there is. And all the films which have come out of that are still using those basic concepts which were set up a long time ago. But that form—the *Woodstock* multiple-screen rock form—has always just been used as a documentary form; no one has ever thought to use it as a dramatic form, and it's just virgin territory!

My next project is called *Phantom of the Fillmore,* and it's a horror/rock musical which will hopefully combine the genres of horror and rock in one Faustian fantasmagoria. And in this film I want to take that whole split-screen rock concert form and really lie with it. I love to deal with the medium of film and bend it all the time!

R R : *What are some examples in* Sisters *of devices which "bend" the medium of film and make people aware that they are watching a movie?*
B D : The opening scene is one example. The audience thinks they are voyeuristically watching people in a bath-house, but then they are suddenly made aware that those people are on a television show and they are watching a television screen. It is also a very unique way of introducing characters, because instead of having them meet on the street and say, "Hi, let's go have a drink together," suddenly you have set up the whole image of the movie: the audience as voyeur which then transforms into what is essentially the character of Grace Collier who sees the murder. And it ends with the detective watching the couch with binoculars, so there is a voyeuristic image at the beginning and at the end. Then there is the TV show, the "Peeping Tom Show," which is an idea derived from "Candid Camera." Also, all the images in the dream scene are very voyeuristic.

In other words, all of this is just a way of making an image for the movie which is essentially candid camera—that is, peering into other people's lives. And that is what Grace does: she is a newspaper reporter and she is the observer of the murder and the one who attempts to unravel it.

And that is what we all do—especially when we watch TV. I really got the idea from watching the Vietnam war on television—watching a war that nobody really knew about except that we watched it every night on the 7 o'clock news. It was really a very voyeuristic war, and I think it says a lot about the way we perceive things. We are very much controlled by the media which present things to us. And those media can be manipulated and they can be manipulated in any way: they can make what is seemingly real false and what is seemingly false real. And that is what has always fascinated me about film—the ability to lie and twist it any way you want.

R R : *Would you say something about the technical aspects of the production.*

BD: *Sisters* was shot in 8 weeks. We used a Nabet crew. They're not like a Hollywood crew, but they work hard and God knows they're earnest. We used a Mitchell BNC with Panavision lenses, an Eclair for the 16mm, and an Arri and two Mitchells for some of the double shots. The film was shot entirely on location on Staten Island except for the stuff on the apartment set and at the Time-Life building. The film was very tightly shot. Our shooting ratio was 8 to 1, and only a couple of scenes were re-shot and only one scene was dropped. Each scene was preconceived and carefully planned beforehand.

The film was very carefully lit in a truly classical style, and it took a lot of time—which is most unusual in a low-budget movie. But that is why it looks so different. The cameraman sometimes took as long as 45 minutes to light closeups, which is especially rare in a low-budget movie, but it makes a big difference because the girls looked good!

The typical low-budget film uses bounced light, gets it up as fast as possible, and then moves on to the next setup. But bounced light, live locations, and moving fast are for a different kind of film with different values. A certain kind of detail is essential in a movie like mine, and it's not essential in something like, say, *Save the Tiger.* The important thing in that film was to get the reality of the places the people were in. *Sisters,* on the other hand, is an atmospheric movie, and we spent time to build a set to create an atmosphere. We even constructed a special cutaway icebox.

RR: *What about special effects?*

BD: The Siamese twins sitting next to each other is a special effect. We photographed Margo as she sat once in the chair and made a mark and photographed one side of the screen, and then we moved her over and photographed on the other side of the screen and made another mark for where we placed her in the frame, and then the optical house joined them together so that she was one piece, just like a Siamese twin. That same sort of thing was done a long time ago in old Bette Davis movies, so it's nothing new; but it's never been done before with a Siamese twin.

On the other hand, the television game show was not an optical but a mask with superimposed lines to give that TV scanline look. And the history of the twins as screened at the Time-Life Building was just old black and white photographs, but they picked up so much grain that it wasn't necessary to go through another optical.

The multiple split-screens were done with set-ups. For instance, in the elevator-hallway sequence we used three set-ups: a pan at the window, one coming around the doorway when they come out of the elevator and the Doctor is hiding in the back, and the two people at the door (when the detective comes in she opens the door and you see it from both sides).

RR: *Had you planned at the outset to use split-screen, or was that something that evolved as you faced the problem of cutting?*

BD: I get strong visual ideas and then I try to develop the story around them. Hitchcock makes drawings for all his films before he shoots them, and that is why his movies are so precise: he has incredible visual ideas and everything is worked out like a Swiss watch. Unfortunately most movies derive from a literary rather than a visual intent. But I always think in terms of what is on the screen, not what is on paper. I am not primarily a writer, and I always have very precise visual ideas and then try to construct a story around them as opposed to writing a story and then trying to figure out how I'm going to shoot it. But most people write stories and forget how they are going to shoot it.

As far as I am concerned, you are dealing with pure cinema—that is, with what is right on the screen—and you should try to think what it will look like. For instance, I had the image of the guy writing "Help" on the window from two points of view years ago, so the problem was how to turn the story so that you could get to that scene. Hitchcock is also constantly trying to find new ways to use original visual ideas. *North by Northwest* was constructed basically from the idea of great locations: how can we have a chase around Mount Rushmore? Or you take the idea of how to kill someone differently and say, well, instead of a dark alley let's try an open field.

RR: *You mentioned that you shot some of the film in 16mm.*

BD: I used 16mm to photograph the doctor when he is talking directly to the camera during the hypnosis scene. I operated the camera myself there because he was looking directly into the camera and there was no other way to see how he was playing it. Also the first dream, where they are going through the clinic with all the freaks, was shot in 16mm.

I happen to like grain if you can use it properly. It has a terrific feel about it. But you have got to put it in the right place so that it doesn't look like a tawdry 16mm exploitation picture. However in this film I was looking for a classical Hitchcock-type look, and when you spend that much time on sets and lighting you have to use Panavision lenses and the sharpest photography you can get—and it's not feasible on 16mm.

But 16mm for other kinds of films is fine. It's the *medium* that you need, and you need that medium precisely for what you are doing. I always choose mediums for the form I am using and not vice versa.

RR: *How do you rise from being an "underground" filmmaker?*

BD: Make a movie that makes money. That's the easiest way. The reason I got financed by a major studio for *Get to Know Your Rabbit* was because *Greetings* made money. The reason that I wasn't financed by a major studio for *Sisters* was because *Rabbit* sat on the shelf for 6 months. After all, it's a commercial industry. Granted *Rabbit* isn't a *great* movie, but it certainly isn't that bad. The point is that people have a very precise memory about where you stand on the *Variety* chart, and the big problem is getting people to believe in you so that they'll finance you. Money you always need, whether you raise it from a studio or from your relatives.

RR: *What is your feeling about the "you don't have to know how a camera works to be a filmmaker" theory?*

BD: I can only speak for myself, but I've done everything involved with making films—I've shot them, edited, taken sound, handled almost every technical aspect. Plus the fact that I come from a good technical background. I was designing computers when I was in high school; I majored in physics and won science fairs. So I am very technically oriented.

But knowing the technical aspects can only help you. That is why I have such an obsession with precision of vision. I can't stand sloppy direction or conception. It disturbs me in my own work and in other people's. The other thing is that once you've made a mistake or been sloppy you will forever see that in your work. I'm not the kind of director who doesn't look at my own films. I'll see them again and again and again, just to remind myself what was wrong with them, where I made a compromise, when I didn't take enough time, what didn't work with the characters or their development or with a shot. It makes me very aware of what I have to do to grow as a director.

I have scrupulously tried to evolve my style organically—I can see what I am weak at and what I need to work on and when I need to bring in a collaborator to strengthen the weakness of whatever I'm working on, whether it be the script, photography, or editing. My first movies were very loose and frag-mented, so I've tried to get very tight and controlled recently. I've also tried to take things step by step, but it's very hard to do that in the film industry. They don't believe in developing talent like that; it's all very hit or miss, get-the-deal-together. It's hard to develop in a system like that, and very few directors do.

RR: *How would you sum up your aims in making* Sisters?

BD: The whole idea of making a tightly constructed film was for my own development as a director. My earlier films had been very loose and all over the place, and as happens in that kind of situation, the parts had been better than the whole. So *Sisters* was a very conscious attempt at making something which was uniform by trying to work within a very tight story form and doing certain stylistic things within that structure.

Basically I wanted to make a movie in the Hitchcock mode in order to work on my own problems as a story-teller. It was also a study in the realiza-tion of precise visualization. I was trying to work in a pure cinematic style—doing everything with drawn shots and figuring out how all the pieces of film were going to fit together, then writing the story and making the story evolve from the images. Then shooting it that precisely and putting it together that precisely and seeing that it worked. It's a great process—and there is no greater craft than that.

De Palma of the Paradise

DAVID BARTHOLOMEW / 1975

I WAS SITTING IN THE LOBBY of Brian De Palma's apartment building waiting for him to show up for our appointment. Suddenly two figures strode in at a gallop, and De Palma, in the lead, nodded in my direction and continued around the corner to the elevator. As I gathered up my tape recorder, clipboard, notes, pens, and coat, a voice boomed out, "Well, are you comin' or not?" I remember reading how an interview with Archer Winston in 1970 had wound up with both of them casually stretched out on the floor, talking and drinking wine, and how he later told a reporter for the *Newark Evening News* that a director "can't believe his own publicity" and that "a director's greatest danger is megalomania." And now this. What's going on here?

I ran for the elevator. Was De Palma changed into a Hyde-ish beast of Hollywood power? We mumbled introductions. Once in the apartment, I set up my equipment while he went to the phone and began calling people in true tycoon fashion. The apartment was nicely decorated, clean, and neatly furnished. I remember reading another interview in which De Palma told the *New York Times* in October 1973, "I've lived in empty places all my life. I don't care where I live or what I look like." Hey, what's going on here?

We begin the interview, and as we get further and further into his career, my suspicions of De Palma's personality change drop away as he loosens up and relaxes, and by the end of an unexpected two-hour talk, we are having a good time. He looks healthier than when I last saw him, at a performance of

From *Cinefantastique* 4:2 (1975): 8–14.

Macbeth by the Performance Group at their garage in Soho. He's put on a little weight, but his tall frame supports it well, and his appearance is now set off by a fine, full beard. I noticed later, almost reassuringly, that his brown sweater looked well worn. And, of course, there wasn't a pair of D. W. Griffith "director's boots" in sight.

De Palma had been in town for a few weeks for the opening of *Phantom of the Paradise,* but when production plans for his new project *Double Ransom* fell into place, he quickly cut short his stay to return to the Coast. De Palma described *Double Ransom,* a George Litto production formerly titled *Deja Vu,* as "a suspense movie inspired by *Vertigo* about a man who has an obsessive love affair with his dead wife." He plans to follow this with a film version of Alfred Bester's science fiction classic *The Demolished Man,* which he is now scripting. Says De Palma, "It's about a murder in a telepathic society. I wanted to do it ten years ago." With his last two films, *Sisters* and *Phantom of the Paradise,* and his future plans, De Palma seems to have found that his forte in cinema lies in cinemafantastique. Actually, his entire career is marked by films that are bizarre, if not wholly genre works, in which he has experimented heavily with new film techniques. And like the character of Winslow, the Phantom in his latest film, De Palma's work has often been frustrated or exploited.

CFQ: *I see real bitterness in* Phantom of the Paradise. *You've had money and distribution problems with all your films. Are you possibly carrying over ideas and descriptions of the film business into the film?*
DE PALMA: Yeah, I think a lot of that is motivated by my own experiences, going into big buildings, bringing in your material that nobody pays any attention to or rips off in one way or another. That's the life of the business. I don't think it is "bitterness" necessarily. That's the way it is and you have to be able to operate within that reality.

CFQ: *How long have you been thinking about* Phantom of the Paradise *and putting it together?*
DE PALMA: Since 1969, about five years.

CFQ: *Have you always seen it as a musical and not as a straight remake?*
DE PALMA: I never had any intention of simply remaking *Phantom of the Opera.* I took its idea of a composer having his music ripped off, endeavoring

to kill the people who are massacring his music and putting on the girl he loves to sing it the way he wants it to be sung. That was the basic concept. I like the idea of a phantom haunting a rock palace as opposed to an opera house, but it isn't simply a matter of up-dating.

CFQ: *The film had a lot of legal problems after completion. How were these settled?*

DE PALMA: We were threatened with court action from three sources: Universal, King Features and Atlantic Records. King Features has a comic strip called *Phantom,* so we changed our title to *Phantom of the Paradise* to get them off our backs.

CFQ: *Originally the film was titled* Phantom of the Fillmore?

DE PALMA: Not really, although the trade reported it that way. We couldn't get rights to use "Fillmore" either, so it was just called *Phantom.* That's where it conflicted with the strip. A subdivision of Atlantic Records is called Swan Song Records, and we had Swan (Paul Williams) name his corporation Swan Song Enterprises. It was never mentioned, it was just that we had the words Swan Song on nearly everything around him and it all had to be optically removed—blown out or other things superimposed over them. We replaced a lot of them, actually, with "Death Records," his record label. Every once in a while, though, you can still see one. Lastly, Universal was finally appeased [with a cash settlement and a percentage of the deal].

CFQ: *Where was it filmed?*

DE PALMA: In Dallas. We had considered using the Fillmore but it really is an uninteresting auditorium. I wanted the most interesting decor I could find, and the oldest available theatre we could get that has terrific interior design was in Dallas.

CFQ: *When and how was Paul Williams brought into the picture?*

DE PALMA: The project went over a period of years from Marty Ransohoff to Ray Stark to Ed Pressman. When we couldn't get any response from a studio, I went to a record company, A&M Records, who liked the material. They had a guy there, Michael Arciaga, who was interested in getting involved in movies for their record performers. And one day, Paul Williams happened to be in his office during one of my visits. He came out as I was going in, and that was the first time I thought of him playing one of the parts and composing the music. He liked the idea alot, and that's how that started. It worked out very well.

CFQ: *He originally wanted the Phantom part?*
DE PALMA: Yes, probably out of identification. The composer who has had his music destroyed by bubble gum groups, the sensitive artist who has had his music commercialized to the point of its being unrecognizable to him but is, of course, fabulously successful by it.

CFQ: *Were the different production numbers done live with music or synced?*
DE PALMA: They were all done to playback. All the people were doing their own vocals except Beef (Gerrit Graham) who was dubbed. Jessica Harper (who played Phoenix) sang all her own material. I cast her because I thought she could really put a song across on-screen. I tested about 15 people and made screen tests for 10 before deciding.

CFQ: *You have a special credit for the wedding sequence. Could you explain why?*
DE PALMA: We wanted the wedding to look like a real rock concert, a kind of *Gimme Shelter* look, a bit chaotic. I wanted it all to be shot *cinema verite,* and I brought in some specialists to give me that style.

CFQ: *Were you thinking of Sly Stone's big to-do at the Garden?*
DE PALMA: But, of course, that came *after* I had shot my scenes [laughter]. Maybe he got the idea from me!

CFQ: *Was the film fully scripted? Did you use much improvisation?*
DE PALMA: It was all fully scripted. All script problems were worked out in rehearsal many weeks before we started shooting.

CFQ: *Since the film poses the entire history of rock music—from beginnings to glitter—as largely the work of the devil, have you gotten any feedback from the music industry?*
DE PALMA: For the most part, they don't like the film. They don't think it is grade A in any one category: Rolling Stones, Chuck Berry, The Beach Boys. This is what they look for. When you do Alice Cooper, they want Alice Cooper and they don't understand any variation of that form. It is a business

without much sense of humor about what they are and what they do. They don't understand that we are having fun with these forms. They also do not like the acerbic view into their world, although some of them do find it quite amusing.

CFQ: *The kinds of groups that have emerged recently—the style that you talk about in the latter section of the film—like Cooper or Mott the Hoople, is it really possible to satirize these people since they seem to be parodies of themselves right in their own acts?*

DE PALMA: It is not a matter of satire. I think the film tries to show what they're actually doing, in a kind of ironic sense. The thrust of that kind of rock is, I think, very serious. What are they conveying to the audience? What is it that they are performing? Why is the audience so taken with it? The film endeavors to show what this tells us about this whole culture. That it is obsessed with death, with destroying yourself, burning yourself up, consuming yourself for entertainment and amusement. That is what the film is about basically. I think it is a culture looking for bigger and better highs, whether it is nostalgia or reminiscing or Armageddon. It is whatever moves them, and the intensity of what moves them is being escalated all the time. It is a very de-sensitized, de-emotionalized culture. They have turned themselves off with drugs and detachment, and they're looking for things to make them feel alive.

CFQ: Privilege *a few years ago took it one step further into politics. Does that interest you?*

DE PALMA: I think that is a very tired concept, just because these people show up in large crowds, that they can be moved into some kind of politically viable movement. A film called *Wild in the Streets* dealt with that too. It's like some older guy's idea of what this culture is like. It's probably the most un-political group that ever existed. Politics is the last thing on their minds.

CFQ: *Did you plan anything for the film that you weren't able to shoot?*

DE PALMA: I had some very elaborate cinematic concepts for some of the numbers that I didn't hve enough time to shoot. The sets could have been bigger, more elaborate, more complicated. The set-ups could have been more intricate. It's all a function of time and money. We had tremendous pressures for time on this film, because we didn't have enough money. To work with what you have, you always compromise your conception to a certain extent. But I think about 80% of it is there.

The picture was, production-wise, a little bit disorganized, because of things we planned ahead that did not work out. But the life of the production evolves from the director, and if he has solid relationships with the key people around him, then that authority, knowledge, and belief in what he's doing goes right to the entire company. On *Phantom of the Paradise* we had everyone turning out for the rushes, even the grips and electricians, the guys who are always most cynical about the whole process, the technicians. They came to see if it looked good, the movements worked, if I was getting what I wanted, and everyone was contributing. I felt that my belief in the production was also being felt by them.

CFQ: *Your film came in for about $1.3 million. Fox plopped down $2 million for it, making it the highest price ever paid for an indie production. Were there others interested in it?*
DE PALMA: Everybody who saw it wanted to buy it, which is how we were able to get the price up. We had lots of bidding, with six studios involved.

CFQ: *Even the people who dislike the film have been floored by the* Psycho *shower reference. The plunger injects a huge surprise.*
DE PALMA: You're playing with a movie sensibility all the time. You set up your audience in one direction, then hit them in another, with the last thing they'd expect. The director always has to be a bit of a magician, pulling a cigarette out of the air or a rabbit out of a hat. It's like Welles says, it's an illusionary thing, you constantly have to surprise them.

CFQ: *You obviously get caught up in the thrill of manipulating your audience.*
DE PALMA: Absolutely. It's a great feeling.

CFQ: *You bring a lot of different horror film references into the film. I take it you are a fan?*
DE PALMA: Yes. I have always been a fan of the horror genre and also of German expressionism. *The Cabinet of Dr. Caligari* has been an influential movie for me. In *Phantom of the Paradise* I was trying to find a new way to enter that world. I thought the rock world is so stylized and expressionistic

to begin with, that it would be a perfect environment in which to tell old horror tales.

CFQ: *I like the bird imagery throughout the film. Is this a function of careful scripting or more of an outgrowth of your vision?*
DE PALMA: A little of both. You try to get your imagery and metaphors organized and let them play through the work. The image of the dead song bird is what the movie is all about. You start with it and end with it. The film is metaphorically consistant all the way through. It's good some people see these things. If you've read my raft of criticism on the film—good and bad—you'll see they've completely missed the underlying themes and metaphors. It makes one wonder what they're seeing up there on the screen.

CFQ: *Are you satisfied with Fox's handling of the film?*
DE PALMA: I think everyone made a big mistake here in New York, which is being rectified and the business will start to reflect it. The reason is that here we sold it to the rock and music audience. We originally used a piece of artwork which made everyone think it was some kind of rock or concert film, like *Gimme Shelter* or *Woodstock,* which is a big mistake. I went along with everyone else, thinking that would be its audience. But the truth is that the audience for it is a movie audience, and now the campaign is changed—we're now using the Phantom surrounded by his consoles—the word of mouth is getting out, and things are turning around for us. In Los Angeles we're a big smash and doing immense business. We got excellent reviews from everyone. Fox is projecting something like $30 million for it, and I think it will do that.

CFQ: *Do you concern yourself with criticism?*
DE PALMA: It does affect the business. I find that critics of my generation, people who have been brought up on film as something very basic, who are knowledgable about the making of movies or may have gone to film school, usually review my films very well. They know how to appreciate the films that are being made by their peers. But the older generation critics, in their 50s or late 40s, come from a whole other place, and you must suffer with their idiosyncratic, out-of-date ways of looking at movies. That's always been a problem with Establishment critics: they seldom see the innovative films as they happen. It is only years later when a kind of revisionism occurs. Look

how *Lolita* or *2001: A Space Odyssey* were treated when they opened. It's unbelievable.

CFQ: *At the end there is a song over a final montage of earlier scenes. Was this planned? It looks a bit tacked-on.*

DE PALMA· Because of time and money there was one song at the end that we couldn't shoot. It was to be done at Beef's graveside, where the record people are recording live as they're burying Beef. Also, I began to think that a number there might slow up the movie too much anyway, so I got to the point that I didn't really want to shoot it. Then I discovered that the ending was so strong and hard on an audience that I could use this song in another way to pull them out of this reality they had been exposed to by recapitulating characters and events. It makes them remember the lighter aspects of the movie and helps your audience bring itself out of the experience.

CFQ: *And the other ending wouldn't have satisfied you more?*

DE PALMA: You can expose a very searing reality. I don't think you necessarily have to brain people with it. Plus you want to get the people out of the theatre so they don't say, "What an ugly thing that was!" You help them remember all aspects of it. Also, it gives you a chance to show off your actors, give them some more time on screen so that people will get to know who they are. The song is also very ironic and serves as a comment on the whole experience. I thought it was effective.

Brian De Palma may have a problem with ending his films, but in this age of bandwagon auteurism, his films and film style seem all of a piece. Underneath their satire and fantasy, his movies are essentially serious forays into the problems, movement, feelings, moods and events of the time of filming. They are about television; De Palma often slyly forces us to sit in the theatre and watch television images. They are also consistently very funny, sometimes painfully so. De Palma has continually experimented with film form and new techniques. And he has also had consistently bad luck in getting his films, if made, then available to be seen.

CFQ: *You're from the same part of Philadelphia that gave us Fabian and Frankie Avalon?*

DE PALMA: And Richard Lester.

CFQ: *And you began making films at Columbia University?*
DE PALMA: Right, in the late '50s. I was interested in theatre first, because I had a way of approaching that. They were doing plays at Columbia and I had been doing skits and things in high school, so I knew something about it. I was much more of a scientist than an artist. I thought science, now *that* was something really important. I was brought up in the '50s when going to the moon was the most important thing man would ever have to do.

CFQ: *One of your first shorts was* Icarus.
DE PALMA: It's not a very good film. I had a whole bunch of ideas, and it's pretentious and slow and stupid in many ways, but it has some rather good things in it, too. It was a beginning, and you have to begin somewhere.

CFQ: *I read an interesting, kind of whacky interview you gave some years ago, in which you told of being disinherited, coming to New York and discovering its street life, working at Hamburger Heaven and the Village Gaslight, being shot by a cop on 13th Street . . .*
DE PALMA: Oh, yes. It's all true.

Woton's Wake, another short film made during the same period, is mainly a spoof of silent films and their stylized form of acting. It ends with a mushroom cloud, pre-dating several of the nuclear holocaust films of the mid-'60s. The film won for De Palma the Rosenthal Foundation award in 1963, and De Palma was described as "exemplifying an American talent that is unusually joyful as well as satirical."

DE PALMA: The prize was $1000, and that was nice. It was nice to get some recognition after making two shorts before that didn't get any notice. It gave me hope . . .

CFQ: *Soon after you began to try, unsuccessfully, to interest Universal in some script ideas. When did you decide to try and make it on your own?*
DE PALMA: In dealing with a studio you build up a certain amount of frustration because they don't pay much attention to you, especially when you are a nobody. You have to have that level escalated to the point where you'll

go out and get the money to make this movie if it kills you! And that's how you get a movie made.

CFQ: The Wedding Party *was your first feature. This was shot while you were doing graduate work at Sarah Lawrence?*
DE PALMA: Yes, the summer after. I did it with my teacher [Wilford Leach] and a girl [Cynthia Monroe] I was in class with. It has a lot of people in it whom I have since used: Bill Finley, Bob De Niro, Jennifer Salt, Jill Clayburgh, people who are now in the industry. We made it over a period of two years, but it was released only after *Greetings.*

CFQ: *It sounds like your most traditional film, as far as form is concerned.*
DE PALMA: No, not really. Technically, it is very bizarre, although it has a fairly conventional storyline. It is about a guy [Charles Pfluger] getting married and the wedding party involved with it. It's based on an experience I had when my best friend got married. But it's full of jump cuts and improvised scenes, fast forward action and slow motion. Of course, I edited the film so it has practically everything in it, as far as experimental techniques. We finally opened it ourselves in April 1969, four months after *Greetings.* It had a tiny run, about 6 weeks, got some nice reviews, and it died.

De Palma's second feature, *Murder à la Mod,* was actually his first film to be released, in May 1968 (also on the same program was Paul Bartel's *Secret Cinema*). It is the first film in which De Palma begins overtly to play with elements of the horror film. The movie is ostensibly a murder mystery, and it is filled with his now-usual flair for cinematics, including slow-motion, a film-within-a-film and title cards. One of its major characters is a sexpo filmmaker, a character (who also may appear as a producer or distributor) who will pop up in nearly all of De Palma's later movies.

DE PALMA: Basically, the idea is that we go through the same murder from three different points of view, the three principal characters. Each of the three sequences are shot in a different style to reflect the different natures and points of view of the same factors and events leading up to the murder. For instance, the girl who gets killed, her section is very much like a soap opera, because her life is like that. Then we go through the murder a second time, from the point of view of a guy, and we did that one like Hitchcock, very eerie, cinematic, suspenseful. The third one is done like a silent comedy because the character, a horror film actor [played by Bill Finley] is a deaf-mute. It's all action, gags, and pratfalls. The guy who was playing the exploitation film director was Jared Martin, who was my college roommate and was in several of my shorts. The sleazy producer of it was played by Ken Burrows, my own producer. [Pause] It's a rather weird movie. I just saw it recently.

CFQ: *Is* Murder à la Mod *resolved plotwise?*
DE PALMA: Yes. It ends with the discovery of who really did the crime. But it's so complicated stylistically that people get lost in it real fast. We had a two-week run with it in New York.

Released in December 1968, De Palma's third film was *Greetings,* a bold and brash blend of mania and anarchy. Made for about $44,000, it follows the adventures of three "heroes;" a draft-dodger (Jonathan Warden), a Kennedy assassination buff (Gerrit Graham) and a porno artist/filmmaker (Robert De Niro). The film seemed to take the critics by surprise. Many hated it, but some compared it to Beat Poetry in its rhythms and another coupled De Palma with Richard Lester as two kindred, wholly original filmmaking talents. *Greetings* was one of the earliest films to earn an "X" rating from the MPAA, and it eventually won a Silver Bear at the Berlin Film Festival in 1969. Most importantly, the film has come to stand for the '60s. Each of three main characters symbolize, or at least work through, the dominant themes of the era. With the hindsight of the seven years since its production, *Greetings* has acquired a double value, as a product of that popular (even Pop) culture and as an acerbic critique of it. The film, although successful, was not a commercial hit.

DE PALMA: I think the film stands up real well.

CFQ: *Were you surprised?*
DE PALMA: It's hard to say. I'm a bad person to judge because I have so many associations with it. It does still work quite well; I think it will probably be around for quite a while. As you say, I think it is the most accurate reflection of what was going down in that era, from middle class kids in college who were worried about the draft—I don't know anybody who actually

went, everybody dodged it in one way or another—and what they felt about what was going on around them: the liberalism of the time, the Kennedy assassination, the sexual liberalism, computer dating, and porno movies, all of that, I think, is reflected very accurately. It catches that feeling better than anything I know, the way it was shot, the free-wheeling-ness of it.

Seven months later, *Easy Rider* would be released (7/69), another shoestring-produced indie and greatly inferior to *Greetings*. And, unluckily for De Palma, *that* was the one that would become a blockbuster and start a whole new trend in Hollywood on which too many feeble talents rode to the major studios. De Palma moved on to an even more uncommercial project, the recording of a performance of the mythic play "Dionysus in 69," an environmental theatre piece based on Euripides' "The Bacchae" and done by Richard Schechner and the Performance Group. The finished film was conceived and completed entirely in split-screen, one side showing the play, the other the audience reaction and involvement It was completed more than a year before Wadleighs's *Woodstock,* often given credit for establishing the technique. *Dionysus in 69* was released on March 20, 1970, for a (forseen) small, and specialized audience.

DE PALMA: I was very strongly affected by the play when I saw it. Bill Finley had been playing Dionysus with the Group for some time. I came to see him and said, "God, this is incredible," environmental theatre, the way it affects the audience and draws them into the piece itself. This was the most exciting thing I'd seen on stage in years. So I began to try and figure out a way to capture it on film. I came up with the idea of split-screen, to be able to show the actual audience involvement, to trace the life of the audience and that of the play as they merge in and out of each other. I wanted to get the very stylized dramatic life of the play juxtaposed to what was really going down in that room at that time. I was floored by the emotional power of it. I shot one of the cameras and Bob Fiore the other. The editing took about a year, because I wanted to play with the different ways to use split-screen. I learned a lot and also about the kind of documentary realism that I would use later in *Hi, Mom!* and even in *Phantom of the Paradise.*

The thing about *Woodstock* . . . I feel that everything is for everybody to use. I do really feel that most of my films have been innovative technically, at least. Other directors are constantly interested in what I'm doing, where I'm going. I am always playing with film form and exposing new techniques.

CFQ: *Did you take the idea of filming it to Schechner?*

DE PALMA: Yes. I told him I thought it was an important work and should be preserved on some level, and that I *had* to find a way to hold this experience on film. He liked the idea, the Group liked the idea, and they allowed me to do it. I put up a lot of the money from my savings when I had been working for Filmways. I always feel that even though the film didn't make any money, it was something that should have been done. I think it will live long, *long* after some of my other movies.

Next was *Hi, Mom!,* which can be described, inadequately, as a sequel to *Greetings.* The film follows Jon (this time played by De Niro) as he returns from Vietnam and tries to slip back into the changed culture. Just as *Greetings* was '60s, *Hi, Mom!* looks to the '70s. It is darker in tone, more caustic and disorganized but again without losing any of the humor. The film cost just above $100,000.

DE PALMA: *Hi, Mom!* was so loose that we had to find a shape for it in the editing room. There were three sections to it: the spoof of educational television, the "N.I.T. Journal" which ended in the "Be Black, Baby" play; the "Housewife's Diary" where a woman [Lara Parker] kind of studies her life from the interior of a co-op; and the returned veteran who was a voyeur following it all about trying to make an exploitation film for Joe Banner [Allen Garfield]. Again, this is like *Murder à la Mod,* with three film realities weaving in and out of each other. This is something I've done in movie after movie, trying to find a way to make it work. Unfortunately, *Hi, Mom!* is too unintegrated; it doesn't work. Like *Greetings,* it is a contemporary statement of what was going on in my life and the lives around me at that period. The producer thought it was another *The Graduate* and opened it on Broadway. I tried to convince him it wasn't, but I lost the argument. The Loew's people thought it was going to make an immense amount of money. It just died in that big cavern of a theatre.

The extended section "Be Black, Baby"—a play within-a-film—takes the ideas in environmental theatre and turns them into a terrifying fantasy of power and rage. Suburban New York City white theatre patrons, off slumming at an Off-Broadway play, are hearded into a small theatre where they are given a taste of the black experience. The play's performers are blacks in whiteface; the whites are soon "blackened." They are degraded and molested, one is raped. The sequences are expertly controlled by De Palma; it ends with the patrons, having survived a harrowing ordeal, that we too have gone through, raving on their way to their taxis and limos about how "Clive Barnes was right!"

DE PALMA: From *Dionysus in 69* I had learned so much about the documentary reality of that type of theatre, so I wanted to show in *Hi, Mom!* how you can really involve an audience. You take an absurd premise—"Be Black, Baby"—and totally involve them and really frighten them at the same time. It's very Brechtian. You suck 'em in and annihilate 'em. Then you say, "It's just a movie, right? It's not real." It is just like television. You're sucked in all the time, and you're lied to in a very documentary-like setting. The "Be Black, Baby" section of *Hi, Mom!* is probably the most important piece of film I've ever done. It also ran away with the movie, destroyed the ending. It became so strong that nobody could go anywhere after that. That's what I tried to anticipate in *Phantom of the Paradise.* I have that "Clive Barnes" line in there, but it doesn't quite bring the movie audience back down. It's funny and ironic and biting, but they've been so emotionally affected that they don't like to be laughed at then.

The film ends with the blowing up of the co-op, a chance for De Palma to spoof *Zabriskie Point* (as he earlier did with *Blow-Up* in *Greetings*). Unfortunately for De Palma, the film opened (April 1970) just after the infamous Weathermen bomb factory on 11th Street blew up—one of the first acid tastes of the '70s for New York. Several critics mentioned it and almost seemed to blame the film for it. But De Palma had been there before.

DE PALMA: The older I get, the more visionary I think I'm becoming. A lot of my work seems to anticipate what's going to happen. With *Phantom of the Paradise,* I truly believe that ultimately, some rock singer is going to be assassinated on stage. I think it's just a matter of time.

*   *   *

The success of *Hi, Mom!* prompted Warner Bros. to entice De Palma to Holly-wood, where, as De Palma puts it, he "got gotten." The project was *Get to Know Your Rabbit,* written by Jordan Crittenden, to be directed by De Palma. It is a fairy tale/allegory about a meek market analyst, Tom Smothers, who drops out of the corporate life to become a tap dancing magician. He is taught the trade by Orson Welles and falls in love with Katherine Ross. He becomes successful, a corporation slowly grows up around him headed by his former boss John Astin, and he finds himself trapped again. As usual for De Palma, the film is loaded with social satire and crazy humor. Problems sprouted on all sides during production between, in differing combinations, the stars, producers, writers, Warner Bros. executives, and De Palma. He was finally not allowed to finish the film.

CFQ: *Warner Bros. originally planned the film as Tom Smothers's film debut?*
DE PALMA: Yes, and that caused problems. He was not a great actor, and he had at the time some psychological problems dealing with his career. He thought the film would change his career around. When he became con-vinced that the film was going down, just like his career, he rode it right to the bottom. And with me on the plane.

CFQ: *He didn't want it released at all?*
DE PALMA: Right. What was so lousy of him was that after promising me, siding with me on all the fights with the studio, in the end, when we wanted to reshoot some stuff, he refused. He said, "Anything you want to do, kid." He was unhappy with the film but he didn't have to lie to me. He said, "I'm going to fight for this, this is the way we're going to do it, it's a great ending, I love what you're doing with the film." Then he went in and stabbed me in the back. So the studio took it over. I will never forget talking to him on the phone and him telling me that.

CFQ: *Warner Bros. treated the film like a social disease.*
DE PALMA: It wasn't really their fault. They had a film that didn't work and had to release it anyway they knew how. They brought in a studio exec [Peter Nelson, a project coordinator] who shot about a day of inserts. They put it together using my concept basically, except for the ending, but the material isn't structured in any way.

CFQ: *What was your original ending?*

DE PALMA: My ending, that Warners would have nothing to do with, was that he tells Astin he wants to go back out on the road. And Astin says, "You're going to play the Big Time—New York, LA, Chicago . . ." Cut to Johnny Carson Show, and Smothers talking about how he's dropped out and his wonderful life. And there's an Abbie Hoffman type beside him who's just published *Eat The Establishment*. And he gets into a big argument with Smothers and accuses him of being a rip-off artist and that the TDM, the Tap Dancing Magician Corporation, is financed by banks and oil companies and he's just a whole new way of exploiting the counter culture. And Smothers is hurt because he's really believed in what he's done. Astin comes on to sell TDM products, and Smothers finally realizes that he's being ripped-off, being used to merchandise products. So he tells Johnny he wants to do a trick, the Great-Sawing-The-Rabbit-In-Half-Trick. Now, on coast-to-coast TV, it looks like he has just sawed his rabbit in half and failed. The rabbit is a bloody, horrible mess, and Smothers rushes off stage. Well, the whole TDM collapses because he's done the worst thing in America that you can do, he's maimed a warm furry animal on TV. He's ruined Astin, again. But he is finally left to his own devices; he's free because no one wants him now. Ross comes up and says "How could you do that? What happened?" And Smothers pulls out the rabbit and you realize it's been a trick. He has finally done a successful trick.

CFQ: *The film ends now with Smothers simply leaving again, with Ross, to go back on the road performing.*

DE PALMA: Yeah, there's no dramatic conflict there. He's not fighting anything. It's arbitrary—one day he's helping Astin with the new corporation, the TDM, and the next day he decides to leave.

CFQ: *It is some indication of the power you get making a Hollywood movie that you were able to get Orson Welles.*

DE PALMA: Oh, yes. Welles started the film as a chore. But he liked me and ultimately got involved with the character he was playing. I felt he gave a very good performance, and he was helpful with the conception of it. He also had many good ideas as far as the writing and directing were concerned.

CFQ: *One critic commented that you had too much of a New York sensibility to succeed with a film set in LA.*

DE PALMA: I believe I directed the material exactly the way it was conceived. I worked with the writer, he re-wrote many scenes and tried to make it work. It was basically his conception, his idea, and I directed it. I don't think anyone could have directed that material, as it was originally conceived, to make it work. Crittenden's idea was you have a very blank-faced character, funny and interesting and exciting things would happen around him, but he was like a reactor, one who smiled a lot. This is very undramatic; it looks great in rushes because you just see pieces of it. But when you string it together, it has no life. This was the conception I had to live with. While I was interpreting the material the way he wanted, we worked fine. But when I wanted to re-write and put in different scenes, then we got on opposite sides of the fence.

CFQ: *The film was trade reviewed in 6/72, but it only played here in 9/73.*
DE PALMA: It was the bottom half of a double-bill. What did they have to lose, they had the prints.

CFQ: *Nevertheless, the film did prompt Canby (NY Times) to say that you would "one day make a really fine American comedy."*
DE PALMA: This is what is so surprising. I thought he would see *Phantom of the Paradise* as that!

CFQ: *How do you look back on the whole experience?*
DE PALMA: Now, it's very instructive; then, it was disastrous. In Hollywood you set the perimeters for your own destruction. I learned what I couldn't control and what I could. I learned you can't overcome certain things that you are strapped with right from the beginning. You can work within the system if you have a strong enough power base and can control all the elements around you. Like Coppola. With that kind of box-office power, Hollywood will let him do practically anything he wants. But if those elements control you, then you're the victim, and ultimately it will effect your work.

CFQ: *Right from the start, you have always said you are not afraid of doing a big, commercial film or being charged with "selling out."*
DE PALMA: Well, what is a "commercial" film? I think people have very stereotyped ideas about it. Are you making this film because it is commercial

or because it is personal expression, and that personal films necessarily are not commercial. It's not as simple as that. I would like to make a film that people like to go to see. So does Fellini, and that doesn't make him "commercial: and not an artist.

You're not dealing with some vulgarian who says, "If we put a nude woman in this scene, we'll gross $100,000 more." You never get in a situation like that. Sometimes you do feel pressures. But if somebody employs a director, for the most part, they will let him have his way, because he's the only one who knows what's going on and can make the movie. If you work in independent production, you get completely to do what you want to do, within the resources you have to work with.

It's good to have people come and see your movies; that means you're touching something in them. It doesn't mean you have to pander to them. At the same time, you have to make films that mean a lot to you, and hopefully they'll mean a lot to others. All great forms of art do that.

De Palma became an independent again with his seventh film, *Sisters*. It went into general release during the summer of 1973 by AIP.

CFQ: *Sisters* was more tightly scripted than your previous movies.
DE PALMA: I think that is a matter of my own personal evolvement. I had made these very structurally loose movies and seen the strengths and weaknesses of them. In *Sisters,* I made a very conscious attempt to make a unified, structurally consistent movie that worked beginning, middle and end. Even though it had some strange stylistic places in it, it nevertheless told a story with characters who went from A to B to C and so on. None of the parts of the film ran away with it. Every shot, every set-up, every thought I have about the material I'm photographing is all carefully worked out. It's all plotted on a large graph that circles my office. I think about it for months and months, move things around, trying to put all the pieces together, which is very much like Hitchcock works. I have a very strong visual conception, and each scene plays in relationship to the others, each image works in relationship to the others.

CFQ: *How much rehearsal was done on it?*
DE PALMA: About a month. I always rehearse material to make sure it works before I think about how I'm going to shoot it. If the story works, the

dramatic flow works, *then* you can think about implementing visual conceptions.

CFQ: *I understand Ray Stark originally bought this project for Raquel Welch?*
DE PALMA: He suggested her to me, once. He bought it because he wanted to make a film with me, and he liked the material. I also wrote *Phantom of the Paradise* for him at that time, but we could never agree on the script so I had to buy it back.

CFQ: *Although there is a lot of comedy in it, it is your first straight horror film.*
DE PALMA: Suspense, I think, rather than horror.

CFQ: *Even though the killings were bloodier than most people will tolerate in a suspense film?*
DE PALMA: Really? You probably know more about this than I do. My father is an orthopedic surgeon, so I have a high tolerance for blood, gore, I guess you'd call it. I've seen my father amputate legs and open people up. So I was used to it at a young age. I tempered that a bit in *Phantom of the Paradise,* in the final cut. I had originally included a longer look at Finley's face, all bloody and steaming, after he came off the record press. But I thought it was too excessive for the movie.

CFQ: *Do you particularly like to do effects like that?*
DE PALMA: I think if you're going to shock an audience, you must expose them to some violence. You can't pull your punches.

CFQ: *You use references to* Rear Window, Repulsion, The Man Who Knew Too Much, Psycho, Vertigo . . .
DE PALMA: Yeah, there are a lot of good ideas in there; they're worth using again.

CFQ: *Did you think with* Sisters *that people would accuse you of simply ripping-off Hitchcock?*
DE PALMA: It doesn't bother me. It's a very eclectic profession, and you draw from whatever sources you can. You can re-interpret good material in different ways, into your own framework. If you have a style of your own

and individuality, you'll take good things from other people and make them better. Great artists have done it, and it sure doesn't scare me.

CFQ: *Do you sketch ideas, like Hitchcock?*
DE PALMA: Yes, very thoroughly. Every set-up.

CFQ: *You had distribution problems again with* Sisters; *at least, it wasn't seen here for quite a while.*
DE PALMA: They went right for the drive-ins, and it played all summer. It was very successful there. Of course, it would be great to have your movie playing in New York for nine months. A lot of movies do that, like *Mean Streets,* and have done no business outside of it. The bottom line is that your movie's got to do business, you have to get audiences in to see it, even if you have to go out of town, to drive-ins, to do it. As long as they show up. It depends on how fragile your ego is. All the good reviews in the world and all the support of the NY audience, and everyone in this town thinking you're wonderful, may not mean anything outside the perimeter of the city. I've made enough films now that it's nice if people come up to me and know me by the movies I've made.

CFQ: *Do you think there are any significant films being made in the genre today?*
DE PALMA: Well, *2001* is the most important, I guess. I think *Zardoz* represents everything bad about the genre; it's pretentious, labored and basically unappealing on most levels. *The Exorcist* is not a very good movie, it's not very well done. I really feel that Kubrick is the only one who has successfully worked in science fiction. He's a real expressionistic director. Very few directors know how to make it work, that when you create another world you have to have strong roots in reality in order to touch an audience, because they're dealing with fantasyland. You'd better be able to draw parallels and emotions an audience can identify with, or else you'll have a netherworld they can only intellectually identify with and have no emotional feelings about.

CFQ: *What filmmakers do you enjoy watching?*
DE PALMA: Hitchcock, Kubrick, Coppola, Lucas, Scorsese, Spielberg . . . Fellini . . . Buñuel . . .

CFQ: *Are you familiar with Pauline Kael's article a few months ago about direc-tors vs. the present distribution system and the possibility of directors distributing their own films?*

DE PALMA: There is an expertise in the selling and exploiting of a picture that a major company has, like Warners or Paramount. AIP certainly knows how to sell the kind of product they create. Better than anyone else. Now to go in there and say you know how to find the audience for your picture is a little naive. You're simply not in touch with the ground floor of exhibitors and audiences. You live your life basically in New York or California and are unaware of what's going on elsewhere across the country. Same with Europe. It's a little presumptuous to feel you know how to sell it better than anyone else. If you have some control, you have a little influence in the selling of it. You get your ideas aired, some may be implemented, that to me is enough. I don't think the present companies necessarily rip you off, although in real-ity, I've never seen any of the profits from my films. Of course, I've never really had a big success, so it's hard to tell. When I make a movie that makes $30 million, and I get a check for $500, *then* I'll ask, "Hey, what happened here?"

CFQ: *Would you give Hollywood another fling if* Phantom of the Paradise *is a hit?*

DE PALMA: Nothing wrong with Hollywood. *If* you're in a position to con-trol your destiny, it's the greatest place in the world.

CFQ: *Many critics consider your movies as downers. Do you consider your view of life pessimistic rather than optimistic?*

DE PALMA: Yeah, I guess so. I usually show the underbelly of the kind of "up" side of everybody else, because I myself have had such a struggle and tried desperately to get unique conceptions done on the screen. And fought tooth-and-nail all the way through only to see them badly received or not opened at all and forgotten. I've yet to be recognized for what my talent is; I have a certain coterie of people, but I have yet to break through in any kind of big way. Even that, though, can be phony. Worse than being dead is being hot, because all these people come out of the woodwork and fall all over you. That is *dreadful*. I'm very suspicious of that.

Everything I do and feel is in my movies. I could leave this apartment tomorrow and never think about it twice—there's no personal part of me here. My view of the world is ironic, bitter, acid, but basically funny, too. I'm a real gallows humorist, I see something funny in the most grim circumstances. Like the line in *Phantom of the Paradise* about coast-to-coast assassinations as real entertainment, and it's *true*. The Kennedy assassination is probably the most entertaining thing I ever saw. It riveted me, held me emotionally, and I watched the television set for days and days, and that is entertainment on a scale that no one could ever come up with. That's what I think the rock world is all about; a world of people killing themselves, consuming themselves, in front of you, and you're sitting there applauding, "Jesus, do it better, do it bigger!"

De Palma Has the Power!

MIKE CHILDS AND ALAN JONES / 1977

MIKE CHILDS AND ALAN JONES interviewed Brian De Palma in London during his visit there for the opening of *Carrie*. De Palma had been attempting to reconcile our request for an interview with his busy schedule and managed the trick by conducting the interview in his limousine on the way to the Heathrow airport to catch a flight to Paris where *Obsession* and a delayed release of *Sisters* were about to open.

Carrie has proven to be De Palma's biggest commercial and critical success to date. Like his work in *Sisters,* the film infuses a new vitality into the horror film genre just when it seemed to become stuck in another repetitive groove—possession and exorcism *ad nauseum.* But the film also garnered the prestige of two Academy Award nominations for the performances of Sissy Spacek and Piper Laurie.

Q: *How did you first get involved with* Carrie?
A: I read the book. It was suggested to me by a writer friend of mine. A writer friend of his, Stephen King, had written it. I guess this was almost two years ago [circa 1975]. I liked it a lot and proceeded to call my agent to find out who owned it. I found out that nobody had bought it yet. A lot of studios were considering it, so I called around to some of the people I knew and said it was a terrific book and I'm very interested in doing it. Then nothing happened for, I guess, six months. When I sold *Phantom of the Paradise* to Fox I found out that they had in fact bought it for producer Paul Monash who had

From *Cinefantastique* 6:1 (1977): 5–12. Reprinted by permission of the authors.

a multi-film deal with the studio. I met him and told him what I had in mind and that I wanted to do it. He listened to me, but nothing happened for another six months because somebody was writing a script from it—some lady from Texas had done the first draft. Then I heard from George Litto, my producer on *Obsession,* that the producer for *Carrie* had called him and asked how I was and how I'd worked with him. George and I had struck up a good relationship on *Obsession.* Now the *Carrie* project was in the hands of United Artists, and the head of production, Mike Medavoy, and the president, Eric Pleskow, were emphatic that they wanted me to direct the film. They didn't think it should be made by anyone else. Paul Monash, however, was not sold on me and it was only because of pressure brought about by the studio people that he came around to thinking that maybe I was the right person for his film. So that's how I came to direct *Carrie*!

Q : *Did you ever have anyone else in mind other than Sissy Spacek for the title role?*
A : Yes. As a matter of fact, I had another lady in mind and had always felt that she would be the ideal person to play the part. Sissy read the book and liked it quite a lot and mentioned to me that she would be interested in playing the part. I knew Sissy quite well because she's Jack Fisk's wife, and Jack has designed a lot of pictures for me. Sissy came in to try it out, and of course she was quite good. She played all the parts—she played Sue Snell, Chris Hargenson, Carrie. She played everybody—and played them all really well—and I was sort of keeping her in the back of my mind, but I was still very much oriented towards this other girl. Then when we finally had our screen tests Sissy tested for the part of Carrie, and made everyone else look silly.

Q : *You won't tell us who the other actress was?*
A : It was . . . It'll come to me . . . [It doesn't.]

Q : *Why did you cast Piper Laurie, when she hadn't worked for so long?*
A : Piper Laurie was suggested to me by an executive at United Artists who lived close to Piper in Woodstock, New York. He told me Piper was interested in acting again and this would be a very good part for her to play. I said fine, I thought she was quite good in *The Hustler* and would like to meet her. So when I came to New York I met Piper and she came in looking like Margaret

White with this red hair and black outfit and I said "My God! This is it!" I liked the idea of making Margaret White very beautiful and sexual, instead of the usual dried-up old crone at the top of the hill.

Q: *Amy Irving's real mother played Sue Snell's mother in* Carrie. *Any particular reason?*
A: I've done this before in *Sisters*. Jennifer Salt's real mother, Mary Davenport, plays her mother and Amy sort of suggested this to me. I knew her mother, Priscilla Pointer, was an actress, 'cause I was familiar with the stuff she did when they were part of San Francisco Repertory, when I met Priscilla. She was ideal for the part and there's something about mothers and daughters playing scenes together that takes on a reality, like a documentary reality, expecially with the relationship between mother and daughter. They've had so many scenes together that suddenly the scenes they play in a movie have the authenticity of twenty years of a relationship that's hard to manufacture by anyone else.

Q: *Did you cast John Travolta because of his popularity on* Welcome Back Kotter?
A: No. I cast him before that. In fact, I never saw that series. He doesn't have a big part in *Carrie*. But John was always the best for the role. He helped immensely. He was very cooperative, very helpful.

Q: *You tried to put across the timelessness of the high school prom.*
A: Yes. I did a lot of research about proms, having remembered my own. They're very much the same as they were. They haven't changed. The Senior Prom is the Senior Prom—it's still the big dance of the year and who's-with-who! I went to a few recently to check out to see if they had changed much—and they hadn't at all. A prom is like your first sexual experience. It never changes. In 1980 or 2001 we'll still be having puberty, adolescence, young manhood.

Q: *It's the same with the actual prom song, by Pino Donaggio.*
A: Pino Donaggio wrote the score for *Don't Look Now.* I was put on to him by a good friend of mine, the *Time* magazine film critic Jay Cocks, who had always liked his music and suggested him to me when Bernard Herrmann unfortunately passed away and I was looking for another composer. I lis-

tened to his records and talked it over with him and felt he was the right kind of combination.

Q: *Margaret White's crucifixion scene has a direct lift from* Psycho *underlying it. Is this part of a tribute to Herrmann?*

A: When we originally put temporary music tracks on the film, we used a lot of Herrmann's music. You know, when you show a film without any music you put in what you think is appropriate for the scene. We first used some of *Sisters,* then *Psycho,* and in the sinking of the house we used some of *Journey to the Center of the Earth.* A whole pastiche of Herrmann. In the end, we used a very famous Italian piece of music for the processional walk to the grave—Albinoni I think it was—a very beautiful piece of music. Then when the hand comes up we cut back to *Sisters.* I think Pino was definitely influenced by *Sisters.* The flexing sound is very *Psycho.* I put in a temporary track and for all the flexes I put in a *Psycho* violin. We couldn't find the right sound, but anyway, it worked. Bernard came up with it, and Bernard, I'm glad we used it again!

He'll probably be very unhappy—he hated listening to his music being played against other films. When he first came to look at *Sisters* I put his music in it all the way through—you know, *Vertigo, Psycho, Marnie* and whatever else I had. He heard it, and went into a rage! "Turn it off, turn it off!" "But Mr. Herrmann . . ." "Turn it off! How can you play that while I'm listening to the film. I don't want to listen to that—oh, don't do that!" He didn't want to hear his music played with the wrong movie. When he first saw *Obsession* he said, "It's a great movie and I can hear the score." He was looking at it and he heard the music in his head.

Q: *The music is brilliant. You obviously admired him a lot.*

A: He was a great man. I loved him. He had a terrible temper. I hope he'll forgive me for using his violins, but they're very effective.

Q: *Is Wendy Bartel, your production secretary on* Carrie, *any relation to Paul, the director?*

A: Yes. She's his sister. She's a very good production secretary. I'd seen her working with Paul at New World Pictures and I got to know her and hired her away from New World. She's very good.

Q : Variety *calls* Carrie *"camp." Any comment?*
A : God, they're still using "camp?" The terminology of ancient persons. . . .
No, I don't think it's camp at all. It keeps very seriously within the realm of
its own world. It has a very adolescent reality and it's very true to it.

Q : *Unlike the novel, Carrie's telekinesis was basically played down in the film.
Why?*
A : I felt the telekinesis was basically a device to trick, and I wanted to use it
as an extension of her emotions—her feelings that were completely trans-
lated into actions, that only erupted when she got terribly excited, terribly
anxious and terribly sad. It was always a little out of control, almost like
Forbidden Planet where the Id monster is an intellectual man murdering people because he subconsciously wants to. I never wanted to use it arbitrarily,
floating stuff around. In a movie that's kind of boring. Okay, she moves
objects. As soon as you've established that, I don't think you can do anymore
with it. Just use it when it's needed and dramatically valid. To play with it,
to me, would be very boring and ultimately it has to do with credibility. If
you do it too much people will say "Come on!" In the cinema it's a trick: "Oh
yeah, they put wires on the lamp and that's why it floats through the air!"
You never want to get the audience to be so analytical and disassemble the
trick. I only ever wanted to use it as an emotional expression of her passions.

Q : *Gregory M. Auer did the special effects for* Carrie. *You used him for* Phantom
of the Paradise, *too.*
A : He's very good. He's a nuts-and-bolts kind of guy . . . very soft spoken.
He used to work for Disney. Special effects are like blind faith—you have to
tell your man what you want to do, and hope to God when you get there
he's figured out how to do it. Otherwise, you get the situation like in *Jaws*
where the shark doesn't work—and if you wait six years maybe it will work!
I was terribly worried about the special effects as I was on a very tight
schedule.

Q : *How much did* Carrie *cost?*
A : $1.8 million. A fifty-day shooting schedule. Everything worked—except
in the book stones hit the house. We had this conveyor-belt with rocks on it
going up and pelting the house. The house that collapses was built to half
scale. Jack Fisk designed it and did a very good job. It's very convincing. This

was the last shot of the film and it's four o'clock in the morning. We had this conveyor-belt and we had fires planted and the house ready to collapse, and the conveyor-belt started and rocks got jammed in it. The rocks were too heavy. Well, it's late already, and the sun's coming up. Everybody's been up all night and the police are arriving due to the noise—they nearly arrested us! So we just went ahead and burned the house up and let it fly apart and sink into the earth. We thought, "Oh well . . ." and went home really depressed. But when we looked at it, it looked great—terrific! "Forget about the rocks!"

Q: *Did the extended slow-motion Prom scene present any problems?*
A: I felt it was a very audacious step to try and shoot that kind of suspense in slow-motion. I had to make a choice to do it or not to do it. So I chose to do it, and hoped to God it would work out! I really wanted to stretch the suspense scene out for as long as I could.

Cutting slow-motion is very tricky—there is a whole different pace to it. It took us weeks and weeks to figure it out, to get the right cutting rhythm. Your editor has to get into the whole slow-motion form. It's really interesting.

The shower scene I always wanted to shoot in slow-motion. I wanted to get involved in this lyrical eroticism before the blood comes, and it's all wonderful, beautiful . . . the steam, Carrie's touching herself . . . and then *wham*! As soon as you cut from slow-motion to regular motion you're already in a jolt, because you're so used to the time sense. But I'd say the trickiest section was the Prom.

The other tricky one was the split-screen sequence. I felt the destruction had to be shown in split-screen, because how many times could you cut from Carrie to things moving around? You can overdo that. It's a dead cinematic device. So I thought I'd do it in split screen. I spent six weeks myself cutting it together. I had one hundred and fifty set-ups, trying to get this thing together. I put it all together and it lasted five minutes and it was just too complicated. Also, you lost a lot of visceral punch from full-screen action. Then my editor and I proceeded to pull out of the split-screen and use it just when we precisely needed it. Each time I use split-screen I continue to learn more and more about it. This worked some ways, but didn't work others. It's the one thing that makes me think everytime I look at the movie and say, "Well, maybe I didn't make the right choice there . . ."

Q : *Sex is kept very low-key in your movies.*
A : I used it well in *Carrie* without going over the top. Straight sex scenes are very hard to shoot because it's been so exploited and shot from fifty different ways. I mean, how many times can you show people getting into bed with each other—what is there to shoot?

Q : *How did you feel about the ending of* Obsession? *Are we to question Cliff Robertson's consequences? The ending is a happy one of sorts, but will he suffer even though LaSalle's murder was in self-defense?*
A : He'd suffered too much anyway; it doesn't matter. Paul Schrader's ending actually went on for another act of obsession. I felt it was much too complicated and wouldn't sustain, so I abbreviated it. Robertson is arrested at the airport and goes into a mental institution for ten years. He gets out, grabs a gun and goes to Florence, goes in the same church, *again* Genevieve Bujold is there! But she doesn't recognize him as she's been in a catatonic state since her attempted suicide. The nuns at the clinic she's in want to try out a new form of hypnotherapy in which they re-enact the kidnapping a *third* time! Bujold thinks it's the first, and Robertson thinks it's the second . . . and it's then she says "Daddy, daddy . . ." as Robertson opens the suitcase with the money finally in the right place. It was an interesting sequence, but it just wouldn't have worked. It made Schrader very unhappy: he thought I'd truncated his masterpiece. He's never been the same since.

Q : *Was this before Schrader wrote* Taxi Driver?
A : No. *Taxi Driver* was written before this, but *Obsession* was shot first.

Q : *When you look back on* Phantom of the Paradise, *can you see why it was the commercial flop it was?*
A : The picture played well in Los Angeles, but not in New York. It did badly in England, but well in France. When we revised the campaign in the U.S. and made it seem more like *The Phantom of the Opera* than a horror/rock film, we got an entirely different response. I think the movie works. It was a very good idea.

I've always thought rock and horror were very close stylistically. I felt I had a solution in combining two separate audiences. Obviously, I didn't. When you look at a film like *Tommy* the audience turned out in force, but in fact the rock in that movie was bad. Divorced from the film the album sounds awful. People went to see images put to music they'd been listening to for years. It was the same with *Jesus Christ Superstar* and *Godspell*. I still think *Phantom of the Paradise* was an excellent idea. It just wasn't sold correctly. The emphasis should have been on a fantastic horror film. I enjoy it. It's one of my personal favorite films!

Perhaps *Phantom of the Paradise* would work better as a play. Horror theatre is something that hasn't been properly explored. People really get scared by things happening on stage more than on film. Horror movies yes, but why no horror plays?

Q: *Give us your views on explicit horror, in the vein of* The Texas Chainsaw Massacre?
A: I haven't seen that. I must see it. I've heard so much about it. I guess I'm getting really disturbed by the fact that movies are getting so cruel and crude—stabbings and choppings—but it's all terrain that's been explored before, and unless you invoke it in a different way a good idea is going to look like all the other stuff that's around.

Q: *Why is* Sisters *only opening now in Paris?*
A: We didn't sell it to all territories at the time of release, and what with interest in *Obsession,* people want to know what else I've done.

Q: *How is your work on* The Demolished Man *progressing?*
A: It's coming together very well. Let's hope in the next ten years I'm going to get it made! Murder in a telepathic society is telling everything in visual terms. I'm going to have to come up with a whole new language for this, which is really exciting. I read the first treatment in '65. I wrote a screenplay in '74. Now I'm rewriting my screenplay in '77. Maybe before I die I'll make this film!

It's somewhat akin to what I'm working on now, a film called *The Furies* for 20th Century-Fox. It concerns a telepathic boy and girl who are involved in some sort of elaborate CIA plot. It's a political thriller with telepathy in it.

Q: *Do you want to remain in the horror genre or not?*
A: I've made so many films and people still keep saying "The Horror Genre." They never seem like horror films to me! Horror films are "Hammer Films!"—vampires and Frankenstein. I love those pictures, but I don't feel

it's exactly what I'm doing. Maybe I'm trying to hammer out a new genre, somehow . . .

Q : *Well give it a name and people will use it!*
A : Yes . . . Hitchcock did it. I don't know what people called it before they coined "Hitchcockian?" They must have had some dimestore novel name for it. You never know . . . De Palmian?!?

Brian De Palma Discusses *The Fury*

PAUL MANDELL/1978

THIRTY-SEVEN-YEAR-OLD Brian De Palma is again back in New York City where he lives a relatively normal life far from the madding crowd of Hollywood. Beside a cigarette-littered ashtray on a table in his modestly furnished Fifth Avenue apartment sits a $50 portable typewriter with a piece of paper rolled through the carriage. On that paper are fragments of ideas for a new project, bits and pieces of a script that will gradually fall into place. Eventually he'll take it back to Tinseltown, show it to the film factories, and some day return to New York again with his imaginings realized on celluloid. "The great disadvantage of living in Hollywood is that you can lose your sense of what you are. Also, I don't think you know the audience you're dealing with unless you get out, walk around, and talk to people outside the industry. It's the only way to get some grasp on why things work and don't work."

One thing that seems to be working is his new film, *The Fury*. The critics appear to like it, and so does De Palma. And as far as he's concerned, the latter's opinion is what really counts.

The Fury is "pure De Palma," only this time lavishly mounted, starts off on location in Israel, and the marquee sports heavyweight names like Kirk Douglas and John Cassavetes. But typical of a De Palma film, there are no holds barred in the more sanguinary sequences. And the finale is literally a mind-blower.

So while *The Fury* is somewhat of a departure from his usual style, the

From *Filmmakers Newsletter*, May 1978: 26–31. Reprinted by permission of the author.

basic elements are still there. Instead of laying out a logical structure in which all the pieces fit neatly in place, De Palma likes to confuse you, leave a lot of loose ends hanging, even throw you into a dreamlike netherworld. "I like to make very stylized setpieces and use them to get you into a whole surrealistic or expressionistic world."

What kind of a guy is this who brews up such bizarre films? I kept thinking as I crossed Washington Square Park one brisk New York morning and headed towards De Palma's apartment building. "I've lived in empty places all my life," I recalled him saying once in an interview. "I don't care where I live or what I look like." Mmmm. I remembered reading how he spent his high school years designing computers and dreaming of going to the moon. I also remembered reading that he had been disinherited; had worked at a Greenwich Village bistro, the Village Gaslight; and had caught a bullet from the NYPD at the age of 23. Mmmm. I rang the bell.

At the door appeared a pleasantly mellow-looking fellow, tall with a short beard. "Sit down and relax," he said as he disappeared into another room. The furniture was quite sparse. "I've never had an interest in anything material," he once said. "I've always found it difficult to buy things. I'm just very bored by the process of going into a store. In fact, it makes me quite uncomfortable." Lining the walls were glass-framed posters of his films. A neon candelabra spelling out *Phantom of the Paradise* blinked at me from a corner of the room.

A photographer from *Us* magazine was also there with his battery of lights and motor-driven Nikon. Brian and I sat at a circular table and somehow communicated between camera clicks . . .

PAUL MANDELL: *What made you decide to film* The Fury?

BRIAN DE PALMA: After *Carrie* I was trying to have several of my projects financed and I was running into some problems. Then one evening I took Jill Clayburgh to see the opening of *Silver Streak* and afterwards to a big bash at the Tavern On The Green. Among those sitting at our table were Frank Yablans and Alan Ladd, Jr. Frank mentioned he was working on a script with a writer named John Farris. It was called "The Fury" and he thought I'd probably be interested in it.

The next day my agent, who it so happens also represents John Farris, sent me the script. I read it and liked it. I saw in it some elements I could extend from *Carrie*, and also liked *The French Connection, Three Days of the Condor* element in it—the cat-and-mouse game with agents chasing each other, big stunts, and elaborate special effects sequences. So I called Frank, told him I liked it, and we sat down and went to work on it.

P M :   The Fury *has two basic themes, espionage and psychic phenomena. Do you think they blend well in the film?*
B D P :   I think it was an interesting mixture of genres. We'll have to see how well it blends together. I like the Kirk Douglas-John Cassavetes "man against man" element and the interweaving of all those story lines in the script. I've never dealt with that before. In fact, I don't think it's ever been done.

P M :   *John Farris wrote the novel and the script. What did you contribute to the screenplay?*
B D P :   I changed some of the dialogue, that's all. One scene was completely improvised: where the two girls are talking at the table and suddenly one's nose starts to bleed. That was a fake nose, by the way, with tiny tubes inside through which "blood" was released.

P M :   *Do you enjoy showing a lot of blood on the screen?*
B D P :   I use blood when it's effective—in other words, in the right place at the right time. The reason it's so effective in *The Fury* is because it happens at strong dramatic moments which viscerally affect the audience. Then again, it's all a matter of how well your audience is set up for it. I'm used to that sort of thing; my father was an orthopedic surgeon and I saw a lot of operations, corpses, limbs, and various body parts hanging around. That influenced me in the sense that I have a very high tolerance for blood. Things that shock other people don't shock me.

P M :   *Are you bothered about the way the color of blood comes off on the screen? At times it seems to look more like tempera paint.*
B D P :   I guess it's all a matter of what you consider looks real and what looks stylized. In *The Fury* I wanted it to be vivid and red. It's obviously redder than what real blood looks like, but that's the effect I wanted. Take a film like *Taxi Driver*. There was so much blood in it they were afraid they were going to get an X rating so they toned it down to a sepia color. I was there when they were timing that sequence. Martin Scorsese wanted a sort of *Daily News* look for it—you know, the look of a gangland killing in a barbershop. Then he

had to pull out the color because he was afraid of getting the X. Sometimes you just don't have any choice in the matter.

P M :   *Most of your films deal with bizarre types of family relationships. Is this any kind of personal statement?*
B D P :   To some extent, yes. The type of manipulation which occurs in familial situations in my movies is the same kind which occurs in the early years of our lives. At least that's what I perceived in my family—a certain amount of manipulation by various family members.

P M :   *Like Hitchcock, manipulation is very much a part of your style.*
B D P :   I really like seeing an audience respond in a visceral way. It gives you a real sense of satisfaction to know you've emotionally caught up your audience. The thing is, when you're effective at what you're doing, you are always accused of manipulating your audience. But I'm not cynical enough yet to feel you can push buttons and know exactly how people are going to respond. If you could do that, everybody in the business would be a lot richer.

P M :   *Other than Hitchcock, what other directors have influenced you?*
B D P :   Stanley Kubrick, George Lucas, and Jean Luc Godard, along with documentary filmmakers like the Maysles.

P M :   *How much did* The Fury *cost?*
B D P : $5.5 million.

P M :   *Was there much studio interference?*
B D P :   Making this picture was good in that sense because I was shielded from any studio interference by Frank Yablans; he handled them very well. They liked the script, liked the rushes, came to see a rough cut, made a few suggestions, and that was about it.

P M :   *Do you have any particular interest in ESP, telekinesis, or the like?*
B D P :   No. I only like to explore that idea because it lets me get into surrealism and expressionism. When you're dealing with the interior of someone's mind, you can do all kinds of stylized things. And that's a form I'm drawn to.

PM: *You used Richard Kline as your DP. How did you choose him?*

BDP: He was available (he had just finished *Dog Soldiers*). I talked to a lot of people about him, got a few recommendations, and liked the way he had lit some of his films. So we sat down, looked at the book, decided what kind of filming style we wanted to use, and then did it. And we worked together quite well.

PM: *Did you have Kirk Douglas in mind for the lead from the outset?*

BDP: I like Kirk Douglas and I've also liked a lot of his films, although in the last couple of years he's been in some not-so-hot ones. I wanted the kind of driven, obsessive character he plays so well. At one point I said to Frank Yablans, "We need a Kirk Douglas type." And he said, "Why don't we get Kirk Douglas?" Kirk had worked with Frank at Paramount before, so the next thing I knew I was talking to him on the phone. Kirk was great! He has a lot of experience and he brings all those years of movie-making to your film.

PM: *Why did you pick John Cassavetes as the heavy?*

BDP: I picked him because John happens to play a sinister guy really well. The trouble with movies like this is the risk of falling into terrible clichés of heavies and heroes. But John is such a good actor, he has a way of turning even a cliché into a style all his own. He wasn't just another guy in a black suit with his arm in a sling.

PM: *Amy's flashback on the staircase with Durning was very effective. Was that a rear process shot?*

BDP: Yes, I used back projection. I was shooting a lot of process and the idea of using it for a flashback came to mind. My first idea was to have the camera move in a 360 degree circle, something like what Hitchcock did in *Vertigo*, but then I realized there was the problem of holding focus on both characters: you couldn't have Durning in slow motion and Amy in regular motion. Then I got the really bright idea of doing it in process, and it worked out quite well.

PM: *How about that beautiful dissolve from day to night taken from a high elevation?*

BDP: That was taken from the observation tower of a building in Chicago. Originally the shot was to have been done at an airport, but I was up on top of this building having a drink with someone and I happened to look out the window and see the view. I immediately called Frank and said, "This is incredible! There's a whole city down there!" But our scheduling was so tight I couldn't do the shot personally. My second unit cameraman Frank Fox was running around shooting a lot of location stuff and I told him to lock the camera off on the observation deck, let the car come up to the parking lot, zoom back to show the Chicago skyline, then sit around for six hours and wait for the sun to come up. It's the kind of shot you've seen done many different ways in many different films; but what made this so effective was the subtlety of this pathetic little truck with the characters inside right in the middle of this huge city. We also had to do some tests to make it work because the observation glass John was shooting through was tinted green so we had to do some color correction.

P M : *Does your editor control the flow of the sequence, or do you lay it all out shot for shot and use the editor in a basically mechanical role?*
B D P : Paul Hirsch is my editor, and we've done six pictures together. When he first worked on *Hi, Mom!* I almost marked the film; but as we progress from picture to picture he almost knows exactly what I have in mind. When he gets the footage back he knows my storyboards and lays it out just like that. So now I leave him alone most of the time.

P M : *I was a bit disappointed with the ferris wheel sequence. I thought it would have been much more dramatic had you intercut some close-ups of the passengers clinging for their lives—as Hitchcock did on the carousel in* Strangers on a Train. *Did you ever consider doing something like that?*
B D P : To me the ferris wheel was very much a throwaway sequence. There were so many disasters and major crises in this picture I decided to simplify the ferris wheel scene and not mount it as a major setpiece. Whenever something is too excruciating or extraordinary, it affects whatever scenes come after it. Also, you can't keep topping yourself; you run out of steam. So I wanted to get that sequence over with as fast as possible without pulling out every stop.

P M : *You really seem to be into slow motion these days.*
B D P : Yes. I think it makes things really poetic and romantic, and it's also very good for making the drama hyper. It's especially great for reaction shots

because it gives them so much force. I chose to use it for the death of Hester because it was the most emotional death in the movie. I also wanted to structure it around her point of view—she's happy and exhilarated and then POW the car hits her.

P M : *Does cutting slow motion shots present a problem?*

B D P : It's very tricky to get in and out of slow motion. In this film it wasn't that difficult because it was basically an isolated section of the picture and it was all shot at 48 frames per sound. But in *Carrie* I used a lot of slow motion against regular motion, and that was quite intricate. Basically you have to know how to use slow motion: when it's going to be 36 fps, when to use 48, 72, and 800 fps. I've shot a lot of slow motion and I have a good sense of exactly how many frames per second it will take to exaggerate movement.

P M : *How many cameras did you have on the exploding dummy of John Cassavetes?*

B D P : 8. Some were rolling at 800 fps and others were going at *1500 fps!* We mainly used the ones going at 800.

P M : *Those are tremendous speeds. Did the cameras ever break down?*

B D P : Yes! The first time we did it three cameras snapped. And they were built by the people who build missiles. Some of them didn't have shutters; the film just ran continuously. But looking at the *slates* was very boring. Three minutes go by before the slate goes out. The editor must have fallen asleep during those rushes!

P M : *Were you satisfied with the ending shot?*

B D P : This head crashing to the floor just seemed the most effective end for the movie. I wasn't going to freeze out the explosion with all the blood and fire hitting the walls. Using two shots of the dummy's head flying up to the camera and falling down was a little risky, but that's the chance you have to take. Rick Baker built the dummy and A. D. Flowers, the Master Powder Man, rigged it.

P M : *Do you see yourself continuing to do psychological thrillers, or do you plan a change of direction?*

BDP: I've learned a lot from the genre, and I imagine that in the next 10 or 20 years I'll start moving into more intellectually complicated things. Ironically, my next film will be a small, low-budget comedy along the lines of *Hi, Mom!*—called *Home Movie*—so I'm actually going back to areas I dealt with 5 or 6 years ago. And the one after that will be an elaborate sci-fi film called *The Demolished Man.* It's about an Oedipal murder in a telepathic society.

PM: *Doesn't that smack of* The Fury?
BDP: Not really. It's more like *Oedipus Rex* and *The Godfather* with strong character relationships. Even though it deals with psychic phenomena the basic theme is a father-son confrontation set in the year 2100.

PM: *To be able to talk confidently of what your next two films are going to be is a sign that you've finally made it, that you're bankable. How does it feel?*
BDP: I've always been very pragmatic about what I'm able to do with the time and the space I'm in. I tend to be very undeluded by hype, and I also know how to make it work for me. You've always got to be aware of how the wind is blowing in a capricious industry. The film business is very much like the circus; and you've got to have that kind of circus mentality in order to succeed.

PM: *Do you feel you've created a new style, almost a new genre?*
BDP: Maybe I'm trying to hammer out a new genre. Somehow. Hitchcock did it. I don't know what people called it before they called it "Hitchcockian." They must have some Madison Avenue-type name for what I'm doing. You never know . . . *De Palmian?!?*

Working His Way through College: Brian De Palma at Sarah Lawrence

GERALD PEARY/1979

W HAT HAPPENED TO Brian De Palma after he blew up John Cassavetes to conclude *The Fury?* He realized that, for now, he had reached the end of the line on bloody expensive melodramas. It was time for a genre and budgetary change, and also a switch in scenery. Very quietly, De Palma holed up at Sarah Lawrence College in Bronxville, New York, and wrote, directed, and supervised a surprise independent feature, *Home Movies.* This goofy character comedy with a filmmaker-on-filmmaking subtext was shot on campus and utilized the talents of the hard-working students from a filmmaking course De Palma taught winter-spring semester, '77–'78. *Home Movies* is being edited at this moment. Negotiations are in progress for an early 1979 release.

De Palma attended the Montreal World Film Festival in September as Guest of the Festival, and he recalled with amusement how just a few years ago he had to sneak into the *Midnight Cowboy* party at Berlin. He was an unknown then, showing off *Greetings,* prior to the Hollywood commercial successes of *Obsession, Carrie,* and *The Fury,* and to the additional cult status of *Hi, Mom!, Sisters,* and *Phantom of the Paradise.*

I talked to De Palma for several interesting hours in his Montreal hotel suite. For the first time, he broke his vow of silence on *Home Movies* and offered *Take One* a candid, exclusive look at how his important new independent movie was made.

PEARY: *Why did you decide to make* Home Movies *outside of Hollywood?*

From *Take One,* January 1979: 14–18. Reprinted by permission of the author.

BDP: I've been sort of traveling around the country for ten years talking about independent features. And whenever I asked who the new independent filmmakers were, everybody gave blank stares. I thought if I showed how it could be done, maybe I could start off new directors. I'll never forget Terry Malick saying that my touring with *Greetings* had inspired him to be a director.

Greetings was financed by friends and relatives of the producer. We had only about $20,000 in cash, $23,000 in deferred payments. *Hi, Mom!* was financed by a small company called Sigma Three for about $100,000. I set out to make a feature in 1978 along these lines.

GP: *How did you settle on Sarah Lawrence College as your base of operation?*
BDP: When I was at Columbia, I wasn't getting much support from the university. But acting in plays, I got to know Wilford Leach very well; and he helped me get this fellowship to Sarah Lawrence. I had a graduate fellowship in the theatre department from 1962 to 1964. It was a great place for me to get started, so I felt very close to the school. I always wanted to do something to pay back the help. Also, I knew they had the flexibility to authorize my project after just a few phone calls. Last November, when I was editing *The Fury*, I called Wilford and said I'd really like to teach a course in low-budget filmmaking. And for the course we would make a low-budget film.

GP: *How was it inaugurated?*
BDP: The course was Independent Filmmaking. We got students together for our first meeting last December 20th. There was a blizzard in New York and they came through this blizzard to a meeting. There was no transportation. There was ten inches of snow on the ground. You had to get there in your snowshoes. I said to myself, "These are tough kids."

We had undergraduates to graduate students, ages 18 to 26. I had this story I had written long ago that I always wanted to do. So we had a discussion about the script and budgets and then we broke up into production people and script people for three or four months. The production people worked on making a board, making a budget, and the script people started writing scenes based on my story. Then we'd have weekly meetings, like student council meetings, and run down all the areas: who would be doing what about what, and how were we going to get financed, and all kinds of schemes.

GP: *So what was your budget?*

BDP: The budget kept rising. It started at $50,000, then it went up to $150,000. It kept going up. But I can't really discuss numbers for the simple reason that when we sell the film, we'll be hanged by the future. A distributor can say, "It costs so much. I read it here." Let's say it cost under one million dollars.

GP: *It hasn't been purchased yet?*

BDP: No. We have all kinds of financial schemes going on. Majors want us, independents, but we are just going to see what would work. I had the students checking all the schemes because that's what happens when you're financing a movie. You send it to studios. You go out to lunch with tax shelter lawyers. It's all part of the course.

Actually we had to turn away a lot of money. At first people within the industry didn't take it too seriously. But then we got some very prestigious people to ultimately invest in the movie, so Hollywood got interested. I was one of the largest investors, and I brought people in with me. Jack Temchin and Gil Adler, who had produced the play *El grande de Coca-Cola,* came in. They raised half the money and we were like executive producers.

GP: *What were the rules of the game about involving your name?*

BDP: I tried to use my name as little as possible because I thought it would affect working conditions. If the students were doing their own movie, they wouldn't have that kind of clout. When we finally got a script together, we put ads in *Show Business* and *Backstage* and had casting calls. We saw hundreds and hundreds of actors off the street, and we didn't use my name in advertising.

But as casting went on, I got into trouble. I needed professional help. A young casting director, Scott Rudin, called up and offered to help us. He brought in some really good actors, and we finally cast his discovery, Keith Gordon, as the young boy lead in *Home Movies.* Keith is also in *Jaws II.*

Then Kirk Douglas called up and said, "Maybe I can help you out." I sent the script to him and he wanted to play a part. Our people were all excited: Kirk Douglas in our first picture! Then I used some actors from my other films, like Nancy Allen from *Carrie* and Gerrit Graham who had done *Greetings, Hi, Mom!,* and *Phantom of the Paradise,* Vincent Gardenia came to me through Jack Temchin, and Mary Davenport from *Sisters*. And that sort of made up the cast.

GP: *And the production staff?*

BDP: One kid had assisted me on a couple of films, and had done gaffing on low-budget productions, and wanted to be a camerman. I made him director of photography. He brought some kids with him from California and the group lived in the dorms at Sarah Lawrence. One kid who had been following me around Chicago became an assistant director. One writer became my assistant, another became a grip, another became head of costumes, another head of casting.

A kid from North Carolina who had brought me out to talk to his cinema class became one of the student producers. All the kid producers were unbelievable. They were just running everything, making deals, heading the production company, handling the money. Art direction was very good. This kid dressed the set and came up with really good ideas.

What happened was an educational experience. The sort of openness and democratic beginning evolved into a real professional shooting unit. A kind of pecking order of authority figures emerged in order to get things done efficiently.

GP: *What about the direction of* Home Movies?

BDP: I tried to let the students direct and write as much as possibly could be done. The irony of it was that we got involved in hundreds of thousands of dollars. It was money which outlined our creative parameters and our flexibility. I had to step in and make sure it all worked. It's so important to make this film a success. Otherwise this kind of film will never be done again.

GP: *How much was directed by others?*

BDP: Some shots, a couple of small scenes. About one-twentieth was directed by the kids. I wouldn't be surprised if you couldn't tell what was not directed by me. Each week there were new student directors. I would assign them if I felt they could handle what was to be done. The biggest problem was that the actors were professionals and felt uneasy with student directors.

GP: *Did you have a second unit?*

BDP: I planned a second unit running all the time, directed totally by the kids. But we couldn't possibly do it. We just didn't have the personnel. We needed all our people right where they were.

GP: *Were there students who dropped the course or were angry because* Home Movies *didn't work the way it had been planned?*
BDP: I don't think we lost one student. We kept picking up students. I do think some were disappointed that they didn't have more creative flexibility; and I was disappointed that I couldn't allow it to happen. But they worked incessantly and a lot of them got very sick while we were shooting. We lost them for a week or so. There was one kid who was very ill and we couldn't stop him from working. He was one of our best student electricians. I don't think anyone realized in advance the intensity of it, 12 to 18 hours a day, six days a week. I mean, I hadn't worked that hard in a long time.

GP: *Did your crew also act in the film?*
BDP: They appear as extras throughout the movie, and are students in the classroom scene. Only two of the crew were actors. The others weren't much interested. They just did parts because we needed people who'd be around all the time to carry through the shots. They'd step out of their departments, put on costumes and play their parts, and then go back to their departments again.

GP: *How did everyone get paid?*
BDP: Everybody was working basically for nothing, $50 a day, but everybody got a percentage of the profits, doled out in points.

GP: *And Kirk Douglas?*
BDP: When we talked about Kirk Douglas, I told the students, "Kirk will do this and this for us. It's nice of him to do it, but I don't really know if we can afford him." They said, "No, no, please use Kirk Douglas." I agreed. "It's important. Kirk is a major movie star; and when we sell the picture to television or to Europe, it means something, a student film with Kirk Douglas in it."

In terms of profits, we had to realign them. Kirk came in as an investor. We knocked out a lot of the kids' investors. I said, "Well, Kirk here wants to put his money in the movie. What are you going to do? Are you going to take Kirk's money? How about your father's money?" Again, I let them make all the decisions. I'd advise them, but they decided what they wanted to do.

G P :   *What is the plot of* Home Movies*?*
B D P :   The story is about a young kid, Denis Byrd, whose older brother, James, teaches a course in Spartanetics, a wilderness type of course. Denis has a love affair with James's fiancee and gathers divorce evidence on his father, Doctor Byrd, by following him around at night taking pictures of his various rendezvous with a Swedish nurse. The whole movie is kind of bracketed by Kirk, who plays the "maestro," a character teaching a seminar in Star Therapy. That's an "estian" philosophy where people must learn to star in their own lives. They mustn't be extras, they must put their name about the title. If they want a studio car, they get a studio car!

Kirk was there for four days, and his scenes were mostly with Keith Gordon, the young boy playing Denis. He finds Denis spying on his father, tells him he's nothing but an extra in his own life, hiding behind trees spying with his binoculars. Kirk gives him a camera and says, "You must shoot YOUR life. You must make YOURSELF a star." In Denis's film diary, he becomes an important figure, a major star in his own life.

All of Kirk's stuff is shot cinema verite, and his own Star Therapy is to have cameras running on him all the time. He's constantly directing the camera crew that's shooting him, telling them to come around for closeups, over here for a medium shot. When the lab saw the stuff, they thought Kirk was directing the movie.

Like in *Hi, Mom!,* there are three different film forms in *Home Movies.* There's the Star Therapy form, which is making the viewer conscious of the film as it is shot. You see the mike and the lights. Kirk talks to the cameraman—giving him directions. Then there's Denis's diary, which is as if you had an 8mm camera and were talking into it. Then there is the body of the film, which is sort of like *Hi, Mom!,* with the character falling in love with the girl and their affair developing throughout the movie.

Denis's diary film evolves into what Kirk's film is, and Denis's conclusion is sort of the ultimate dramatic conclusion of the film itself. I mean all the films come together in one big resolution, when he finally gets the girl and takes over his own life.

G P :   *Is this film based on your personal experiences?*

BDP: Well, there are a lot of autobiographical things. The Byrds are somewhat reminiscent of my own family, the brother, the parents. I've never done an autobiographical movie before, but this is a very, very zany look at the family.

GP: *What was the fanciest shot you tried?*
BDP: We have a 6½ minute tracking shot. It took us a day to do, and we stopped at Take 28 or something. But I was amazed that we pulled it off. It's a scene where the girl comes to the family's house and she walks from room to room, running into one member of the family after another. The dialogue had to whip along, everybody had to be in the right place as the camera moved around, hitting these marks. It wasn't the greatest tracking shot in the world, but it played.

I have a very good shot of James lecturing Spartanetics theories to his students by a fire in the woods. That's done in one long shot with very funny material there. I just have a few cutaways to break it up, in case I want to go from one take to another.

GP: *You have said you learn something specific and pragmatic with each film. What about* Home Movies?
BDP: I hadn't done just a straight-out comedy in a long time, just letting an ensemble do really good character acting, having them carry the movie as in my earlier pictures. I like the kind of mad story of this lunatic family, something I haven't ever done before. *Hi, Mom!* and *Phantom of the Paradise* are the most idiosyncratic of my movies and this one, too, is very idiosyncratic. But I think we made a fabulously funny movie. I think *Home Movies* will be very successful. And I think it might start a new generation of low-budget filmmakers.

GP: *Can you compare the experience of making* Home Movies *with university training in filmmaking?*
BDP: I did take a one semester course at NYU in production, but that was the only real film school experience I had. The biggest mistake in student films is that they are usually cast so badly, with friends and people the directors know. Actually you can cover a lot of bad direction with good acting.

The real trouble with film school is that the people teaching are so far out of the industry that they don't give the students an idea of what's happening. Students should be exposed to the best people in the profession. If you study surgery, you study with the best doctors working in the hospital. You don't study with the ones who couldn't get a job.

Techniques of the Horror Film

RALPH APPELBAUM/1980

DRESSED TO KILL, Brian De Palma's most recent contribution to the horror genre, has been lauded by critics around the country for its exquisite capacity to deliver the chills and thrills sought by horror buffs as well as the subtler titillations enjoyed by the sophisticated movie-goer who rarely deigns to see such pictures. David Denby, writing in *New York* magazine, called *Dressed to Kill* "the first great American movie of the 80's." And *New York Times* critic Vincent Canby proclaimed it "a witty, romantic psychological horror film" and the work of "unmistakable talent."

Horror films have always had their own following of cultists who can make or destroy a picture primarily on the basis of their word-of-mouth. But it is exceedingly rare for a horror film (other than one by Hitchcock or a proven master like Stanley Kubrick) to merit critical space in the nation's prominent media, let alone garner rave reviews. Even more interesting, *Dressed to Kill* is an obvious re-make (rip-off?) of Hitchcock's *Psycho*—a sexual/psychological murder with a pathological twist—although Director De Palma vehemently denies there are any but genre similarities.

My course of action was obvious. It would be impossible to write an overview of the contemporary horror genre without interviewing its currently reigning king, Brian De Palma.

RALPH APPELBAUM: *When you were first working on* Dressed to Kill, *were there certain shocks you knew had to be in it in order for the film to be successful?*

From *Filmmakers Monthly,* September 1980: 35–41. Reprinted by permission of the author.

BRIAN DE PALMA: Absolutely. *Dressed to Kill* is really an exercise in different successful sequences, and it works with very traditional genre gambits which have been practiced for years and proven tried and true.

RA: *What do you feel are the most effective techniques for shocking an audience?*
BDP: The genre has been so well mined and refined over the years there is almost a codex, a list of every classical horror or suspense set-piece that has been used. And *Dressed to Kill* probably has every one of them in it.

First, the film has the idea of Hitchcock's *Psycho*. Not the shower murder per se, but the underlying notion of setting somebody up and then killing them—which is a brilliant stroke because you can thereby terrify an audience by annihilating the very identification they have with the character they think is going to take them through the film. So that's number one: psychological surprise.

Then *Dressed to Kill* has such classic bits as the sexual intimations and overtones leading up to the murder. The use of sex is a common feature in many horror films, and particularly those made today. A character who achieves sexual gratification is usually killed; and the murderer is often portrayed as sexually deprived.

There is also stalking: that is, the killer coming slowly, surely, determinedly toward the victim. In *Dressed to Kill,* it's basically Nancy Allen being chased by cars and in subway stations. A corollary here is urban paranoia, because the subway provides a dark, confined space with nowhere to run. Being on a subway train surrounded by the usual scary and threatening urban types is capped off by the presence of a genuine lunatic and then gone one better by the rescue-in-the-nick-of-time trick.

Another set-piece is placing the naive, unsuspecting audience identification figure in a situation where he or she is actively arousing the lunatic without realizing it. In this case it's Nancy Allen wandering around in her underwear in front of Michael Caine. But here too she's saved in the nick of time.

There is also the tactic of having a maniac on the loose while the victim is home, alone. The implication being of course that the maniac is coming to get said victim.

So *Dressed to Kill* is really one set-piece after another.

RA: *Would you say the story was actually secondary to the set-pieces and the need to absolutely incorporate certain techniques in the final product?*

BDP: No. I've gotten a lot of criticism about the story not making sense, not adding up, having too many coincidences, etc. But at the time that never occurred to me. I think the story is a perfectly logical construction of who did what to whom and why. The story must work on a rational level first. All the classic suspense tricks then function within that story. But everything is deliberately, consciously worked out. I think audiences just have to see my film a few times in order to figure out how all the pieces fit together.

RA: *I must admit that I thought the blonde policewoman working on the case was a plot contrivance that didn't work. It was as though she existed sheerly to throw suspicion away from Caine.*
BDP: Remember, there are only so many people in the movie you can work with to completely misdirect the audience—which is another important rule in horror films. To me it seemed perfectly logical that the police detective would have somebody follow her. And instead of a policeman, it turned out to be a policewoman.

RA: *What about Angie Dickinson leaves the apartment and goes down the eleva-tor. Then she remembers she left her ring upstairs and goes right back up. When the elevator door opens the slasher is standing there with a raised razor. How could she know Angie was coming back? And if she didn't know, would she have slashed whoever was in the elevator?*
BDP: Possibly. Who knows? Remember, you're dealing with a psychopath's point of view, so the kind of logic you're trying to apply just doesn't obtain here. Of course maybe she should have been sitting there going through her purse; then she sees Angie, grabs the razor, and starts to slash at her.

But whereas that may be right logically, it doesn't work at all on a subconscious level. To say nothing of a horror-film level. Because when that door opens, she's got to be terrified: the sight of that person wielding a razor has got to be like the worst nightmare in your life.

In other words it's one thing to open the door and see somebody standing there with a razor; it's another thing entirely to see somebody with a purse and then they take out a razor. The latter is *not* the kind of effect you want to generate in a horror film. Granted you may have to stretch the logic a bit in order to achieve the effect, but you can get away with it because you're dealing with Angie's point of view, so you're operating on a very visceral level.

RA: *Was that also the purpose of the nightmare at the end?*

BDP: The ending in the psychiatrist's office is very unsatisfying, but it was meant to be that way. It's a kind of *deus ex machina*—you know, just as you're about to get it the policeman shows up in the nick of time and saves you. But it's really a set-up for the audience who says, "Oh god, they got me all stroked up and this is what happens. The cop grabs her and she doesn't get killed."

You see the audience wants Nancy to get the s--- slashed out of her then and there. They've been primed for something to happen—and then nothing happens essentially. So when they see that first shot of the lunatic asylum they're caught completely off-guard because they're already packing their things up to go home.

RA: *Yes, but there's a tip-off that it's a set-up because a lone nurse wouldn't be walking through an unattended ward.*

BDP: Yes, but you forget you're dealing with a very stylized form of film-making done by a director who interprets reality in the most bizarre ways imaginable. Take Fellini's 8½. Now you wouldn't exactly call that film realistic. But for him that's realistic, and the audience understands that and they go right along with it. They don't just sit there and say, "Gee, this is sort of strange looking. It must be a dream." Rather they accept the logic of it immediately because they're used to seeing that kind of stylized work.

RA: *Then you don't consider* Dressed to Kill *a kind of nightmare?*

BDP: The whole thing works on such a subconscious level I'm not sure even I understand what a lot of it means. When you direct a film so many of your decisions are intuitive. Directing is a constant process of subconscious decisions. Granted there are things which bother you, disturb you. But you'd have to sit down with a Freudian analyst to figure out what they really meant.

RA: *And yet I've read that you work out your movies very, very carefully, planning in exact detail the shots for a sequence.*

BDP: True. I lay out all the shots and I shoot exactly what I'm supposed to have. And they usually hold together and they don't change too much. In this film we only dropped one scene.

RA: *What qualities were you looking for in the* Dressed to Kill *score?*

BDP: I wanted a very sensual, erotic score. *Psycho* has the best score ever written for this form, but still it's too crazy, there's something mad about it and it has no heart, although I'll admit it's perfect for *Psycho*. But I felt *Dressed to Kill* had to have an emotional, sensuous, feminine sound to it. And of course in the terror sequences it should be abrasive, disturbing, etc. So I decided that Pino Donaggio, a very romantic Italian composer, would be perfect for this movie and would throw a slightly different light on my suspense sequences.

RA: *What is your opinion of* The Shining?

BDP: In *The Shining* you're dealing with a director who is working for the first time in this genre and who seems to have a bit of contempt for it. He is obviously not interested in the conventions of the genre he's chosen; in fact he seems to feel there would be something cheapening or demeaning in drawing from the wellspring of the normal genre conventions. Instead you sense that he wants to revolutionize it and make it something profound or significant. But the result is inevitably heavy-handed because what he has actually done is failed to realize the intrinsic beauty of the basic form per se.

The real trick is not to ignore the conventions but to take them and then personalize them. For instance, in *Dressed to Kill* we're dealing with the whole world of women's erotic fantasies, which to my knowledge has never before been done in a horror film. Also my movies are full of surrealistic imagery, which also isn't seen too often. To me the scariest thing in the world is a nightmare—scarier than life itself—yet few of today's horror films use it.

RA: *What about those horror films that are cranked out for a preestablished audience. Do you feel the audience is so hooked on sensationalism that they will overlook a poorly made film so long as it can provide lots of grizzly murders in the course of 90 minutes?*

BDP: I think that audience is still discriminating. The low-budget films which have been successful, like *Halloween* and *Friday the 13th,* may have been crudely made and done on a shoestring budget, but they are in fact suspenseful; they do kill people in very effective ways; and their plot twists are often very ingenious. But for every *Halloween* and *Friday the 13th* there must be 150 which have the exact same elements and yet they don't work.

R A : Friday the 13th *has a scene where a guy gets skewered through a bunk bed with a giant drill. It seems to me that's what an audience leaves the theater talking about and not whether the cinematic values were good.*

B D P : I disagree. I think it's got to be effectively done—well set up, the maniac stalking, the way the people are dispatched, etc. There has got to be something more than run-of-the-mill horror in order for a film to be successful. Repetition is anathema to the genre. You can no longer just decapitate people or slice them through the gut or whatever. You've got to give the audience something new and striking if you want them to walk out talking about your film.

R A : *Do you feel the ad campaign plays an important part in selling a horror movie? For instance,* Friday the 13th *had a $3.5 million ad budget from Paramount and spent it on very effective TV spots.*

B D P : I don't think that's what makes a film successful. True the horror-film audience will go to see the picture; but if it doesn't deliver, they won't talk about—and that means it will be gone the next week.

TV spots, no matter how well done, no matter how they blanket the tube, can't sell something that doesn't really exist. I've seen films with $10 million ad campaigns go rapidly into oblivion. The only thing you can say about the horror genre is that distributors will rarely spend a lot of money unless they feel the film truly is effective.

R A : *The* Dressed to Kill *ad art was changed from a shot of a shadowy figure in a doorway and a shapely girl's leg to one of a maniac wielding a razor. Why? And do you feel it's had any effect on the film's earnings?*

B D P : Filmways decided the ad art was too classy. Though we were attracting the audience which doesn't usually attend suspense and terror films—i.e., the 25-and-up audience—we weren't penetrating as deeply as we should into the real market which is the black and the youth audiences. So Filmways felt they needed an ad which would address itself directly to the kind of audience that depends on ads for making their decision to see a movie. Or to put it another way, an audience that doesn't care terribly much who's in it or what it's about, but is interested in knowing that some lunatic is running around chopping people up. Traditionally suspense and horror films have ads displaying someone or something with a sharp, lethal instrument glaring out at you from the mysterious shadows. The posters themselves are a convention, and if you look at them you'll see they're all more or less the same on one level or another.

Interestingly in the case of *Dressed to Kill,* after the new ad appeared that missing audience came in almost immediately. Although whether it was word of mouth filtering down or the new ad no one really knows for sure since the picture was a success right from the start.

RA: *Why do you think horror films are so popular today?*
BDP: Because the genre is one of the few forms that hasn't been invaded by television. The stations have picked up the situation comedies and the political stories and all the other forms you used to go to the movies to see. But they're avoided the horror and suspense genre because these works lose their scariness when they're broken up by commercials. Also because the networks can't portray graphic violence or things like brutal murders—even though people like to see lots of action and killings and don't seem to care whether you slice up someone in a horror movie, or shoot them in a western, or strangle them a la *The Godfather.*

Personally I think the horror genre is a very filmic form. Certainly it's the closest thing we have today to pure cinema. And the fact that most horror films are so badly made doesn't mean there isn't a tremendous amount of artistry in this genre. I sometimes feel compelled to work in it just to show what can be done.

Brian De Palma: The New Hitchcock or Just Another Rip-Off?

JEAN VALLELY / 1980

IN LESS THAN TWO MONTHS, *Dressed to Kill* has grossed $30 million, making it one of the few solid successes of an otherwise disappointing summer. And most people would probably agree that it was one of the summer's most talked-about films. But here the consensus ends. *Dressed to Kill* has provoked an intense, divided reaction that has some critics proclaiming it a masterpiece and others dismissing it as junk. At the center of the controversy is the film's writer-director, Brian De Palma. Is he the new Hitchcock, the new "master of the macabre," as he's being touted, or is he just another rip-off artist?

Sitting in his homey Greenwich Village office, Brian De Palma does not look much like a master of the macabre. Relaxed and obviously enjoying his latest success, he looks more like a big, cuddly bear than anything else. But at the mention of Hitchcock and charges of rip-off, his mood darkens.

"The critics sort of split on *Dressed to Kill*," he says, lighting a Montclair. "The Andrew Sarris-Richard Corliss school feels it's comparable to necrophilia to take any of the visual grammar Hitchcock pioneered, or any of his ideas, his music." De Palma's voice trails off. "In their minds, anyone who does this is the lowest form of embalmer. The Pauline Kael-Gary Arnold school doesn't take such a sanctimonious approach to the master."

He shrugs his shoulders and adds, "The other reason *Dressed to Kill* got so much attention was that there was really nothing much to talk about all summer.

"My style is very different from Hitchcock's," he continues. "I am dealing in surrealistic, erotic imagery. Hitchcock never got into that too much. *Psycho* is basically about a heist. A girl steals money for her boyfriend so they can get married. *Dressed to Kill* is about a woman's secret erotic life. If anything, *Dressed to Kill* has more of a Buñuel feeling to it." De Palma lights another cigarette, getting a bit fidgety. "I mean, *Psycho* came out in 1960. I was twenty years old. What the fuck do kids who go to see movies know about *Psycho*? Even the term *Hitchcockian* is a bit arcane now."

De Palma takes a long sip of coffee. "It's like pop art, in a sense. When pop art first came out, the academic, mainline critics just dismissed it as shocking and ridiculous. How could anyone find anything artistic about a painting of a Brillo box? And when people started writing seriously about rock & roll, they were called nitwits. Suddenly pop art and rock & roll had to be taken seriously. Same with my movie. It can be dismissed on so many levels: the genre is dimestore stuff, it's dirty, it's bloody, what does it have to do with art?" He takes a deep breath. "But you always have to fight that. Older generations of critics are always talking about films, great masterpieces made twenty and thirty years ago, and they tend to dismiss anything new or contemporary as not serious. I just don't think it has anything to do with the audience."

De Palma slumps back in his chair and says he expected to get creamed a lot worse than he did. He acknowledges his debt to Hitchcock and certain obvious similarities to *Psycho,* but he insists on the originality of his story. He claims he got the idea of the transsexual murderer from watching trans-sexual Nancy Hunt on a *Phil Donahue* show (portions of which appear in *Dressed to Kill*). De Palma was fascinated, and he began to read extensively about transsexuals. "They have this wonderful term for it," says De Palma, leaning forward. "Gender discomfort." He shakes his head. "Gender discomfort! Can you imagine? I was at a dinner party, and I asked, quite innocently, 'Wouldn't it be terrific to dress up in women's clothes and go out and see how people related to you?' And everyone looked at me like I was a lunatic."

The freewheeling sexual world we live in, where you can be in a bar one minute and in some stranger's bed the next, fascinated De Palma as well. "I basically got the idea of cruising around and what can happen from *Looking for Mr. Goodbar*—the idea that it's dangerous and exciting at the same time."

De Palma gets a puckish look on his face when asked if he agrees with those critics who consider *Dressed to Kill* a masterpiece. Placing his hand over his heart in mock seriousness, he says, "It is difficult for a man to evaluate his own masterworks." He laughs. "I think *Dressed to Kill* is the best film of this kind I've done so far. And I consider myself one of the best at this form. I'm not shy about that. But 'masterwork' is a very heavy term to use on anyone who isn't dead." He laughs again. "You never want to feel that you've come to the end of what you're doing."

Nevertheless, De Palma feels he is going through a particularly creative period, the result of what he calls a "major breakthrough." "I discovered the pencil!" he laughs. "It took me days to type a page, by the time I had corrected all the mistakes." But once he began writing on big yellow pads, "I wrote like a lunatic," he says. "I can write ten pages in a day. I wrote *Dressed to Kill* very quickly and then started *Personal Effects,* my next project. Then I had two other ideas that I started writing, and *another* idea started haunting me."

De Palma records ideas as they come to him—in pictures. The walls of his office are covered with little stick-figure sketches on index cards. "Once I get a good idea," says De Palma, "it doesn't let go. I walk around, doing my normal activities, but I'm in a daze, because I'm trying to figure out how to get this character over to that point so he can meet this other character. In the last couple of months, I've had a bunch of ideas. I almost wish it would slow down a bit. It's getting a little crazy, waking up at four in the morning and trying to get it all down. But on the other hand, it's wonderful, because there are times when you just don't have any ideas. This is better.

"Directors in their forties—I just turned forty—move into high gear; they get to use all they've learned. But the tragedy of the profession is that so many directors make their best pictures in their thirties, and because of the corrosive aspects of this business, they suddenly go out of control." He pauses. "I would hate to think I made my best picture four years ago."

De Palma's mood grows serious. "This is a terribly destructive business. When you become successful, you lose your critical peer group. You're off living in a mansion somewhere, surrounded by people who think you are wonderful. This is so dangerous to artistic growth." He pauses. "You know, everyone has an image of himself that, in fact, really isn't true. When you're successful in one area, you tend to say, Hey that's not me. They think I'm a horror-film director when I'm really a . . ." De Palma searches for the right word, "'. . . a poet.'" He grins. "Suddenly I want all my poetry on the screen, so I start shooting scenes with horses running across fields.

"If I had been Truffaut," he continues, "and had made *Home Movies,* it would have been infinitely more successful, because the critics are used to Truffaut making this sort of movie—about his youth, a kind of sweet, personal, sentimental, quirky, ironic, funny film. But they're not used to me doing it." De Palma sighs. "You've got to know what you do well and not be embarrassed by it—even if it brings you great wealth and success," he says, smiling.

De Palma isn't ambivalent about what it is he does well. "I can tell a story in visual images probably better than anybody. My weakness is that I've never done a great character story. I should probably direct somebody else's material if I am going to grow as a director. I can direct actors well. But I'm usually so involved in the visual storytelling that the slow rising and falling of the characters' relationships just doesn't interest me. But it should. I should do it.

"See, the problem in this business is that in order to grow, you have to make lots of pictures. And fail a lot of times. We're going through a wild budget syndrome at the moment, where a young director will make a big score on some small-budget picture, and then whatever he says and does is right. The problem with this is that your failures won't be half-million-dollar ones but $30 million ones. And those can be devastating. The critics start reviewing your budgets, and the distribution companies, who have lost a lot of money, become reluctant to let you experiment. I had the advantage of being able to fail many times on minuscule budgets early in my career, and I wasn't wiped out. With most directors, ten-to-one their first couple of pictures were disasters." De Palma pulls on his salt-and-pepper beard. "Right now, if I wanted to make a story about a porpoise and Benji, I could probably get it financed. And that, of course, would be my undoing. Because when it failed, I would be in terrible, terrible trouble."

De Palma blames this treacherous situation on the Hollywood system. "There is a danger to living in that community," he says. "It affects your standards, because what they think is successful isn't at all. I don't think I have failed if I'm making a picture for a small company or one that is financed independently. But in Hollywood's terms, I have.

"I'll give you two examples of what I mean. I was in California to mix *The Fury.* Frank Yablans [a producer] told me he could get me a million dollars to direct *Hurricane.*" De Palma laughs. "Now, normally I wouldn't even have considered directing *Hurricane.* It's not exactly my cup of tea, you know, shooting on Tora, Tora, Tora or wherever, but the fact that Frank said he could get me a million dollars made me think about it enough to read the script and take that meeting. I kept thinking, 'Well, Roman Polanski was involved, and he's a great director, right?' I kept saying, 'A million dollars . . .' I didn't do it, but the fact that I even considered it, that I could be bought. . . ."

De Palma tells his second story. "I was in California, at the bottom of my career. I had a picture on the shelf, *Get to Know Your Rabbit.* I couldn't get arrested. I was trying to get *Sisters* off the ground, but it was hopeless and I realized I'd have to raise the money independently. Then Marty Ransohoff [a producer] offered me *Fuzz.* It was a funny New York cop picture, and I thought I could do something with it. We started to pick the cast; I went after Burt Reynolds and got him in the picture. Then I was told the studio heads wanted to cast Yul Brynner and Raquel Welch for the foreign market." De Palma's eyes light up. "Yul Brynner and Raquel Welch in a New York street-cop movie! I went to the writer and producer, and we met with Ransohoff. He said, 'I've got United Artists on the phone, and if you don't put those fucking people in the picture, United Artists won't finance it. You guys better go back and talk it over.'" De Palma shakes his head. "Anyway, I ended up not doing the picture, but it's that kind of thinking—you're in a desperate situation, you gotta have a job, you're offered a lot of money. . . . It affects you. I think the only way not to be affected by it is to try to keep away from that kind of crafty, commercial, capitalistic world as much as possible. The key to that kind of system is, 'What's his price? How can he be had? How can we get him interested?' And there are a lot of people a lot smarter than I am who think about nothing else twenty-four hours a day. I'm smart enough to know they might find some way to get me. You just try to keep on a different road."

Personal Effects, De Palma's next project, will not be about a porpoise and Benji but about a film sound-effects editor who witnesses a political assassination. "It goes back to my assassination-buff years and Watergate, and how things get covered up. It's about explanations that don't explain anything. I think it will be quite original. I don't think the audience is aware of the sound-effects process. At the same time, it'll be a detective thriller, you know, putting together all these clues."

De Palma leans back in his chair. "I think I'm headed in more of a political, ethical direction. I am fascinated by things like Watergate and the Joseph Yablonski murders. I watch a lot of television. I loved the conventions." He pauses. "When I made *Greetings*, I found myself on talk shows, talking about the revolution, and I realized I had become just another piece of software that they could sell, like aspirin or deodorant. It didn't make any difference what I said. I was talking about the downfall of America. Who cares? In my experience, what happened to the revolution is that it got turned into a product, and that is the process of everything in America. Everything is meshed into a product."

He shrugs his shoulders. "I'm interested in why things happen. For instance, why did the Billy Carter affair break the week it did? Why didn't it happen a year ago? I mean, something's going on there. Those things don't just happen. Why did Deep Throat emerge at just the right time to lead Woodward and Bernstein on?

"I'm dealing with things close to me more than I've done before. *Home Movies* dealt with my youth, my family. By taking that character and moving him into *Dressed to Kill*, I'm building a character very close to me. As you get older, you know more about life. You're emotionally susceptible. For me, I had to develop a skill in order to express what I had to say. And now I'm getting to the point where I'm able to express what I'm feeling," De Palma says, rolling his eyes, "no matter what perverse street it takes me down."

Travolta and De Palma Discuss *Blow Out*

CARMIE AMATA / 1981

AMATA: *Was the script written with John Travolta in mind?*

DE PALMA: Actually, the kind of people I had in mind to play Jack were [Richard] Dreyfuss or [Al] Pacino. But one day John called to say he had this story—a kind of adventure thriller about planes—that he was interested in doing with me. I told him that I wasn't intersted in doing that kind of picture right now because I was working on *Blow Out*. He asked me what it was about and if he could read the script, so I sent him a copy and five days later he called and said, "I like it, I want to do it."

TRAVOLTA: My script was a suspense film about a man who wants to steal Howard Hughes' Spruce Goose and successfully does. They were moving the plane at the time I proposed the idea to Brian and I thought if we timed it right we could work something around that. But Brian said he was working on *Blow Out* and I said, "Take a look at it anyway and maybe we can mock it up for the future." I suggested that we exchange scripts and after I read *Blow Out* it took dominance over my airplane thriller. I've abandoned that project, at least for now, because I'm so pleased with the way *Blow Out* turned out. I think, for now at least, I've done my genre thriller.

AMATA: *The original title of* Blow Out *was* Personal Effects, *wasn't it?* Blow Out *seems dangerously close to* Blow-Up.

DE PALMA: Basically the title was my idea, because I just didn't think *Personal Effects* was a strong enough title. Of course, I knew that by taking the

From *Films & Filming*, December 1981: 8–10. Reprinted by permission of the author.

title *Blow Out* I'd run into big problems with people comparing it to *Blow-Up* but I felt that commercially it wouldn't make too much difference, because *Blow-Up* came out in 1966 and audiences wouldn't be getting them confused.

Both pictures deal with a kind of technical way of finding out about a crime. You know, the use of very photographic tools in order to solve a mystery. This was also done in *The Conversation*, which is very much a cheat because they re-read the line: they don't really use all those filters to pick the line out. Ultimately, they re-read what she said: it's a different reading. It's a very terrible cheat.

AMATA: *The whole thing about Jack having been responsible for the murder of his friend, the undercover cop—I had a feeling that it was tacked onto the plot, like something left over from* Prince of the City *that you just couldn't get out of your system.*

DE PALMA: You're absolutely right about my not being able to get *Prince of the City* out of my system. I spent a year with Bob Leuci working on that script and that material is ultimately not in *Prince of the City*—they never used that sequence of the taping of the undercover cop.

Bob Leuci had a million stories: a lot of them never appeared in the book, nor did they get to the screen in Sidney Lumet's *Prince of the City.*

That area really fascinates me. In fact, I'm going to make another movie that deals with that kind of police corruption and that period. I just spent so much time with that and I got filled with a million anecdotes. The thing in *Blow Out* is basically a Bob Leuci idea, that's definitely true.

AMATA: *And are you bitter about your treatment by Orion over* Prince of the City?

DE PALMA: Oh, yeah, *very* bitter. But that isn't why I used that wire thing in *Blow Out*. I did that because I wanted to give John's character a background of having used it before he uses it again on Nancy's character. Still, you're right to assume that I'm bitter about what happened with *Prince of the City*. It was awful and I'm very unforgiving in that area because David Rabe and I wrote a very good script which will never be seen.

AMATA: *Is your next project the one that's rooted in the stuff you got from Leuci?*

DE PALMA: No, although I'm going to be in the same sort of realm of non-fiction, which has strong dramatic and historical roots. I'm developing a script that Scott Spencer is going to write based on a book called *Act of Vengeance*, about the 1969 murder of Joseph Yablonski and his family. With the Yablonski project, I'm moving into a more documentary type of thing—dealing more with real people as opposed to things that are more fantastic and involved with the suspense genre.

AMATA: *(To Travolta) And your next project?*
TRAVOLTA: I don't really know for sure although I kind of like the idea of doing the Jim Morrison story. But there's no script yet or anything like that.

AMATA: *What do you find appealing about Morrison's life?*
TRAVOLTA: He seemed like such a really complicated individual and it would be interesting as an actor to play that. I mean, he seemed to vary in his personality and that would be fun to do. Although maybe it's just that I'm interested in doing a rock kind of character.

AMATA: *The fact that you'd have to sing doesn't put you off any?*
TRAVOLTA: Oh no. I do have training in singing—I did sing in *Grease*. I don't think there should be any problem.

AMATA: *Is there any other genre you'd like to do?*
TRAVOLTA: Oh yes, a comedy! God, I'd love to do a good sort of old-fashioned screwball comedy.

AMATA: *What has been your favourite role so far?*
TRAVOLTA: I don't have an absolute favourite. What I have is specific memories for each role. Like, the most fun I had was doing *Urban Cowboy*—it was a new thing for me. The most electric for me was *Saturday Night Fever*. And *The Boy in the Plastic Bubble* is a gem of a picture—it works and it has a very, very special place in my mind.

AMATA: *Since that was made for television, you must be unique having had such a wonderful experience. Many serious actors don't look upon television as a very rewarding medium aesthetically.*
TRAVOLTA: I absolutely did feel great about *Plastic Bubble,* right from the start. It was a lovely script and I knew it could work and that I could make it work. I don't think people thought I'd be as convincing in it as I ultimately

was. I think they cast me because I was in a hit series on television (*Welcome Back, Kotter*) and they figured they'd get a good rating if they used me. I really think I surprised them with my interpretation of that character.

I would never put down television. I probably would never do another series but I'm a sucker for a good script and I'll do whatever's good whatever it is. I wouldn't mind doing a play again. The last play I did was four years ago. I did *Bus Stop* on a tour. We played Boston and upstate New York.

AMATA: *What about* Blow Out? *How do you feel about your work in it?*
TRAVOLTA: I'm so proud of this picture, of my role in it. It was like a group effort on the part of a lot of wonderful artists. The role was so different for me—I've always played characters that always go directly from the heart. Jack is so very analytical that it seemed like a real challenge.

AMATA: *What are your political feelings about the picture?*
TRAVOLTA: I'm not a very political person. I wouldn't choose a script for its politics. Quite simply. I just loved Brian's script and I wanted to do it.

AMATA: *At the end of the film, is there any room for optimism in Jack's charac-ter? Has he totally given up at the end and accepted the insanity of the situation, or dare we hope that he will bounce back and fight to prove the murders?*
TRAVOLTA: I feel that the character is basically a strong person, but you don't get over a thing like that right away. I mean, he feels responsible for two deaths. He's murdered someone. It's going to take some time—several years maybe—but I wouldn't like to think that he's totally done in. He's got too much character and strength to ultimately feel like that. It's just too black a picture to paint of his future.
DE PALMA: I don't think he's ever again going to try to prove anything. I think his is a hopeless situation. I think when you have a truth that does not fit in with what people want to accept you are an odd man out and you will be driven crazy or totally ignored or killed. I really believe that. If you read about the [John] Kennedy assassination and the witnesses that vanished, you realise there's all kinds of paranoia.

AMATA: *I take it then that the picture is a reflection of your own political pessi-mism and feelings about things like Watergate and Chappaquiddick.*
DE PALMA: Yes, over the years I've read a lot about the political calamities we've had in America. There are obvious historical references to Chappa-

quiddick and the Kennedy assassination in Dallas. What I've gleaned from all my reading is that a conspiracy sort of happens by accident. What I wanted to do in this film is to show how haphazard—as opposed to precisely worked out—a conspiracy is. What I wanted to show was how some over-zealous guy—in *Blow Out* it's Burke (John Lithgow)—goes a little too far at the start and things just grow more and more illogically.

In the film, the car wasn't supposed to go into the creek and kill the guy. Burke's people just wanted a little blow out, a little Chappaquiddick-like scandal to cloud his political future, but Burke went overboard.

AMATA: *And that whole fascinating idea of capturing the blow out/gun shot on sound—what inspired that?*

DE PALMA: I've spent lots of time in mixes with my sound effects editors. Over the years they've been telling me all kinds of anecdotes about what they have to do to get exact sounds for the movies I make. One told me once he had to go to the zoo and wait nine hours for the owl to open up so he could record it for some mood or other we were after in the scene. And I got to thinking, what would happen if somebody just by accident recorded a murder and what if someone else got a picture of it? If you sync up the two, I figured that you could actually see where the shot was coming from.

AMATA: *Isn't that what was eventually done with the Zapruder film of John Kennedy's assassination?*

DE PALMA: Yes, something like that and it was just one more thing that inspired me to write the film.

AMATA: *Was there any discussion of allowing Sally (Nancy Allen) to live?*

DE PALMA: Not on my part. That would have been awful—John Travolta to the rescue! Besides, there's no way she could get away from Burke—he's just too good at what he does.

AMATA: *But she does manage to break away for a few seconds . . .*

DE PALMA: That was only in order for her to get the scream out. We needed to have Jack get her scream recorded.

TRAVOLTA: There may have been some outside input about having me save her but there certainly wasn't among the inner group. It was always written that she dies in the end and I liked that. All of us who were making the film knew that was the only way for Sally to end up.

AMATA: *But does he have to use that final scream in something as base as a sleazy porno flick?*

DE PALMA: Sure, it's a crazy thing to do, but I don't think he really knows what he's doing at the end. And I also think it has to do with the whole idea that all of those very critical events can be reduced to dirt in the end. That this whole thing can be reduced to just an effect in a movie is essentially what does happen.

TRAVOLTA: I really believe that, at that point, anything goes. He's crazed and in that state of mind anything goes. Nothing's rational. He feels responsible for two deaths and he's just murdered someone himself. He's in a cold sweat and he doesn't even realise he's got a cigarette burning. You have to take all of these awful things that have happened to him and the people he cared for and put yourself in his shoes. As an actor that's what I did and I played it like "What does it matter? It's all anarchy!" Also, if you want to see it as a positive gesture, it's a way of keeping Sally alive, the way he's continually listening to that tape at the end.

AMATA: *Mrs. De Palma—Nancy Allen—went from playing a smart hooker in* Dressed to Kill *to a dumb call girl in* Blow Out. *How does she feel about her husband casting her as prostitutes?*

DE PALMA *(laughing nervously)*: Well, Nancy would like to play other parts. Originally, she was not going to play Sally but John felt so strongly about her doing it, he convinced me to ask her to play it. Of course, I never doubted that she could play it but we both agreed that she should follow up *Dressed to Kill* with something other than another prostitute. But John convinced both of us that she should do Sally.

TRAVOLTA: When I read it, I just thought of Nancy immediately. Sally was perfect for her. But Brian and Nancy had made this pact not to work together so soon after *Dressed to Kill.* I just said to Brian, "I really feel it's a mistake for Nancy not to play Sally." At first, when Brian was thinking in terms of Pacino or Dreyfuss, he figured to cast someone like Dyan Cannon or Julie Christie in the part. But with me playing Jack, it really did make more sense to bring Sally's age closer to mine. Nancy and I had worked together before [*in De*

Palma's Carrie *in 1976*] and the chemistry was so good between us, I just knew we'd be perfect together in *Blow Out*.

AMATA: *When was it decided that* Blow Out *would be made on location in Philadelphia?*

DE PALMA: Right in the beginning. I come from Philadelphia and I wanted to play this sort of contemporary political story against the old conceptions of liberty and independence and truth. We invented that whole Liberty Day theme, that parade and big finale—fireworks, costumes, everything—to give that kind of patriotic air.

AMATA: *Actually, you staged the Liberty Day parade with Jack's chase in the van twice, didn't you? I'm referring to the theft of part of the film which must have sent you into a frenzy.*

DE PALMA: That's putting it mildly. I just went crazy when I heard it was stolen. It was all cut and we were mixing it and I got this call on Monday that two boxes had been stolen the previous Friday while the film was being shipped from New York to Los Angeles. It was the stuff we shot on the first two days of shooting, which constituted the parade sequence. We had to recreate from scratch that entire sequence.

AMATA: *I read that the budget for* Blow Out *was $18 million. What did it cost to re-shoot the parade sequence?*

DE PALMA: It cost $750,000. We had negative insurance. All companies carry it. Still, it was just awful. The driver of the truck just stopped to pick up something else and somebody broke into the delivery truck and figured the boxes the film was in contained television sets or something. When I heard about it on Monday—I only wish they'd told me rightaway, when it happened on Friday—I found out where the truck had stopped and looked on the street and all around it to see if the robber just didn't dump it when he saw it wasn't anything he could sell easily. Of all the different boxes—a total of fifty in all—the boxes that were taken were of the most expensive scenes we shot.

AMATA: *In that case, could those particular boxes have been deliberately stolen?*

DE PALMA: I'd have been happy to ransom them, but we were never contacted to do so. No, I'm sure the robber figured he'd stolen something he could sell outright. It wasn't planned, it was a ridiculous event that just occurred. It's like *Blow Out*—it was a very haphazard accident.

Brian De Palma's Death Wish

LYNN HIRSCHBERG/1984

PARAMOUNT IS BURNING and Brian De Palma is calling for blood. "The New York street set's on fire," someone says. "*Star Trek*'s in flames." De Palma nods, unconcerned. He's at Universal Studios directing *Scarface*, and there are immediate worries here: an actor hanging from a rope looks, somehow, wrong. "They'll save Paramount," De Palma says. "What I want now is more blood."

You'd think De Palma would be thrilled about the fire. A real-life horrific event! A piece of Hollywood destroyed! De Palma loves horrific events (murders especially), and he certainly hates Hollywood ("the land of the devil"), but he doesn't seem to care about the Paramount fire. It's just a nuisance interfering with *his* reality, *his* self-created horrific event. The hanging man, bloody and dying, is just as De Palma imagined him. An actual fire would never be De Palma–perfect; it couldn't be visually controlled. Reality just ends up being too . . . *real*.

De Palma has never had much interest in reality. His films—*Carrie, Dressed to Kill*, the whole lot—are full of highly improbable plots and characters; they're flashy, creepy, packed with remarkably brutal deaths. That suits his personality: De Palma, soft-spoken, placid, has what appears to be an almost psychotic interest in violence.

This makes Hollywood nervous. "Uh, his early movies?" one studio executive says. "You mean, like, around *Carrie?* Well, I didn't really understand those pictures." *Scarface*, cut from *Godfather* cloth, is a movie the executive

From *Esquire*, January 1984: 79–83. Reprinted by permission of *Esquire*.

would understand, which makes it hard to understand why De Palma's involved. The film has a conventional script, written by an Academy Award–winner (Oliver Stone), a big budget (at least $21.5 million), and a big star (Al Pacino). *Scarface* even has a novelization! The project is big Hollywood all the way. And yet, if Brian De Palma has always seemed a bit sick for the mainstream movie business, there's a reason for all this sudden cooperation. De Palma wants a hit, and *Scarface* has great on-paper hit potential. De Palma realizes that hits mean money and money means respect. And respect, well, respect means more freedom to realize his daydreams. Or nightmares. More psychotic visions revealed. If *Scarface* is a hit, Hollywood will immediately "get" De Palma; they'll give him money to do anything.

Or so De Palma thinks. He may be wrong. On the set of *Scarface* he's still calling for more blood. "I want blood in his mouth," De Palma tells his crew in a calm, steady voice. "I mean, what are we making here? *Cinderella?*"

Brian De Palma sits behind his desk dressed in a khaki safari suit, sporting a beard and looking very much like a large stone. He registers no emotion, except for an occasional laugh, which is extreme: loud, wild, crazed. De Palma only laughs when the talk turns to Power, Sex, or Controversy. These are De Palma's favorite topics, and they are important De Palma themes. They connect to Fear and Violence, and eventually, to Movies, *Brian De Palma's* Movies. De Palma loves his movies, he loves thinking about them. He doesn't care much for people, but he loves movies. "I don't care if people like me," he says. "If they do, fine, but if not. . . ." De Palma shrugs. He lights a cigarette and stares into space.

De Palma isn't much interested in talking. He regards any interruption with a sort of bemused contempt. Any interruption: a phone call, a message from his secretary, a question. Brian De Palma hasn't much use for interruptions. For example, a typical exchange:

So, Brian, before you make a movie, do you see the whole thing in your head?
Yes.
Do you have problems re-creating the movie you see?
No.
Is it difficult, say, to write the script? To cast the actors?
No.
How does the actual movie measure up to what you originally imagined?
[The phone rings.] It measures up.

And so it goes. De Palma stares directly at you while he delivers these monosyllabic answers, but it's as if he were concentrating on your nose—no eye contact is made. He's clearly thinking about something else. "Images run through my brain all the time." De Palma says, finally answering a question. "Lately I've been thinking about rearview mirrors. You can see people in the next car out your rearview mirror. They're always doing the most personal things—putting on makeup, fighting, kissing, *whatever.* I want to put that in a movie. Someone could see a murder in their rearview mirror. The car murderer or something."

It's a perfect De Palma scenario: a few steals from Hitchcock (*Rear Window*), a lot of flashy camera work, and a psycho on the loose. Perfect. De Palma laughs. He loves to think about his movies. He reads all his reviews, both negative and positive. He watches *Donahue* regularly, knowing Phil and his audience would condemn his work as immoral and evil. He flies to screenings of his movies in the Midwest, sits in the first row with his back to the screen, and gauges the crowd's reactions. He has listened to audiences boo his films. Yet De Palma seems to enjoy their hatred more than their adoration. No criticism really affects him—it just interests him. Or at least that's what he says. For Brian De Palma, it seems, has unlimited faith in himself, and he clearly loves the controversy he generates. "Hey," he says, lighting a cigarette, "you have to be happy with someone."

De Palma puts his feet up on the desk. The desk is borrowed. It, like this office, belongs to Steven Spielberg, an old De Palma chum. Spielberg and De Palma (and George Lucas and Martin Scorsese) met at Warner Bros. during the early Seventies. "We were all having our movies recut by the studio and badly distributed," says De Palma. "We've managed, somehow, to all stay friends." There's a certain amount of healthy competitiveness within this boys' club ("We're all each other's best critics"), but De Palma seems honestly fond of his friends and impressed with their work.

Still, he does appear to envy the freedom Spielberg's and Lucas's hits have assured them. And while it's impossible to imagine De Palma directing *Star Wars* or *E.T.,* it also seems odd to find him in this particular office. The room, which De Palma has dubbed "the *Jaws* Memorial Office," is covered with *Jaws* junk: shark teeth, letters concerning sharks, framed shark photos. The room is a shrine to Hollywood success, to everything Hollywood stands for. There is no sign of De Palma—except for a photo taken with Spielberg—

anywhere in the office. This is clearly temporary: De Palma's just visiting this planet, soaking up the atmosphere.

"I'm currently very hot because the advance word on *Scarface* is good," says De Palma. "But that situation won't last. It never does. There's a whole school of De Palma criticism that says I'm absolutely terrible, that I've never had an original idea in my life, that I'm just a poor man's Hitchcock. And, actually, I do get all the knocks Hitchcock used to get before critics decided *he* was a genius. They say this isn't literary material, that my themes aren't serious. I can give all the answers Hitchcock gave. Like, What is the content of a still life? *Nada!* But artists paint them anyway."

De Palma is excited, this topic heats him up. "They say I'm violent," he says. "They say violence is immoral. In painting, artists deal with grotesque images constantly. Crucifixions are pretty grotesque, yet painters have painted them for centuries. If those painters were around now, they'd be putting them in movies. Nailing someone to a cross, letting him sit there— *hmmmmmm,* that's pretty grotesque. To me, violence is just a visual form. It's very exciting. Movies have physical motion and you can get violence that has a visceral effect. Slashing someone with a razor is a very visceral image. What are you going to do? Hit them over the head with a sponge? In the book version of *Carrie,* Carrie gives her mother a heart attack. Well, just imagine what that's going to look like. It's not an effective visual image. So I crucified her with the kitchen utensils." De Palma issues his laugh. "Violence is extremely beautiful."

Extremity appears to be a long-standing personality trait, but films themselves were not his first passion. As a kid De Palma, who is forty-three, was interested in physics. He built computers and rarely went to the movies. De Palma also had an interest in medical procedure. His father, an orthopedic surgeon, would let his son watch while he operated. "I have a high tolerance for blood," says De Palma now. "But I never liked scary movies. Who wants to be scared? When you're scared, you're out of control. Who wants to be out of control?"

He enrolled in Columbia University and, shortly thereafter, discovered film. It made sense. Making movies was the ideal pursuit for De Palma. He could control the action, the plot, the visuals—*everything.* Film so absorbed him that he sold off his electronic equipment to buy movie equipment. "I traded one obsession for another," De Palma says.

In 1964, after completing the masters of fine arts program at Sarah Lawrence, De Palma shot his first feature, a comedy entitled *The Wedding Party*. After two more features, the anarchistic *Greetings* and *Hi, Mom!* (like *The Wedding Party* they starred Robert De Niro), De Palma hit Hollywood with a movie called *Get to Know Your Rabbit* which told the lighthearted story of an executive (Tom Smothers) who leaves the business world to become a magician. "*Get to Know Your Rabbit* didn't start out as a terrible experience," recalls De Palma, "but that's the way it ended up. Tom Smothers became very difficult to direct and was ultimately instrumental in creating a totally unworkable situation. I said to the studio. 'Either you do it my way or no way.' I was taken off the picture."

"The thing I learned from that experience," De Palma continues, "is that when you can't control things, you gotta walk away from them. Now when I get in situations where people are trying to undermine me. I say, 'Hey guys—*you* do it! You think you're so smart? *You* make this turkey.' If you're making your own mistakes, fine, but it's too difficult when other people make your mistakes for you."

De Palma's next few films, *Sisters* (about a pair of Siamese twins), *Phantom of the Paradise* (*Faust* to a rock beat), and *Obsession* (*Vertigo* redux), veered away from the lighthearted and established the director's reputation as a master of the gruesome. Blood-drenched movies tend to sell well, but Brian De Palma had a little problem. His problem was that he was a great director. His movies were bright, flashy, and clever, as well as junky, rather funny, and very energetic. Brian De Palma emerged as perhaps the greatest visual stylist in the business. "De Palma's visual style," Pauline Kael later wrote, "is smoothness combined with a jazzy willingness to appear crazy or campy; it could be that he's developing one of the great film styles. . . ." Kael remains one of his most persistent defenders.

But De Palma's talent was a problem because his movies, as berserk as they were, couldn't be dismissed easily. And his expert wielding of the camera tended to create movies that were too complicated for the typical horror junkie. As a result, De Palma was not a box-office draw, and as a result of that he was not allowed the freedom he coveted. "They wouldn't hire me for *Carrie,*" De Palma states about what would become his most successful movie. "I had to beg for the job. I pleaded, *pleaded,* to be allowed to direct it. Frankly, I was more than ready for big-time success. All my best friends in the business—Martin Scorsese, George Lucas, Steven Spielberg—had already made it in a huge way, and there I was, after eight or nine pictures, still struggling."

Carrie wasn't *Jaws*, but it did establish De Palma in Hollywood's eyes. He might have been thought a touch mad, what with his extensive use of blood, and his fondness for "visual quotes" from Hitchcock and others, but *Carrie* was a hit, nothing else mattered, and De Palma was offered every suspense and terror movie that found its way to a production executive's desk.

In addition to opening doors for him, *Carrie* introduced De Palma to his future wife, Nancy Allen. "I was the one who told Nancy that Brian had a crush on her," says John Travolta, who played Billy Nolan in *Carrie*, his screen debut. "I said, 'I can tell when a man's in love.' She said, 'You're *crazy!* He doesn't even *like* me!' We went through the whole shoot like that and then, at the end, she said, 'You're right. He does like me.'"

Nancy Allen didn't appear in her husband's next film, *The Fury*, a movie about a telekinetic girl that one critic labeled "bloody and violent. The ultimate litmus test for those who prefer form over content," but she did star as a prostitute in De Palma's subsequent venture, a film entitled *Home Movies*, which he wrote, produced, and directed with a group of students at his alma mater, Sarah Lawrence. *Home Movies*, which prompted one of De Palma's former students to remark, "I got through *Home Movies*, so I feel I can get through anything in life," was, however noble an experiment, a huge disaster.

So De Palma went back to making bigger films. The result was *Dressed to Kill*, a very sexy, very chilling movie. "There's something terrifying about sexuality," says De Palma regarding one of his most prominent cinematic themes, a theme that dominated *Dressed to Kill*. "It's one of the few mysteries around these days. A pickup, for instance, is a very sexually dangerous experience. When a woman decides to go home with a man she's just met, it must occur to her—'If I go home with this guy, is he going to kiss me or kill me?'" De Palma laughs hysterically: "Sex is terrifying."

For *Dressed to Kill*, Nancy Allen obliged her husband by parading about scantily clad, cast once again as a prostitute. De Palma put his wife in lingerie, sent a razor-wielding transvestite schizophrenic after her, and then filmed the scene, knowing it would be shown to thousands, possibly millions, of people. This was troublesome to many. How could you perpetrate such violence on your wife? Why display your wife nearly naked, and so consistently? Why your wife, why not some other actress? *Why?* De Palma laughs. "I put her in a car roll in *Carrie* before I even knew her," De Palma explains. "She looked good in *Dressed to Kill*. It worked in the movie."

It did, and *Dressed to Kill* made money. *Blow Out*, which was released in 1981, didn't. Starring John Travolta ("I always felt that Brian adored me. He seemed to get pure joy out of watching me work") and Nancy Allen, in the bimbo role she had grown accustomed to playing, the film, which had a production budget of $18 million, made only $9 million in domestic rentals. It's hard to say exactly why—the movie was certainly thrilling, and thought by some to be his most accomplished. Travolta thinks the ending—an illogical chase through the streets of Philadelphia—is to blame. De Palma doesn't know. "It frustrated me that *Blow Out* didn't do well, but I saw *Lolita,* and I thought that was a good movie, and it closed in three weeks. You've gotta realize that when you've made a movie that may be commercially disastrous, it may also be the best work you've ever done."

But *Blow Out* was greeted by a snarling press, ready to pounce. They attacked the film's violence, the putting-one's-wife-in-lingerie routine, and, worst of all, the stealing from the Great Directors. Not even Pauline Kael's usual praise (she compared Travolta to a young Brando and called the film "hallucinatory, a great movie") could soothe Hollywood's rumpled nerves. They were convinced: Brian De Palma was *mad. Saturday Night Live* summarized the *Blow Out* backlash in a "commercial" for a Hitchcock-esque (De Palma–esque) film entitled *The Clams (The Birds)* by announcing at the close: "Once a year Brian De Palma picks the bones of a dead director and gives his wife a job." "No one would answer my phone calls after *Blow Out,*" recalls De Palma. "It was a very bad time."

Bad for his marriage as well. All the negative press, according to mutual friends (Nancy Allen will not comment), helped to ruin the De Palmas' marriage. A woman he dated before Allen has her own thoughts about the matter: "How would you like to be married to someone who keeps a book on Nazi atrocities next to his pillow?" Whatever the reason, a divorce is imminent. "A lot of people were attacking me through my wife," De Palma explains. "And it caused a lot of problems. My wife was being attacked because she was Mrs. Brian De Palma. I've been through that before. I'm used to it, but she wasn't. I've answered all those questions over and over, but when they start focusing on your wife and she gets hurt, it ends up affecting you. It can bring a lot of pressure to a marriage."

Maybe so, but De Palma is a difficult man. His energies are directed toward

one end—making *his* movies—and that fact must have had negative reper-
cussions in his marriage. As long as Nancy Allen was in his films—being
killed off (or nearly so) in movie after movie—she was in his life. And perhaps it was also easier for De Palma to deal with his wife as a fantasy creation
in a De Palma–directed reality. Real life was much more difficult. Now he's
cold to the topic, closed off. His movies are all that interest him.

Paramount is burning and the man at Universal is still hanging, quite
bloody, from a rope. "Don't die until I tell you to die," De Palma says to the
actor. "You need to die a little faster."

The man's head droops, his mouth opens, he dies. "Let's do it one more
time," De Palma says. "I want it even faster."

More blood is applied to the man's face and De Palma looks pleased, very
pleased. Brian De Palma is wild about this movie. "*Scarface*," he says, "is the
greatest movie of the last ten years. Think about it: CUBANS! COCAINE! AL
PACINO! MACHINE GUNS! GIRLS! WOW! That's what I want to see."

For all of De Palma's enthusiasm, *Scarface* was a project he originally
turned down. Producer Martin Bregman suggested the project, then a remake
of the original *Scarface,* during the filming of *Blow Out.* De Palma said yes,
then no—he was too busy with *Blow Out. Scarface* was offered to Sidney
Lumet, who accepted, then rejected the assignment. By this point, several
years later, *Blow Out* was a commercial failure and De Palma wasn't having
much luck selling one of his pet projects, a movie about the Yablonski murders, to any of the studios. He had even signed on as the director of *Flashdance.* "I knew it would make a lot of money," De Palma says, "and, naive
fool that I was, I believed the producer would consider my script on the
Yablonski murders if I just made *Flashdance.*" De Palma quit the movie after
two weeks. His star was not ascending.

Bregman then reapproached De Palma with a lifesaving package: AL PAC-
INO! CUBANS! COCAINE! etc., etc. *Scarface,* rewritten and revamped, was
not only a marketable property, but the script had enough controversy—the
lead was a violent, power-mad gangster—to appeal to De Palma. "I always
look for the corrosive side of everything," he says. "Very few people seem to
transcend that. And those that do are either executed or crucified or shot.
For the same reasons, megalomania also fascinates me. Howard Hughes.
Elvis's last years. They all seem to wind up in hotel rooms with the drapes
drawn, staring at movie screens or TV sets. Those people want everything to

be an extension of their own reality. I can identify. Making movies is a lot
like that."

All this extended De Palma reality may turn out to be too intense for
Christmas merrymakers, but *Scarface* looks as good as any De Palma project
could as a vehicle for big box-office and Hollywood credibility. As soon as
filming began the movie became weighed down with production problems—an expensive location change from Miami Beach to Santa Barbara,
shooting delays, a last-minute ratings panic—but it was the equation of De
Palma and *Scarface* that Hollywood bought right from the beginning.
Enough so that after a year and a half of unemployment, De Palma was being
hailed as a hero just for having signed with the project. And in no time at all
he had financing for what was to be his next picture, a movie called *Fire,*
starring John Travolta as the unheard-of: "I play," Travolta says, "a cross
between Bruce Springsteen and Michael Jackson." Actually, his character
sounds a good deal more like Jim Morrison, what with an onstage obscenities
arrest ("Jim just exposed himself," says De Palma. "We're going to have the
guy arrested for screwing onstage. Who wants to look at a penis when you
can see someone screwing?") and a tragic finale. De Palma and Travolta spent
years trying unsuccessfully to secure the rights to a Morrison movie, but even
a Morrison roman à clef sounds like a perfect project for De Palma—Morrison
being the ideal embodiment of all the director's sex-and-violence imagin-
ings. But De Palma also wrote the script for *Fire,* which worried people, particularly one person—Keith Barish, who was to have put up the money, then
pulled out at the very height of the De Palma hype, reportedly because he
hated what De Palma had written. If *Fire* still happens, it won't be for a while.

De Palma isn't likely to forget the slap. He doesn't forget *anything.* "I never
went out to be famous," he says. "If you just want to be famous, it's better
to go out and shoot somebody. This takes a lot of work. Killing someone is
easy, and *instantly* you're famous. I want to be *infamous.* I want to be *controversial.* It's much more colorful."

In the end, *Scarface* and *Fire* both pale next to De Palma's dream movie, a
project that will serve as the sum of all the projects that went before it. Brian
de Palma is dreaming of . . . porno. He is now planning to follow up *Scarface*
with *Body Double,* a hard-core, pornographic suspense film. "As soon as I get
this dignity from *Scarface* I'm going to go out and make an X-rated suspense
porn picture," De Palma says enthusiastically. "I'm sick of being censored.
Dressed to Kill was going to get an X rating and I had to cut a lot. So, if they

want an X, they'll get a *real* X. They wanna see suspense, they wanna see terror, they wanna see SEX—I'm the person for the job. It's going to be unbelievable. I've been thinking about this for years: BRIAN DE PALMA'S *BODY DOUBLE!* I can't wait."

De Palma laughs his most crazed laugh. What could be a better joke on the system? A hot director making psychopathic porno! How wild! How . . . *controversial!* De Palma laughs. "This is going to be *Dressed to Kill II*," he says. "I'm already thinking of casting. I don't know if there's any good young porno stars out here, but the older ones—Annette Haven, Seka—some of them can really act. And Annette Haven has a terrific body. This is really exciting. *No one* is going to stop me from making *Body Double*. I can't wait."

This is what *Scarface* may wreak, an opportunity for De Palma to thrust upon us a multimillion-dollar projection of all our worst fantasies about what goes on in his mind. For the moment, though, *Scarface*, De Palma's ladder to porno fame, is calling. The hanging man is about to die again. "Okay," De Palma says, "when I say die, you *die*." The crew is silent. "DIE!"

The man dies perfectly. Not too fast and not too slow. Brian De Palma congratulates him. "It's not easy to die convincingly," he says. "I should know. I've had a lot of experience."

Double Trouble

MARCIA PALLY/1984

IT WOULD BE EASY TO SAY Brian De Palma hates women. He goes after them in the most grisly ways. Carrie impales her mother with kitchen utensils, gets pig blood dumped all over her (De Palma's idea of a prank), and is transformed into a monster to make your skin crawl. Angie Dickinson in *Dressed to Kill* is cut up with a straight-edge razor in the now-famous elevator scene. And in De Palma's latest effort, *Body Double,* a guy takes an electric drill to his lady and drills her to the floor. You gotta wonder about the mind that conjures such delicacies. If that's the upchuck, what's churning around inside?

"I like women," says De Palma. Let's say he does. But he told *Esquire* in a January '84 interview, "Sex is terrifying." Put them together and you have the straight man's burden: how to get laid when the experience is so flattening. (What an ironic worry it is: women's fear of sexual adventure is supported by the assault stats—and the *New York Post*—yet look who invents *vagina dentata*.)

De Palma does not like to be terrified or, in fact, to have the slightest thing out of his control. Perhaps his oeuvre should be seen as part exorcism, part conquest of unruly effects like lights, props or camera angles, or women. Especially sexually eager women. Carrie is trying to "find herself" in spite of a repressed religious nut of a mother, and the women in *Dressed* and *Double* aren't getting enough.

From *Film Comment,* September 1984: 12–17. Reprinted by permission of the author and *Film Comment.*

So it's fear rather than hate behind this update on the wages of sin, on bad-girl-gets-it-in-the-end. There are people out there upon whom such subtleties are lost. To the folks in the antiporn movement, De Palma's images are up there on the screen inciting people to sin (the new right), or teaching violence against women (feminist antiporners). That's damaging—and damning—enough.

The antiporn crusade didn't start with De Palma. Oh, he gets its attention when he unleashes a film redolent with the bouquet of sex and violence—which nevertheless gets an 'R' and the serious discussion of critics to boot. But the various churches have been warning us against the dangers of carnality since Augustine, and the born-again refurbishing of Christianity that got rolling 15 years ago is just making the cries of brimstone and hellfire louder, slicker, and brought from their sponsor. The feminist protest took off in the mid-Seventies when women, fresh from the abortion victory, turned their energies to rape and battery—the catastrophies possible to us all, the "single issue" capable of rousing the female masses.

Along with rape crisis centers and reckoning with cops and judges who considered rape the deserts of women who asked for it and the understandable restlessness of (white) men, came an analysis of violence against women. Susan Brownmiller's *Against Our Will* was one of the earliest and best known explorations of the subject, but in consciousness-raising groups and Take Back the Night rallies in town and country an ideology was gaining consensus, often distilled into the slogan "Porn is the theory, rape is the practice." With that, feminism launched upon its antiporn journey: WAP and WAVPM began their organizing efforts; other books hit the stands (Andrea Dworkin's *Pornography: Men Possessing Women,* Susan Griffin's *Pornography and Silence: Culture's Revenge Against Nature,* and the Laura Lederer edited anthology, *Take Back the Night,* among others).

The antiporn argument—greatly simplified, *pace* Dworkin—runs something like this: Men may or may not be born with murderous instincts, but at the very least they have developed a culture of misogynist mayhem bequeathed father to son. One of the prime conduits of transit is pornography. From porn, men learn to hate women (or hate them more), to rape them, and that such violation is erotic. So much for the catharsis theory. Freud, eat your heart out.

As though it had been planned, the film industry of the mid-Seventies provided the antiporn movement with fuel for its fire: snuff films and the slasher flicks like *Halloween, The Texas Chainsaw Massacre,* and *Friday the Thirteenth* that followed. To be sure, there had been precursors: the relatively small, underground porn industry of the Hays Office years; the art films such as *I, A Woman, Straw Dogs, The Devils, A Clockwork Orange,* and *Last Tango in Paris* which conflated sex with violence; and the porno flicks like *Deep Throat, The Devil and Miss Jones,* and *Behind the Green Door* that were so sensationalized they nearly qualified for date-night outings. But *Snuff* was in another league. Here we saw porn itself raping and murdering; it is the perfect (if horrifying) reduction, the worst (if self-validating) fears of the antiporn movement. *Green Door* by the way, is about S/M, a sport feminist antiporners began to tackle a few years ago. Consensual violence is no better than out-and-out force, they said: it recreates and reinforces the pernicious power imbalances that make women and minorities suffer in real life. No more "O"; no more of that letch of a marquis.

Except for the ERA debacle and Geraldine Ferraro, the antiporn protest has been the most visible—and seemingly uniting—of women's issues. After all, dueling with Hefner, Guccione, or Calvin Klein is a lot sexier than organizing the pink collar professions—or, for that matter, the women in the sex industry. (COYOTE, acronym for Cast Off Your Old, Tired Ethics, a group run by former and working prostitutes to help women-in-the-life, is perhaps the only operation of its kind.) But in the spirit of the democratic process, opposition has spoken up. Obviously, the producers of porn rebutted immediately. Civil libertarians cried censorship and set the movement a step or two back, smarting. (Having been burned, however, most antiporners steer clear of the First Amendment by calling, at least in their public appearances, not for the end of porn but for the enlightening of the citizenry.)

Less obviously, women who don't buy the antiporn line have begun to challenge its hegemony in feminist thought. The matter of consent should be brought to discussions of S/M, they argue, and the matter of context—of the difference between fantasy and reality—to discussions of porn. They worry about the defensive premise of the antiporn argument: men are lusty brutes, women their nice but helpless victims. Kept busy warding off attack, women will hardly have the time for their own pursuits, for finding out what they like or want. And some women don't want to wait till after the revolution. They are wary of prior restraint and the boundaries of government: if the state can interfere with the running of an adult bookstore, is that not a precedent for its closing gay bookstores or bars, abortion clinics or Planned

Parenthood? The social climate need shift only a little . . . And they wonder about our ability to define porn: is Brooke Shields in jeans porn, is a nude Rubens art? Or better yet, if an oil campus of a nude hanging in a gallery is stolen and the thief jerks off to it, is that painting art or pornography? Implicit in the problem of definition is the question of who gets to decide.

So much for the pulpits of the Christian right, for intrafeminist or intraleft quarrels; the porn debate has gone mainstream. ACLUers and WAPers have at each other on *Nightline,* Indianapolis passes antiporn legislation under the aegis of civil rights law, a woman immolates herself as a protest in a Minneapolis porn shop. And this past winter, the Justice Department awarded Dr. Judith Reisman $800,000 to research the connections among testosterone, pornography, and violence. In all this brouhaha, Brian De Palma's films don't stand a chance of simply being packaged as genre horror flicks and left at that.

In August, De Palma and I talked in his very white, very clean, very spare, very air-conditioned office, about what's going on in the antiporners' minds and what's going on in his. And about Vanessa Williams, voyeurism, the women's movement, Son of Sam, Hitchcock (again), the Sixties left, capitalism, government repression, the media, and (briefly) his taste in porn.

M P : *Do you think the hardcore fucking will get you an 'X'?*
B D P : There is no hardcore fucking. There's making love but nothing verging on hardcore.

M P : *What about the masturbation scenes?*
B D P : We'll see if they make an issue of it. I've had good luck with the ratings board before and I'll have good luck again.

M P : *Where'd you get the image of drilling a woman to the floor?*
B D P : I do a lot of murder mysteries; after a while you get tired of the instruments. Agatha Christie must've dealt with this day in and day out. You can use a knife, a rope, but now we have electrical instruments—which are truly terrifying.

M P : *But why the drill?*
B D P : Because he's using it to crack a safe.

M P :   *Did you start with the theft or with the idea of murder-by-drill?*
B D P :   The theft.

M P :   *Where'd you get the razor for* Dressed to Kill*?*
B D P :   I read somewhere that the most terrifying thing for a woman is disfigurement, that disfigurement is worse than death—that a woman would rather be stabbed than have her face cut up. It seemed to me a particularly terrifying image.

M P :   *Do you consider your work pornographic?*
B D P :   No. But now you're getting into what is and what isn't pornography. The stuff that is shot and sold as porn is meant to get you aroused and to climax. I don't think my movies have people coming in their seats . . .
     When you're dealing with an art form, you shouldn't be drawn into all kinds of social and political issues. People can comment on your work and write about it, but I think those making the form should not be bound by these things. If we had people saying you can't use certain words, or have violence, or shoot women in this way, what kind of world is that?

M P :   *Some women feel it's a safe world where women aren't made into playthings.*
B D P :   Does that mean that nude portraits should be eliminated, should we tear down all those paintings?

M P :   *That's the question of what is art or erotica and what's porn.*
B D P :   Who's going to decide that?

M P :   *People in the antiporn movement insist that they can distinguish, that people can tell what is respectful and what's "dehumanizing."*
B D P :   I'd hate to live in a world where art is left in the hands of the political people. I'd leave the country if it came to that—sounds like Russia.

M P :   *In previous interviews you've said that the crucifixion is a fairly gruesome sight, and no one goes around pulling crucifixes off museum or church walls or off the walls of bedrooms—God only knows what's going on there. Do you think there's a difference between a still life of an action and an enactment of that action?*
B D P :   No. Moving pictures is a Twentieth Century art form. If they had film when Rubens was painting, he probably would've used it.

M P :   *The antiporn argument makes an analogy between misogyny and racism: we would never allow pictures with sexual violence done to blacks or Jews, and the body politic does impose restraints on its citizens for the good of society.*

B D P :   But that's film as advertising . . . and I don't remember any great Nazi art forms or socialist art forms.

M P :   *You mean high quality anti-Semitism in cinema is okay but low quality isn't?*

B D P :   No. I'm saying in politically restricted societies where politicians control artists, you don't get interesting works of art.

M P :   *I think the antiporn people would agree that Nazi films were advertisement and the intention behind your work may not be, but the effect on the viewer might be the same. Do you think people learn values or perspectives or even how to act from watching film?*

B D P :   You're being put in contact with the sensibility of one person and you're either attracted to that sensibility and you find connections with your own experience or you don't.

M P :   *But art is said to affect its audience; art that contains racism or misogyny could be just one more thing in our culture that adds weight to them.*

B D P :   If you have a misogynist outlook a sexist film could strike a chord in you, but I don't think it engenders sexism. I don't think women are beaten or raped because the rapist has been affected by the entertainment industry. If there were statistics to prove that, they'd be on the front page of every newspaper in the country.

M P :   *One of the projects of the antiporn movement is to get those statistics, to prove that men learn to rape or assault from porn. The line of thinking goes something like: boys learn to be contemptuous of women, and every time they go to a porn film or a Brian De Palma film that attitude is stroked. It snowballs till it leads to violence.*

B D P :   Makes no sense to me. I've seen a lot of movies and a lot of porn, and it's not made me violent to women in *any* way. Anybody who's had contact with true violence knows there's absolutely no connections with artistic violence . . .

I was just reading a book about Son of Sam. The first time he tried to stab someone, he hit her and nothing happened. He expected her to fall over and be dead like in the movies, but it was nothing like the movies. The difference is so profound. It's the antithesis of the antiporn argument.

MP: *What about statements by rapists in prison counselling groups who say they learned how to do it, or that it was in some way okay to do it, from porn?*
BDP: I hate to give you this tired answer—I must've said this a thousand times . . .

MP: *I've probably read it as many times as you've said it.*
BDP: . . . but motion pictures are a kinetic art form; you're dealing with motion and sometimes that can be violent motion. There are very few art forms that let you deal with things in motion and that's why Westerns and chases and shoot-outs and killings crop up in film. They require one of the elements intrinsic to film: motion.

MP: *Rapid motion, percussive motion, emphatic motion may enliven the screen, but then there's the content. You can have an arching motion by itself and you can have that motion be used to slash someone's throat. You can use deep red and silver as a color combination or you can have a razor cut someone's face. Why do you choose the violent content?*
BDP: It interests me. I don't know why. I'd have to be on the couch a long time to figure it out. I seem to be attracted to it.

MP: *You said in an interview in* Macleans *a few years ago that you didn't go into medicine like your father because it wasn't precise enough for you. When you direct, you control a whole world, particularly events which, if they happened in life, would be terrifying because you would have no control—like meeting a razor-slashing crazy in an elevator.*
BDP: I don't like to be out of control. I don't see scary films. That's like getting on a roller coaster, you're out of control. I never get on roller coasters; I'm amazed at people who do. Who wants to be scared? Why would you put yourself in a situation where you were out of control?

MP: *Are you amazed that people go to your films?*
BDP: I certainly wouldn't go see them. But there's a difference between being the marionette and being the puppet master. One is a director because one wants to be the master.

M P : *Do you think men feel women are dangerous?*

B D P : They're used to mothers taking care of them and to a woman being that nurturing partner she had been for so many centuries. Now when she has her own concerns, career, men have trouble with that. And women are more sexually demanding now: "Where's my orgasm buddy. You call that an erection?"

It was never a problem for me but I think men find women's intelligence and aggression, their ambition, threatening. Women aren't going to make the terrible bargains they made in the past; they're too well educated. Why should they?

M P : *That's the modern problem. I wonder if there's an older issue. First mothers—women—control little boys' lives. And then, as if getting out from under the mother's control weren't enough, when boys grow up they have sex with women so the fears one has about sex—about that moment of being overwhelmed or out of control—becomes associated with women yet again.*

B D P : Sex is out of control . . . and love is out of control. Having your emotions in the hands of someone else is more terrifying than strange, wild sex. It's the nature of love to be out of control. But I *like* women. I get along with them; I went to school with a lot of them. I have long-term relationships. I use women in my films, and they tend to be strong women. I like directing women. I'm not Sam Peckinpah, you know, down in Mexico screwing whores. So I'm a strange kind of guy to be making the films I make.

M P : *Then why do you make them?*

B D P : Because of an aesthetic interest that I don't have much control over.

M P : *An* aesthetic *interest?*

B D P : I'm a visual stylist. I like interesting visual spaces, architecture. I like photographing women because they're aesthetically interesting. I'm interested in motion, sometimes violent motions because they work aesthetically in film. I like mysteries and plots with reversals. I have a dark image of society in which people are manipulating each other. Maybe that has to do with the world I work in.

M P : *But that's formal stuff again. You haven't said why you use violence.*

BDP: I said I'm a visual stylist, a VISUAL STYLIST (bangs on the table). I'm dealing with a white canvas up there and I may be one of the few practitioners doing that today. Sometimes I feel like Eisenstein; he was a great montage stylist.

MP: *But you don't make abstract films.*
BDP: The content of my films is a secondary issue. I don't start with an idea about content; I start with a VISUAL IMAGE (more banging).
    (De Palma starts to smile—oddly, I think. Is he feeling out of control? Is he going to want to do something about it? Am I crazy to be wondering where the drill is? No, razors would be better for the office.)

MP: *In the Jan. '84* Esquire, *one of the women you dated before you married Nancy Allen said you keep a book of Nazi atrocities by your pillow. Is that true?*
BDP: No. I read nonfiction about murders and if I'm doing a film about the cocaine industry I read about that. I keep most of my books here—you can go look.

MP: *What are you smiling at? Why are you looking at me that way?*
BDP: (Chuckling) Uh, it's just that a person's face changes when you get to know them. I'm starting to see how you think.

MP: *In your camera-work, you use the protagonist's or voyeur's point-of-view almost all the time—you've got to stop looking at me like that.*
BDP: (He laughs. I'm getting pissed off; he's just getting off.) Film is one of the only art forms where you can give the audience the same visual information the character has. I learned it from Hitchcock. It's unique to cinema and it connects the audience directly to the experience—unlike the fourth wall approach, which belongs to the Xerox school of filmmaking.

MP: *By connecting the viewer to the experience, the sex becomes hotter, the violence more frightening.* (He's peering at me again.) *I'm going to ignore that. The viewer flirts with losing control . . .*
BDP: You couldn't be a good director if you didn't also feel the arousal, the fear . . .

MP: *. . . but inevitably regains it. When you direct from the protagonist's POV,*

isn't that what happens to you, standing behind the camera, behind the eyes of the character? Don't you get aroused or frightened and then rein in your feelings, get on top of them?
B D P : That's the nature of directing. Taking control.

M P : *Did you see the* Times *story on the woman who set fire to herself in a porn shop in Minneapolis? She lit herself up as a protest against pornography, and then was hailed as a martyr by the antiporn feminists there—that was the group that tried to get the city of Minneapolis to pass the Cathy MacKinnon-Andrea Dworkin antiporn bill. It takes pornography out of the obscenity area into the civil liberties bailiwick and makes porn illegal by claiming it violates the civil rights of women. The mayor of Minneapolis vetoed the bill but in Indianapolis, the city passed a version of it.*
B D P : That woman is someone who made an extreme personal sacrifice to dramatize her political views, but I don't think we should encourage this—whether it's for no-nukes or to stop the war in Nicaragua.

M P : *I was struck by the difference between attacking porn stores—going after whoever you think the enemy is—and attacking yourself.*
B D P : It's almost a kind of terrorism, and unless it has a strong base behind it, it doesn't have any effect. It just looks like some single crazy event, like assassinations.

M P : *Assassins try to get somebody else; this woman went after herself.*
B D P : That depends on one's psychology: do you direct your anger out or in. It's safer to kill yourself than to kill somebody else, there's no question about that. But it doesn't accomplish anything.

M P : *Except the media blitz.*
B D P : That's a problem—that people do things for the sake of media attention. And the media tends to be attracted to violent, explosive, pornographic acts.
    I'm getting very interested in doing a movie about this media circus. I'm working on a script now. When I'm on a talk show, there's a montage of every violent scene from movies and life before we even begin to talk. People interpret that as news. Then everybody asks me how I can make violent movies, and the television program is doing the same thing—except they're pre-

tending it's news. They put sensational things on the air in order to sell advertising space. People don't understand that both presentations are entertainment. And news shouldn't be entertainment.

MP: *Earlier you said audiences didn't learn to be violent from your films and yet now you say viewers are affected by the news, which you say is entertainment just like your films.*
BDP: The media affects people because they can become stars. They do things in order to get on TV. You don't become a star by watching my movies . . . Take the street riots at the Democratic convention: if you turn on cameras and lights, people perform. The media is creating its own "news" events—and it's a monster because it needs stuff all the time.

I think there are a lot of psychopaths out there watching television—I don't think they're watching my movies, particularly—and when they see someone like Gary Gilmore giving press conferences, they say "Hey, what am I doing sitting in this motel room when I could be out there killing people, writing books, and being a celebrity." It's the *Taxi Driver* idea, the *King of Comedy* idea. And television has a much larger audience than movies.

MP: *You don't think people get the message from your films that if they take a razor to some woman in an elevator they'll become a star?*
BDP: No. If you're worried about violence against women, stop buying *Penthouse* magazine. That's the simplest way to deal with that problem—and the media is selling it all over the place.

MP: *What did you think of the Vanessa Williams business?*
BDP: She's very young, and I thought she handled those reporters like a seasoned anchorperson. I believed everything she said—until I saw the pictures. They were obviously carefully posed—this was no poor young girl wandering into a studio—specifically pornographic, created for a hardcore male market.

MP: *But they were rather standard, tame shots.*
BDP: Uh, that's pretty hardcore stuff, I think.

MP: *The lesbian shots?*
BDP: And the split-crotch shots.

M P : *Do you think she should've had to return her crown?*
B D P : Well, after all, she's a spokesperson for a lot of products and obviously it embarrasses the manufacturers. Come on, any public company would bail out of it in ten seconds.

M P : *Do you think the pageant is being a little hypocritical?*
B D P : Because the pageant exploits women in bathing suits and what's the difference between that and *Penthouse?* I think it's a matter of degree. We don't like to think of Miss America as a sex object, it's more the image of a pretty girl. There's a big difference between girls parading around in bathing suits and posing for *Penthouse,* just like there's a difference between love scenes in movies and hardcore porn.

M P : *What's the difference between a nude scene in one of your films and the shots of Vanessa in* Penthouse?
B D P : One is constructed to arouse and the other is constructed to enhance, or beautify, or whatever. I don't think pictures of women with their legs spread is aesthetically pleasing. I guess it's in the eyes of the beholder, totally subjective.

M P : *Who gets to decide what's art and what's porn?*
B D P : You do, each individual.

M P : *So you're not for closing down* Penthouse.
B D P : Absolutely not. I don't want to be in a bureaucratic situation where some people can decide what the rest of us should read and what we shouldn't.

I was on a program once with those guys who did a study where they showed a group of college kids a bunch of violent movies and then did a mock rape trial. The researchers concluded that the people in the test group were de-sensitized to violence, did not empathize with the girl who was raped, and in fact thought if they could rape somebody and get away with it, they would. It makes no sense at all to me—that I am such a brainless fool that if I see a few violent movies I'll feel it's perfectly fine to go out and rape somebody. Are we that impressionable? That's the whole process of growing up. You're supposed to be able to discriminate.

When you're dealing with someone like Son of Sam who thought if he hit someone like they do in the movies she would fall down dead, you're talking about someone who obviously can't distinguish between a movie and really trying to get a knife into someone—which is a very difficult process, especially if she's wearing a heavy coat. That guy is crazy.

I think the antiporn movement is dealing with duplicitous arguments. They're worried about walking into one of my films when in their neighborhoods there are stores selling pornographic cassettes hand over fist, and their six-year-old can turn on cable TV and see a hell of a lot more than is ever in my movies.

M P :   *The antiporn people are worried about that, too.*
B D P :   I should think they would be. That's a huge business. The history of radical movements in this country has been that the media addresses itself to the minor issues because there's no way they can deal with the major ones. If people are worried bout aggression, then we shouldn't live in a capitalist society. Capitalism is based on aggression, and violence against women has to do with aggression. That aggression is fanned constantly.

M P :   *The antiporn people think pornographic cassettes and cable and magazines and your movies are all dangerous.*
B D P :   Then we get into where you draw the line and the effects of drawing that line. Cigarettes are death and we still sell them. If you can't prevent me from smoking cigarettes then you can't prevent me from buying porn. People have a choice: nobody has to walk into my movies . . . Why not have an economic boycott of films they don't like?

M P :   *Do you think they'd be successful?*
B D P :   If they got enough support they could probably . . . if that's the way society is going to go then I'll have to stop making movies. But to me that's like the revolution of the Sixties—trying to create a revolution in a society that doesn't really want a revolution. I don't think too many people want to burn down the banks; they have car payments and mortgages.

Profit has become the moral justification for selling cigarettes. If you say that capitalism is the best system and free choice is necessary, you're going to have to accept that cigarettes and porn are going to exist. They make a profit, and people have the choice to buy them.

Margot Kidder and William Finley, *Sisters*, 1973

Geneviève Bujold and Cliff Robertson, *Obsession*, 1975

Sissy Spacek and William Katt, *Carrie*, 1976

Amy Irving and Kirk Douglas,
The Fury, 1978

John Travolta, *Blow Out*, 1981

Craig Wasson and Melanie Griffith, *Body Double*, 1984

Andy Garcia, Sean Connery, Kevin Costner, and Charles Martin Smith, *The Untouchables*, 1987

Sean Penn, Don Harvey, and Michael J. Fox, *Casualties of War*, 1989

Tom Hanks, *The Bonfire of the Vanities*, 1990

John Lithgow, *Raising Cain*, 1992

Al Pacino, *Carlito's Way*, 1993

Tom Cruise, *Mission: Impossible*, 1996

Nicolas Cage, *Snake Eyes*, 1998

Jerry O'Connell, Tim Robbins, and Connie Nielsen, *Mission to Mars*, 2000

MP: *You seem to be pro-free-choice and critical of capitalism.*
BDP: Capitalism has to be tempered by your own sense of morality. There are certain things you just shouldn't do in order to get ahead and those things need to be engendered by your family, by whoever brings you up.

MP: *Not by society?*
BDP: I don't think it would work. Going to a communist country isn't going to do it either. You have to balance the freedoms of a capitalist world with a sense of what's good and bad.

MP: *That means people will develop different moral codes. You smoke but other people think smoking is polluting the air and killing them. You don't think men learn to cut women up from your films and other people do. What's your "sense of morality"?*
BDP: I hate to get Biblical, but the Ten Commandments work perfectly well. 'Do Unto Others' seems to make a lot of sense. To me, the aggressive aspects of man come from profit being the most important thing in life.

MP: *Are women affected by the profit motive?*
BDP: Of course. I think it's behind a lot of the women's movement. Women want a piece of the pie too—and why should they be deprived of what we've had?

MP: *Do you think women are aggressive?*
BDP: Sure. They're being affected by the same system that men have been. If you want to change all of society you have to protest porn and General Motors simultaneously. I want to see WAP take that position.

MP: *I think a lot of them would.*
BDP: Then they have to start trying to get legislation against both industries—and they will get nowhere. So they focus on porn. They get a lot of attention because the media loves to put antiporn stuff on the air . . .
You get the jollies of porn and you get to feel righteous at the same time . . .
And you get to sell General Motors too. You can go live in places in this country where the profit motive is not so important. I'm sure I can go out and live in Maine and get a job in a mill and earn $200 a week—or maybe a

month—and I'd be totally unaffected by the profit motive of this country. But if you're going to live in one of the power capitals . . .

MP: *Unless they closed the mill.*
BDP: Then you'd have to go someplace else. But don't come into Manhattan and talk about pornography—it's ludicrous.

I think this antiporn business is a tempest in a teapot. When I was making *Dressed to Kill,* suddenly there were three books out on transsexuals, and transsexuals were on all the talk shows. One was on *Phil Donahue,* one on *Good Morning America.* You'd think they were all over the place. Same thing with the gay movement; people think they're going to take over. Then the craze passes, and we move on to the next thing.

There's also something else. We are human beings; we have certain kinds of drives and things we're attracted to that don't get educated out of us. And I don't think I'd want them to get educated out.

MP: *One last question. You've often been accused of lifting from Hitchcock . . .*
BDP: Richard Corliss is a big one on that . . .

MP: *Given all those accusations, why do you still put bathroom scenes—lifting from* Psycho, *they call it—in every one of your films, including the new one?*
BDP: I throw it right in the face. I refuse to be censored by a bunch of people who have the wrong perceptions of my movies. I should listen to these nitwit critics? I don't cater to the public, why should I cater to the critics?

MP: *Do you put those scenes in as a jab?*
BDP: No. If I'm attracted to something I shouldn't refuse to use it just because Hitchcock was attracted to it too.

MP: *What's the attraction of the shower scene?*
BDP: Hitchcock discovered that people feel safe in the bathroom with the door shut.

MP: *Not any more . . .*
BDP: It's a place that when someone comes in, you really feel violated. To me it's almost a genre convention at this point—like using violins when people look at each other or using women in situations where they are killed or

sexually attacked. You know, the woman in the haunted house—I didn't invent that. Women, over the history of Western culture, seem to be more vulnerable than men. It has a lot to do with their being physically less strong. They made a movie with Roy Scheider being stalked in a basement. Roy Scheider is the guy who killed Jaws. Now who is going to jump out at Roy Scheider? Obviously children in peril is also something you'd connect with, but there's something too awful about that. I don't particularly want to chop up women but it seems to work.

(Picking up pen and paper and holding them out expectantly, the way a priest motions for his congregation to rise.) So, Marcia. Can we have a drink sometime?

Cool Head, Hot Images

BRUCE WEBER/1989

IN THE MINUTES BEFORE the first public test screening of Brian De Palma's new movie at a theater in Boston, a young man approaches Steven Spielberg, De Palma's friend and fellow director who is sitting in the audience with a baseball cap pulled down over his brow, and asks him if he is Steven Spielberg.

"No," Steven Spielberg says, though as the man begins to walk away, he changes his mind.

Ambivalence—and nervousness—are prevalent this evening. De Palma himself, who believes this movie, *Casualties of War,* unequivocally to be his best, is nonetheless aware that it is not a romping entertainment. "It's so intense people may get up and leave," he said earlier in the day. At the moment, he's in the front row, and will spend the evening with his back to the screen, watching the audience.

Farther back, seated with Spielberg, are the film's producer, Art Linson, and several Columbia Pictures executives, including Dawn Steel, who approved the project in November 1987, shortly after she became president of the beleaguered studio.

Casualties of War had been abandoned by Paramount, Steel's previous employer; she rescued it for Columbia, upped the budget to a reported $22.5 million and made it her first "green light."

Columbia finished 1988 last among the nine major movie studios in

From the *New York Times Magazine,* 21 May 1989: 24–26, 105, 116–17, 126. © by the *New York Times.* Reprinted by permission. All rights reserved worldwide.

domestic market share, and Steel, charged with effecting a resurgence, is now awaiting summer, when the first movies produced at the studio on her watch will be released. Though *Casualties of War* features Michael J. Fox and Sean Penn, and is thus compatible with Steel's predilection for star packages, it isn't *Ghostbusters II* (which is due next month). As the lights go down, Steel is visibly on edge.

Based on the true story of an atrocity committed by a squad of American soldiers in Vietnam, *Casualties of War* is immediately recognizable as a Brian De Palma film. In its opening sequence, a nighttime battle in the jungle that is photographed in the glossy, hyperbolized mode De Palma has frequently favored in his depictions of threat and chaos, Daniel Eriksson, a "cherry" who is seeing his first action, falls through a hole in the jungle floor and finds himself wedged in the earth up to his armpits, his legs dangling into a tunnel dug by the Vietcong. Played by Fox, Eriksson is plainly terrified, but he is spared a bit of suspense that the audience, which sees that the tunnel is occupied, is not. As Eriksson is yanked to safety by a comrade, an enemy guerrilla swipes at his legs with a knife—and misses.

It is a typical De Palma manipulation, a macabre joke played both for the audience and at its expense. It is the only one in the picture: Though the film is bursting with De Palma's inventions, the grim truth of the material is no laughing matter. When the squad members, sent on a scouting patrol, kidnap a young Vietnamese woman, rape her and kill her, Eriksson is unable to stop them and bears excruciating witness to the crime. For the remainder of the movie, he is at the mercy of his conscience.

In the middle of the screening, half a dozen people do pick up and leave. And when the lights finally come up the theater is silent. Not a rustle. Eventually, as opinion cards are distributed, Steven Spielberg leans across Dawn Steel, whose fists are not yet unclenched, and murmurs a judgment to a man sitting on her opposite side.

"You'll be thinking about this for a week," he says.

"Maybe the ending could be made simpler," De Palma says. It is the following morning, and he doesn't look well. A large man—his girth, like many of his movies, is reminiscent of Alfred Hitchcock—he is devilishly bearded, and can be imposingly stone-faced. But today he is pale with apparent sleeplessness. After the screening, he attended a focus group discussion, examined the audience opinion cards and went to bed. Dawn Steel and Art Linson have expressed a wary satisfaction at the results of the test, but sipping cappuccino in the lounge of his hotel and speaking in his oddly reedy voice, De Palma is more forthright. The focus group had been impatient during a key expository sequence, he says, and he now wears the aspect of a man who, at the end of a long and grueling effort, has just discovered there is more work to be done.

"We were disappointed," he says, acknowledging that the majority of the audience graded the picture in the good to very good range. "What you really want," he says, and then stops to distance himself from the studio executives. "What *they* want is to have it tipped way high in the excellent area." He points out that, unlike a comedy, in which you can actually gauge what the audience thinks is funny, *Casualties of War* is supposed to leave the audience stunned, disturbed, introspective—and silent.

"In a movie like this, I'm not sure testing has any relevance," he says. "Still, you have to consider the problems when you read the cards and listen to the focus groups. You have to consider what's bothering them. Why aren't they reacting more strongly? It unnerves you. Everyone is unnerved. No question about it."

It's an unusual admission for a director who, by all the available evidence, is at the height of his career. Now 48, De Palma has directed 19 feature films, including *Casualties of War,* a long-held ambition, the making of which was engendered by the critical and commercial success of *The Untouchables,* his 1987 film about gangsters in Chicago during Prohibition. That film garnered nearly $80 million in domestic sales for Paramount Pictures. And he has recently landed what likely was Hollywood's most coveted assignment, having signed on with Warner Bros. to adapt *The Bonfire of the Vanities,* Tom Wolfe's celebrated, darkly comic novel about class stratification in New York.

For De Palma, it has been a long, evolutionary climb. He has always been a virtuosic technician, equally deft with a moving camera and a still frame, a muscular stylist who until recently has been little interested in conventional narrative development. His films—often, in the past, built on preposterous or bizarre plots (two revolve around characters who are telekinetic)—are rife with contrived angles and shifting points of view. And murder in *Casualties of War,* for instance, takes place in a corner of the frame, behind a close-up of Michael J. Fox—he will use the frame as a three-dimensional space and juxtapose images in the foreground and background, thus wordlessly dramatizing a moment of conflict.

A student of film history whose work has quoted unabashedly from familiar masterworks, he is probably best known for the relish with which he has used the medium to convey anxiety, horror, and shock. Many of his films have made an almost gleeful use of sex and violence for their natural evocation of tension and release. He was once quoted as saying, "Violence is extremely beautiful." He amends that now. "Violence is cinematic," he says, adding that film is a medium in which "you can explore very strong, violent emotions."

In *Scarface* (1983), he cuts off a man's arm with a chainsaw. In *Body Double* (1984), before finally murdering a woman with an enormous power drill, he engages in a savage, phallic joke; initially, at the moment of penetration, the killer accidentally yanks on the electric cord, the plug comes out of its socket, and the drill bit withers. Both scenes are agonizing in duration and excruciating at their peak, yet in both, the killing is ultimately accomplished just beyond the frame, and thus in the mind of the viewer. It's wicked excess.

De Palma has been frequently and vehemently chastised for his willing portrayal of brutality—both in general and, in particular, toward women—but his vivid imagination for the humorously gruesome has won him admirers as well. They include Pauline Kael, film critic for the *New Yorker,* and Jay Cocks, the former film critic for *Time,* now a screenwriter and friend. Cocks remembers an unproduced script they worked on together that De Palma opened with a scene in which a man is killed in a park by a murderous model airplane, a fondly sinister parody of the famous scene in Alfred Hitchcock's *North by Northwest,* in which Cary Grant is chased by a crop-duster.

It is only lately, De Palma says, that he has become interested in character development, and it is no accident that he has worked, in his last two films, with scripts by established playwrights—David Mamet on *The Untouchables* and David Rabe on *Casualties of War*—rather than pen his own, something he did frequently in the past. "I'm good with story ideas and visual ideas," he says. "But I'm not good at writing characters. There are 8,000 quotes of me saying, 'Form is content.' Well, it's true. Form *is* content. But other stuff is content, too."

A cerebral, pragmatic man, De Palma, figuring blithely out loud, says a film maker can probably expect a four-decade career. Nearing the end of his third decade himself, he says, he should be at his peak, a time when his experience and creative energy are at maximum confluence, and when his work ought to be making use of every element of the medium.

"What a camera does is essential to being a film maker," De Palma says now. "But when you do it all—when you have a great story, a great script, great characters, great actors, and a director who has an incredible visual sophistication—that's when you're going to make a truly great movie. I'm at the point in my career where I want to push it as far as I can."

Many critics have noted that, in the midst of a De Palma film, there is typically a sequence that can almost stand by itself—the lolling, lascivious sojourn in a girls' locker room that opens *Carrie* (1976), for instance; or Angie Dickinson's dangerous flirtation in the Metropolitan Museum of Art in *Dressed to Kill* (1980)—set pieces, really, in which the film maker seizes on a setting or a narrative situation and uses it to parade his capabilities. The most virtuosic of all, perhaps, serves as the climax to *The Untouchables,* and it is a nice illustration of De Palma's deftness at solving problems, as well as his ambition to incorporate his expanding concerns.

In the scene, two Federal treasury agents, played by Kevin Costner and Andy Garcia, have a gun battle with henchmen of Al Capone. Their aim is to capture Capone's bookkeeper, who has the information that would convict Capone on charges of income-tax evasion. As scripted by David Mamet, the scene was elaborate, yet according to De Palma, not interesting enough visually. So he seized the initiative and reconceived the scene in the midst of production. "Writers don't have good visual ideas. It's my job to give them ideas to work with," he says, adding that he would have asked Mamet to rewrite it himself, but Mamet, in the midst of making his own movie, wasn't around.

Ultimately, the scene was shot at Union Station in Chicago, much of it in slow motion to heighten the drama of its complex choreography, and with suspense provided largely by the soundtrack. In the vast, echoing chamber of a train station at midnight, with Costner poised and waiting, various sound elements—a music-box lullaby, footsteps and then softly dissonant strings—are introduced one after another, entrances as dramatic as characters'. The key visual element was a baby carriage bouncing down the station steps that De Palma simply lifted from the famous "Odessa Steps" sequence in the Sergei Eisenstein classic *Battleship Potemkin.*

"You try to get all your story and character elements merged in a physical action section of the movie," he says. "You develop your characters, you develop your story, then suddenly you bring it into a total cinematic confrontation. The greatest example of this, I think, is *The Bridge on the River Kwai,* where all your characters come to this huge metaphor—the bridge.

And everybody is doing something to the bridge that is a development of their own character line. That, to me, is a perfect movie.

"*The Untouchables* is essentially about how the innocent get slaughtered in the conflict of the gangsters. That's the story idea," he continues, and thus, in the climactic scene, he was looking for a way to dramatize the central theme.

"It's something I thought about all through the movie, coming up with an idea for getting the bookkeeper. Eliot Ness"—played by Costner—"has to get the guy and protect the innocent simultaneously. And suddenly, some-how, *Potemkin* popped into my head. Of course, the image of a baby carriage bouncing down those steps in the midst of a crossfire is an image that's very strong.

"Ordinarily, I storyboard everything, but this time I didn't have a chance. The most important thing was location. We needed a set of steps. And they had to be period steps. And we looked around and looked around, and we finally came up with the train station. And when I looked at it—it's very important to see the actual location—I had all of it in my head. I could see the baby carriage going up and down in the crossfire. I could see sailors pass-ing through."

As the scene draws to a close, Andy Garcia flips a gun to Costner, then slides across the slick marble floor and stops the baby carriage at the bottom step with his body. Costner, meanwhile, dispatches another bad guy with his new gun and grabs the carriage from above. It is meant as a symbolic moment. "I wanted to bring them together as a unit," De Palma says.

The scene took six nights of shooting. De Palma smiles slightly at a satisfy-ing recollection. "Mamet, by the way, didn't like it," he says.

In *Home Movies,* a low-budget feature De Palma made in 1980 with some students at Sarah Lawrence College in Bronxville, N.Y., Keith Gordon stars as an introverted teen-ager who is largely ignored by his mother and who lives in the shadow of his older brother. It is, De Palma says, reasonably autobiographical.

He was born in 1940, the youngest of three boys, and grew up, after the age of 5, in Philadelphia. His father, now retired, was an orthopedic surgeon. Young De Palma attended a private high school, where he spent much of his time designing computers and participating in science fairs.

"I was one of those science types who was always up in his room with all these parts," he says, an image that recalls another character played by Keith

Gordon, Angie Dickinson's computer-nerd son in *Dressed to Kill.* "Oh, boy, that was me," De Palma says. "I remember being on that set and feeling very at home." It also recalls, indirectly, the locker-room scene in *Carrie,* which, it has been suggested, is every adolescent boy's fantasy.

"No kidding," De Palma says.

It was in the late 1950s, after he entered Columbia University, that De Palma started going to the movies seriously, and he edged out of the sciences and into drama. He acted in a few plays at Columbia, poorly, by his recollection, and after graduating he studied direction and film making for two years at Sarah Lawrence.

At Columbia, like most of those around him, De Palma was in the thrall of the French New Wave directors François Truffaut and Jean-Luc Godard. He had also discovered Alfred Hitchcock; watching Hitchcock's films, he says, is like going to suspense school.

"Take *Dressed to Kill,*" De Palma says. "That has a great idea that's taken from *Psycho.* You take a character, a leading cast member that the audience is involved with, and you bump her off 30 minutes into the movie. That's a great idea. The audience can't believe you're bumping her off. You don't want your audience to know where the story is going."

De Palma doesn't volunteer a great deal, but what emerges, when he talks about his life, is a curious self-awareness. He'll tell you the facts when you ask about them, and communicate, with an acknowledging shrug or a snicker, that they are somehow relevant to the movies he's made. But he engages only privately in self-analysis.

He was married once, in 1979, to the actress Nancy Allen, whom he had cast in several roles; they divorced in 1983. His frequent companion for the last year has been Kathy Lingg, an executive at Tri-Star Pictures. He has a home in Los Angeles and an apartment in New York. He is a software junkie, he says, who spends off afternoons cruising the computer stores in Los Angeles malls.

The distinction between his outer quietude and garrulously sinister imagination is evident even to those who know him. "There's just a part of him that's unknowable," says one woman friend. "But I've always thought that the Keith Gordon characters were standins for him, the insecure outsider who wants to save the girl but fails."

"He scared me at first, to tell the truth," says Thuy Thu Le, the 22-year old Vietnamese woman who plays the victim in *Casualties of War,* her first acting experience of any kind. "Brian, if he has one fault, it's that he's shy. He's a big man. He looks mean. He doesn't talk to anybody. People misunderstand."

De Palma himself says simply that he likes women and, in particular, likes working with them. (His track record is good; he has provided important roles for Jill Clayburgh, Amy Irving, Sissy Spacek, Melanie Griffith, and Michelle Pfeiffer.) And though some of his films, particularly *Body Double,* catalyzed the ire of feminists, the critic Carrie Rickey, now with the *Philadelphia Inquirer,* points out that though he may victimize women in particularly gruesome ways, "they are never as dumb or as psychically tormented as the men in his films."

"Brian is a true eccentric," says Jay Cocks, who has known him since the early 1970s, and in whose household De Palma is known as "the Bear." Cocks says that Sam, his 8-year-old son, treasures the recording, made for him by De Palma, of De Palma doing a voiceover of the Otis Redding song, "(Sittin' on) The Dock of the Bay," in a British accent.

Often, because of his steely demeanor, De Palma has been perceived by journalists as cold. And owing to the brutal imagery in his films, many moviegoers consider him to be something of a calculating beast. "Gratuitousness is a relative call," he says. "Is *Clockwork Orange* too violent? Some people are going to say, 'It's too much.' But violence is cinematic. It can, of course, be misused and done clumsily, but I'm very good at it."

It is evident that he regards film making as a complex task, a job for the intellect, and he prefers to talk about it that way, as opposed to confronting the emotions that seed the work. Yet eventually, he tells two stories that begin to give him away. His first successful film, *Greetings,* (1968), was an X-rated antiwar comedy about the draft that starred a young Robert De Niro. De Palma himself was a draft dodger. "I pretended I had asthma," he says. "I did have asthma, actually. But I really had a case when I went to the draft board. I could hardly breathe. I had taken everything in the world to make me . . . asthmatic." Which is particularly interesting given the concerns of *Casualties of War,* a movie, he says, "that epitomizes the Vietnam experience. To me, the Vietnam experience is the sore that will never heal. So many things happened to these kids, and marred their lives forever, and there's no rational way to explain it."

The second story is especially, though not exclusively, pertinent to the movie he will make next, *The Bonfire of the Vanities.* The script is now being revised for him by the screenwriter Michael Cristofer, but since he read the novel, De Palma says, the central scene in which the Wall Street blueblood, Sherman McCoy, is thrown unceremoniously into a crowded jail cell, has chilled him with remembrance. "Anyone who's spent a night in the Tombs, which I've had the *privilege* of doing"— he says, and then pauses, laughing nervously. "You get it real fast."

According to De Palma, it was in 1963, when he was 22 and "feeling very sad about myself," that he got drunk and stole a motorcycle and began driving around Manhattan. "Some cops pulled me over, and I was feeling a little self-destructive. And I knocked one down. And they ran me down and shot me.

De Palma recollects being treated for a leg wound at St. Luke's Hospital with a police guard at the door. He says he ultimately pleaded guilty to grand larceny and assault and was given a suspended sentence. But in the interim, he remembers spending a night behind bars.

"I understand that moment Sherman has very well," he says. "When you're brought up as a middle-class kid from Philadelphia, you've gone to private schools and Columbia, and suddenly you're in the tank? Whoa! You're in there with people you've sort of read about in the newspaper. And you realize you're just one, and everybody is equal before the law. And they said, like, 'What are you in for?' And I remember one guy handing me one of those sandwiches they give you, two pieces of bread and a piece of cheese? Fortunately, I was, like, the guy who knocked down a cop, so they treated me with a certain amount of respect." He laughs again.

"But I was terrified," he says. "I'll never forget it."

De Palma's latest film is gravely and potently distinct from all his earlier work. Daniel Lang's account of the rape and murder of the Vietnamese woman, and the court-martial of those who perpetrated it, first appeared in the Oct. 18, 1969 issue of the *New Yorker*. "But there was no way for me to get control of it then," De Palma says. "A couple of screenplays were written, but no one could get it made, and it kind of vanished."

It was in 1979 that David Rabe, who is a Vietnam veteran, mentioned it to De Palma as a project worth resurrecting and said it was a script he'd be eager to write. Still, it wasn't until the Hollywood clout De Palma had gleaned from *The Untouchables* kicked in that he pursued the movie in earnest. The package he put together, with Rabe, Michael J. Fox (whose agency, Bauer, Benedek, is the same as De Palma's) and Sean Penn, was initially given the go-ahead by Paramount. But Paramount executives are said to have become doubtful that Fox, known as the fresh-faced teen-ager from the television sitcom *Family Ties,* could shoulder the burden of such an intense dramatic role.

Dawn Steel, meanwhile, had left Paramount, where she was president of production, and had arranged to become an independent producer in partnership with none other than Michael Fox. When Victor A. Kaufman, the president and C.E.O. of Columbia Pictures Entertainment Inc., hired her to replace David Puttnam as head of his flagship studio, she jumped at the chance to make *Casualties of War.*

"It's very simple," Steel said in an interview last fall. "Historically, Vietnam movies have been profitable. All of them. *Platoon, Full Metal Jacket, Apocalypse Now, The Deer Hunter.* You're looking at movies that have been not pretty successful, but very successful. The foreign numbers have been extraordinary."

Still, Steel also said at the time that she did not want the film portrayed as being about a rape and murder, which is, of course, what it is centrally about. And in April, after the screening in Boston and an additional test in Houston, she canceled another scheduled interview.

With major studios planning to release two other Vietnam movies this fall, and with Michael J. Fox's *Back to the Future II* due in November, Columbia will forgo positioning the film later in the year for optimum Academy Award consideration. The nationwide release date is currently set at Aug. 18, to capitalize instead on traditionally high summer movie attendance.

Casualties of War, is, in fact, different from the other celebrated movies about Vietnam, largely because it makes presumptions about what audiences have learned from them. It is not a "journey" film, or an allegory of good and evil, that uses the war to track its characters' descent into inhumanity. Nor is it a surrealist portrait of the horrors of combat. Rather, almost from the start, it asks the viewer simply to accept the fundamental amorality that our soldiers embraced in order to survive.

Then, too, its focus is on a single event and a single young man. For a while, Eriksson shares the agony with the young victim. But after her death (she is murdered during a battle scene shot on a trestle, a sequence whose complexity matches that of the "Odessa Steps" in *The Untouchables*), the film becomes the story of a personal ordeal. It depicts a situation, as De Palma puts it, "that any of us could have been in," in which a 19-year-old—one reason, De Palma says, that Fox, who is actually 27, was suited for the role—

"cannot do anything that is right and will spend his whole life haunted by it." Indeed, according to the director, the real Eriksson has read the script and signed a release, but he has never talked with De Palma and wishes to remain anonymous and unaffiliated with it.

It is a different movie, De Palma concedes, than it would have been had he made it two decades ago. "It's not really political. It's very emotional, and full of sorrow," he says, adding that he does wonder about the war experience he chose to avoid.

"I think I was lucky I didn't go to Vietnam," he says. "Maybe it would have given me an understanding of some things I only understand second-hand. But I think you'd be so horribly scarred by it. I mean, the people I know who have been there, like David Rabe, there's something that's behind their eyes that isn't behind mine. How close do you want get to the fire in order to be able to write about it?"

"We were in hell for five months," said Michael J. Fox. Speaking during the filming of the movie's final sequence in a San Francisco park last summer, Fox had, along with the rest of the crew, just returned from the jungles of Thailand, where the bulk of the movie was shot, and where temperatures had been routinely over 100 degrees.

"You're physically exhausted, and because of the material, you're emotionally in a bit of a state," Fox said. "It was really important to watch Brian getting out of his Volvo every day, and to know that he knew exactly what was going to happen. He inspires confidence."

Indeed, as technicians, setting up one last shot, built a track on the park grass for a camera to dolly on, De Palma, supervising, was an enormous, composed presence amid the commotion. De Palma would explain later that the scene had been storyboarded long ago; it was already in his head, and because there were no grave problems afforded by the location, the only problem left, really, was the technical one—matching his vision.

In the sequence being filmed, Eriksson, years after his discharge, confronts a young woman who reminds him of the woman he saw killed. And in the final shot, the young woman emerges from a bus, followed by Eriksson, who pursues her into the park and calls after her. As the cameras rolled, De Palma, seated in a director's chair and watching the scene through a viewfinder, hunched his shoulders, becoming aggressively more attentive, like a cat who'd heard a distant, unidentifiable sound. Fox approached the camera; the camera dollied toward Fox, so that, in the end, they were inches apart, his face in close-up, the actress Thuy Thu Le offscreen. The whole thing lasted less than a minute.

De Palma ran the actors through eight takes, consulting with Fox after each, and finally, the last couple of times, hustling just to the edge of the confrontation himself, so that he, Fox, Thuy Thu Le and the cameraman were all huddled together under the sound boom as if it were an umbrella.

It was the acting that hadn't satisfied him—Michael Fox's final expression. "It's a difficult scene to bring off," he said afterward. "You know, you run into a stranger and she looks at you and understands something about you that no one's ever understood. In a sense, she's the forgiving angel. And he's got to show that he's been forgiven. In the initial takes, it just wasn't there."

Eight months later, sitting in his Boston hotel, De Palma is asked if this is the scene that befuddled the screening audience. "No," he says, "they seemed to like that. They thought the movie was paced very well. And they were not disturbed by the violence, which in a movie of mine is remarkable." The problem, he explains, was in the court martial scene, which the audience seemed to feel reiterated dilemmas that had already been resolved.

"I think it's important to see the squad members on the stand," he says, "see what they have to say, see them confronted with what they've done. But you are taking the risk of dragging the audience back through material they are familiar with, in order to get the true emotional thrust of the movie—which is that these are *all* casualties of war." He admits that he's thinking of dropping the trial scene, or at least editing it down.

It's an interesting moment, the film maker listening in his head to several different voices at once. He looks as if he wished they would all shut up.

How, he is asked, will the decision be made?

"Everyone will give me an opinion," he says. "and then I'll do what I want."

Brian De Palma, Through the Lens

PAULA SPAN/1989

LUNCH WITH BRIAN DE PALMA. You half expect him to order a very rare steak, slice into it with a large serrated knife, and watch the blood form visually striking patterns on the china.

You have, after all, spent several increasingly jittery days watching his movies on videocassettes, seeing people artistically dismembered with chain saws, drilled to the floor, slashed with straight razors, attacked in showers. Entering an elevator behind a perfectly ordinary-looking businessman now gives you pause.

But no. He asks the waitress for an endive salad. Then he pulls a high-resolution video camera out of his canvas shoulder bag and turns it on his interrogator. "Introduce yourself, please," the director of *Carrie* and *Dressed to Kill* and *The Untouchables* instructs the reporter, calmly, from behind the viewfinder. "What's going to be your first question?"

Then he turns off and stows the camera, folds his massive hands on the tablecloth and answers the question. But how can you launch into a discussion of his new Vietnam movie, *Casualties of War,* after a stunt like that? Especially given his series of stylish suspense movies in which being watched was often a prelude to sex or death (in De Palmaland, these frequently amount to the same thing).

He may enjoy briefly turning the observers into the observed; he has been victimized over the years by the press (and by critics and Hollywood studio

---

types and the film ratings board and certain feminist anti-porn groups, and he doesn't sound forgiving about a single skirmish). But his primary motivation, he insists, is more personal: Since the mid-70s he has videotaped "what I did today, who I met, an idea that occurred to me . . . you note something down in your diary." Overturned trash cans on East Eighth Street, a drive to Florida with his brother to visit their parents, publicity junkets for *The Untouchables*—they're all on cassettes, an ongoing video memoir.

"It makes you kind of examine your life," De Palma says in his quiet tenor, an unexpected voice from such a bear-like man. "You juxtapose one thing against another to figure out what kind of river you're swimming in."

De Palma's life looks to be flowing more smoothly these days, after a period of struggling against the currents. He first read about the tragedy on which *Casualties of War* is based in the *New Yorker* in 1969, and the story has hovered in his brain ever since. "It told, in a very contained, tight form, a kind of parable about the war," a war that always triggered his mistrust. But finding financial backing proved a tough task for years, until *The Untouchables* connected at the box office in 1987. Suddenly the frustrating drought between hit movies ended (the 1980 thriller *Dressed to Kill* had been the last big moneymaker), bringing not only the go-ahead for *Casualties of War* but another plum directorial assignment: Next year, De Palma starts shooting *Bonfire of the Vanities*, adapted from Tom Wolfe's stinging bestseller.

You note the evolution here. These latest films leave the confines of De Palma's eccentric imagination and move out into the world, where characters are driven by social forces as well as their own murky psyches; the scripts are written by playwrights (David Mamet for *The Untouchables*, David Rabe for *Casualties*, Michael Cristofer for *Bonfire*) instead of by De Palma himself.

What of the genre that over 20 years often drew him into cinematic voyeurism and violence, sexual compulsion with brutal consequences (particularly for women), arrestingly photographed psychopathology? Enough. De Palma did it too masterfully to be dismissed but too disturbingly, in most cases, to draw a mass audience. (Twenty-two-year-old Thuy Thu Le, who plays the Vietnamese victim in *Casualties*, recalls her audition for De Palma: "He asked me to look scared and yell and scream, but I expected that from him.") In any case, "I've sort of plowed that field over and over again," he says. Unless he encounters "something that can push that form a little further," he's had it with horror.

"I'm attracted," he announces seriously, "to ideas dealing more strongly with character, dramatic storytelling, ethical issues, things that make you think."

Of course, *Casualties of War* both differs from and harks back to his previous work. A taut recounting of how a patrol of young Americans raped and murdered a Vietnamese woman, and how one soldier felt bound to bring the others to justice, it is an exploration of moral struggle. "Take human beings and they wind up committing atrocities; there's got to be some reason for that," he says. "How can this happen? Why did it happen?"

It also reflects "an era when a lot of us learned to doubt our leaders. . . . The assassinations, the Vietnam War—you sense you're being lied to, and sure enough, you are."

De Palma avoided the draft in the early '60s, as the troop buildup loomed, with a doctor's note explaining that he was asthmatic. He has suffered no second thoughts about his choice: "It was a misguided policy; thank God I didn't have to go." And the doubt has stayed with him. Talking of Nixon's lies about Watergate and, he thinks, Reagan's about Iran-Contra makes him more animated than anything except excoriating film critics.

"The generation that has not been brought up with all this is probably not as skeptical as we are," says De Palma, who's about to turn 49. "It's always important to make movies about this particular section of our history, so people will know what it is. . . . 'No more Vietnams' has kept us out of Central America."

Yet *Casualties of War* incorporates a number of De Palmic elements: the assaulted woman, the witness, the paranoiac dread of not knowing friends from enemies. Assigned to come up with a war movie, De Palma might almost have envisioned this scenario, mightn't he?

"Obviously you are attracted to certain things: they're themes that reoccur in your work," he responds, cautiously. From long experience, he was able to call on "certain technical skills—how to visualize people in peril, make action vivid and heart-rending." But, he adds, wanting to draw the line, "I don't think I've ever made a movie that had such a strong ethical conflict."

This is the tricky part, trying to signal a change in direction without repudiating his earlier movies. Plenty of others have already trained their scopes on films like *Dressed to Kill* and *Body Double* and *Scarface,* complained about the gore, protested the female body count. "I'm tired of answering questions about violence against women and horror," De Palma complains without being asked, the sores evidently still raw. "I stand by the movies I make. If someone wants to challenge me, I say what I feel."

He returns to the subject, unbidden, several times. Violence is "an aesthetic tool," he argues, "part of the palette. . . . Many movies are exciting and exhilarating because of their use of violence. Chase movies. Boxing movies. Stalk-somebody-and-kill-them movies. That's why it exists."

Casualties of War, which is comparatively restrained anyway, will be less subject to this debate; no one can argue that savagery and the slaughter of innocents were not part of Vietnam. But De Palma won't take that defense. "That's like giving yourself a moral justification for something that's part of the aesthetic: 'It's immoral in suspense movies but moral in war movies because it serves a greater need.'" No go: "I think it's dishonest."

Besides, he doubts that realism will protect him from the usual charges. "If I have put a woman in jeopardy, no matter what the context, believe me, it'll crop up. . . . 'Why did you choose this incident?'" It's a legitimate question, given all the other possible stories to be told about Vietnam. De Palma may be providing fodder for his critics when he describes the Vietnamese woman victim as his story's catalyst, her plight less central than the clash it sets up between her murderers and her avenger.

"I thought it was more about our own conflict than the Vietnamese," he says of the story he filmed. "That was the tragedy of the war: we wound up sort of biting ourselves."

Part of his weariness, and wariness, probably stems not just from the controversy engendered by the films he's made but from the extended warfare over the films he wanted to make and couldn't. Hollywood inflicts its own kind of mayhem. Years back, De Palma says, he "pleaded" fruitlessly to direct the film version of *Dog Soldiers,* the Robert Stone novel. He was fired from *Prince of the City.* During the years-long effort to make *Casualties of War,* studio types argued first that nobody would want to see a Vietnam movie and then, after *Platoon* had proved them wrong, that nobody wanted to see *another* one. What gets him through, De Palma says, is "a great sense of humor."

A case in point: De Palma had long yearned to direct *Act of Vengeance* based on the 1970 murders of United Mine Workers leader Jock Yablonski and his family. Some years ago he took a script written by novelist Scott Spencer to executives at Paramount, who announced that it was the best thing they'd seen in 10 years and were clambering aboard. "This never happens. Normally they say, 'Wellll . . .'" De Palma mimics a stalling veep demanding another rewrite. Not this time, though. "I thought, 'My God, a miracle, we're going to make this movie.'"

And then? "I sit around. I get a call in my hotel; I'll never forget it. The executive says, 'I want to say one word to you.' I'm expecting, 'Go.' Or 'Congratulations.'

"And he says, *Flashdance.*"

Yes, Brian De Palma was invited to direct the movie that introduced pre-ripped sweat shirts to malls across America. He didn't, of course, but he never got to make *Act of Vengeance,* either. What is there to do but giggle?

Flashdance happened to be on television the night before this steak-less lunch; De Palma watched about 15 minutes of it. "It looked as silly as it always had. This girl with a blowtorch, who then goes to a nightclub and does these crazy dances." He shakes his head, still laughing.

He probably could've done a little something with the blowtorch, though, it's suggested. He smiles, thinly.

End of lunch. He shoulders the bag containing his video camera. Not long ago he shot hours of tape of himself getting lost in the Tokyo subway, along with "lots of shots of plastic food" in Japanese shop windows. He's never edited his growing collection of cassettes, but the thought has some attraction.

"What I should ultimately do, when I retire to the Will Rogers Old Age Home, is get them all together," De Palma says, exiting. "And maybe I'll come up with some shattering insights into my life."

De Palma Comes Back, Sort Of

RYAN MURPHY/1992

LOS ANGELES — It is a Friday night in a darkened Hollywood movie theater, and the air is thick with anticipation. A sneak screening of Brian De Palma's *Raising Cain*—billed in advance as a spooky psychological thriller and a return to form—is about to begin. More than just a movie, it is a comeback after the fall from grace that was *The Bonfire of the Vanities,* the 1990 critical and commercial disaster.

But De Palma—the man who gave us *Carrie, Dressed to Kill,* and *The Untouchables*—still has his fans, and many of them are assembled here. As John Lithgow, star of his new film puts it: "After *Bonfire,* I think everybody is really rooting for Brian."

And so the lights dim. The movie unwinds. And then slowly, the 150 or so viewers begin to . . . titter. Then they laugh. Finally, by the end, it's belly-laugh city.

De Palma, sitting in the back row, strokes his beard thoughtfully as the giggles spill out of the theater.

Outside, after the screening, viewers gather to talk this one over. Was this De Palma in rare form, spoofing himself and the thriller genre that brought him great attention and fame? Or was it just an unintentionally campy movie about a tortured split personality (Lithgow) who turns against his wife (Lolita Davidovich) after he catches her having an affair?

"Oh come on!" De Palma barks during an interview the next day. He points to a scene in his movie (a favorite) where a doctor (Davidovich) begins to make out with the husband of a dying cancer patient who's in a coma. Suddenly, miraculously, the patient's eyes zing open. She sees her husband with her physician, has a heart attack and dies. "I think that's very intentionally funny," he says with a wry smile. The audience gets it immediately.

When it is pointed out to the director that confusion reigned after the screening (after all, there was no advance hint that the film was supposed to be funny), he sighs and says, "Yeah, well, they've been arguing about that for decades. There are conventional thrillers, where hatchets come out of walls. That's fine. But I don't see it that way.

"This is my particular sensibility," he says. "And you either like it, or you don't."

A week after the press junket for *Raising Cain,* De Palma rewrote the press kit himself, changing the "terrorizing" angle to "wickedly funny." In a *Hollywood Reporter* article, this maneuver was classified by one insider as "damage control." De Palma's PR people deny this. So does De Palma.

Is critical and commercial acceptance important to him? The answer at first seems obvious. Before the $45 million *Bonfire,* De Palma had never played the Hollywood game.

He has never gone out of his way to make mass-market-friendly flicks; his greatest money-maker, *The Untouchables,* was a sleeper hit. His is an auteur talent—one that, like Robert Altman's, seems predisposed more to winning eye-popping reaction than big box office.

But confront him with this, and he says solemnly that being embraced by critics and audiences "is very important. Because you make too many bombs in a row, and you stop working."

If this comment seems to spring from pain—disillusionment, even—it's because it does. The vicious reaction to *Bonfire,* he acknowledges, shattered him. He took a year off, married producer Gale Anne Hurd, fathered a child, worked on the $11 million dollar *Raising Cain* (which Hurd produced) and basically reevaluated his career and life. Still, it seems he has not come all the way through the *Bonfire* bonfire, and with little pressing, he acknowledges as much.

"It's always hard to tell when you're in the middle of a car crash what the reasons are for the crash," he says, "but you know you're in the wrong place at the wrong time. That's something that's going to take me years to sort out."

Although other big-budget films have bombed, *Bonfire* became an industry whipping boy, a symbol of everything that is wrong with Hollywood today. How could they write that nonsensical script? And spend all that money? And cast Tom Hanks in the role of Sherman McCoy when the part had William Hurt's name written all over it?

These questions, and more, were addressed in Julie Salamon's *The Devil's Candy*, a book that—along with covering the cinematic blowout in hyperdetail—cataloged the bottoming-out of a big talent.

"I didn't read the book," De Palma says. "It was too much like rereading a chapter in your life that was too painful. Julie probably did a great job." The book was done with his full cooperation, De Palma says. "My idea was to show what it's like to make a big movie in contemporary Hollywood." He shrugs. "But if you open up and be as honest as possible, everybody dislikes you for it."

De Palma takes full blame for the movie's failure. What he was trying to do, he says, was make a cartoony epic—one quite different from his trademark thrillers—that would please audiences and executives instead of himself. "I made a terrible mistake," he says. "I liked the book very much. If I would have just made the book, I would have been a lot better off."

The experience and the blistering press, he says, only proved what he always suspected. "That's the process of the American dream. They build you up, then they run you out of the country."

But Hurd says her husband handled the failure well. He still keeps in contact with Hanks, Melanie Griffith, Bruce Willis and the other *Bonfire* actors. And he chose to throw himself back into work, into *Raising Cain,* she says, instead of pouting in St. Croix.

Although looser and (as De Palma clarifies) more humor-minded than any of his previous pictures, *Raising Cain* is familiar ground in that it was inspired by real-life events. Dissecting the thin line that separates the sane from the insane is a trademark De Palma angle.

The story—in which Lithgow's character is intentionally driven crazy by his psychotherapist father so the warped doctor can study his son's split personalities—came about, as De Palma tells it, "because I had a friend who was a child psychologist. He took off from work to record his child's growing habits. He would say, 'Now, if I did this here, what's going to happen six years down the line?'"

Along with his usual brand of stylized gore, the film contains other

De Palma trademarks such as bouncing baby carriages (remember *The Untouchables?*), infinitely long tracking shots (the one thing he borrowed from *Bonfire*), and elevator confrontations (*Dressed To Kill*).

When talking about his films, the usually stern De Palma, 51, becomes a jolly Buddha. Talk of Hollywood and how it works, however, turns his mood quite foul.

Most of the movies made today, he says, leave him cold. He sees mostly foreign films (a recent fave was the Australian *Proof*) because "I get tired of all the American clichés."

"The big change in the system," he says, "is that everybody got really rich in the '80s. . . . It used to be, executives worked for the company. Now, you're dealing with executives who are worth $20 million. That changes how they deal with you. The big hurdle now is getting them interested in what you're doing. They're not very interested in movies out here anymore."

De Palma begins a dead-on impersonation of a whiny, modern-day studio suit. "It became, 'Who is this guy who wants to make this movie? Why should I have to sit and listen to this egocentric director babble for a couple of hours? I'm more interested in hanging out in the Bahamas!'"

Despite his clear disdain for Hollywood, where everybody has an opinion that must be listened to and where a clear, singular vision almost always ends up being homogenized, De Palma is, in a way, a part of the establishment. With Hurd, he has a multipicture deal at Universal, which is releasing *Raising Cain.*

A major director known for genre work who flames out with an unspectacular spectacular, learns his lesson and returns to the slightly familiar—it seems like a story plucked straight from *The Player,* Altman's acid portrait of Tinseltown.

De Palma's eyes brighten, and he corrects himself. *The Player* is one American film he did enjoy.

"It's a terrific movie. Its perceptions about Hollywood are very accurate."

Out of the Ashes

PETER KEOUGH/1992

WHEN THE CRITICS HOOTED at the Los Angeles press screening of *Raising Cain,* Brian De Palma must have smelled the smoke of another *Bonfire of the Vanities* in the air. The story of Carter Nix, a child psychologist bedevilled by a twisted, and possibly imaginary Norwegian father, by an evil twin named Cain (all three roles played by John Lithgow), and by an adulterous wife (Lolita Davidovich), the film is a non-stop romp involving kidnapping, child abuse, multiple personalities, cross-dressing, murder, flashbacks, dream sequences and baroque violence. It is further addled by De Palma's trademark visual kineticism, narrative convolutions, and allusions to films ranging from Hitchcock's *Psycho* to Michael Powell's *Peeping Tom.* It assaulted the preview audience with scenes so excessive and implausible that many concluded that it was a deliberate—and hilarious—self-parody.

Whatever the original intention, that's the line De Palma and the marketing people have taken as well. Originally described in press kits as a "romantic suspense thriller" and a "return to a genre made popular by Hollywood classics," after the disastrous screening the film was promoted as "a departure from the traditional suspense thriller . . . a devilishly funny film which combines wry humour with shocks and thrills." "It's my sensibility," De Palma insisted. "I mean, I think it's funny and scary. I've just got a black sense of humour. You disarm audiences when they're laughing. They feel like everything's under control. And then you can really nail them."

As it turned out, the film didn't nail them. Grossing a modest $21 million

From *Sight and Sound,* December 1992: 14–15. Reprinted by permission of *Sight and Sound.*

in the US and receiving mixed reviews, it was hardly the comeback De Palma might have wanted after the debacle of *Bonfire*. Although it cost $10 million to make, and will after its European and video releases undoubtedly make a profit, this modest showing would seem a negation of the kind of ambitious, challenging, often infuriating film-making that has distinguished De Palma's career—and of which *Raising Cain* is a near-hysterical summation. But every time the director goes down in the flames of another *Bonfire,* he seems to rise again from the ashes. His resilience is due in part to his inventiveness in expanding and reconfiguring the language of film. And much of his enduring appeal lies in his preoccupation with themes essential to cinema and the human spirit—the nature of duality, the mysteries of memory, guilt and desire, and the allure of the forbidden image.

De Palma's work is known for other qualities, however, that are less appealing, such as his taste for violence to women. A woman is brutally assaulted with the first ten minutes of *Cain,* and accusations of misogyny have long dogged De Palma, not without reason. His films have shown women as dehumanized objects of voyeuristic pleasure *(Greetings, Hi Mom!, Body Double),* demonic agents of evil *(Sisters, Carrie, The Fury),* and victims of sadistic male violence *(Dressed to Kill, Blow Out, Casualties of War).* "You know you're going to be bored again with my stock answers," De Palma sighs when confronted with the familiar question. "Usually I put women in jeopardy because I think they are more vulnerable. It became very unfashionable in the 80s to put a woman in jeopardy. You were immediately accused of being sexist, so that went out of the genre. Now you put men and machines in jeopardy, or children."

In short, De Palma is saying that he uses women as objects to ogle and violate because it works. For De Palma, women are tools to manipulate an audience, which gives rise to another criticism of his movies—that he directs merely for effect, with little heed to the integrity of the work as a whole. Critics contend that he indulges in showy mannerisms to conceal a lack of content.

Certainly *Raising Cain* could provide plenty of evidence to support that contention. In one sequence, Frances Sternhagen plays a psychologist rattling out a long-winded, *Psycho*-like explanation of a suspect's murderous, multi-personality malady. Sensing a lull, De Palma indulges in a steadicam tracking shot lasting about five minutes. Isn't this just a gratuitous trick, a distraction from the story and a reminder of the artifice?

De Palma agrees, but feels that stylistic novelty is of value for its own sake. "It's like that Orson Welles thing," he says. "What a toy train set you've got. You've got all these things you can do. Do you really want to go to work every day and shoot two-shots of people talking to each other? Is that directing? I could take a script out and photograph it and I can be called a director: the story's all there, they walk in the door, they sit down, then they get in the car and there's a car chase. But to me, that's not directing, it's being asleep at the switch. When you can put that camera anywhere and you can make it do anything, it's like you can put anything on that canvas. Well, why not think about it a bit?

"I don't think it should be so showy that it takes away from what's going on," he adds. "But you shouldn't have that awful scene that happens in every thriller where you bring the audience up to speed. Should we sit them in an office and have them drink coffee, and have her talk for five minutes? How do you make that interesting? So you figure out some way. Most stuff is just xeroxed and shown over again, and that's when it becomes very boring. Anything inventive and new is something you can't pigeonhole but you have to take that risk."

Not that everything De Palma does is inventive or new—he's notorious for borrowing not just motifs but whole movies from other directors, most often from Hitchcock. *Sisters* (1972) reworks *Psycho* and *Rear Window; Obsession* (1975) takes its lead from *Vertigo* with apologies to *Rebecca; Psycho* is reprised in *Dressed to Kill* (1980); *Rear Window* makes a return in *Body Double* (1984). In *Raising Cain,* De Palma's allusions seem more playful and self-conscious; he refers not to the original film, but to his own previous allusion to it (a killer in drag refers back to *Dressed to Kill*'s allusion to *Psycho;* an endangered baby carriage to *The Untouchables'* allusion to *Potemkin*). Is De Palma attempting a cinematic intertextuality, a post-modernist deconstruction of film language? Or was he just lazily plagiarizing techniques that work for cheap thrills and perhaps a pretension to cinema literacy? For De Palma, neither applies—imitation of other film-makers is a practical inevitability.

"These are tired perceptions—that because somebody's wearing a wig it's *Psycho,* or *Dressed to Kill*," he says. "Hitchcock made fifty movies and explored every kind of visual grammar of suspense and action. So somewhere, if you're working with this type of visual storytelling, you're going to be using material Hitchcock has used before. You have somebody walking down a corridor, or going up a flight of stairs—he's used that shot somewhere before. It's almost impossible not to fall into his grammar, which is, of course, the best.

"But Hitchcock only made *Psycho* once," De Palma concludes. "His career ranges over a whole bunch of other obsessions. I've spent a long time making movies about doubles and twins and psychological characters that are driven by good and evil." It's this obsession which suggests that something deeper lurks beneath De Palma's seeming superficiality. Even in those films most obviously conforming to the requirements of a genre—the bland *The Untouchables* (1987) or the overwrought *Scarface* (1983)—this motif gives a meaning beyond the obvious. In *The Untouchables*, Kevin Costner's Elliot Ness is a whitebread family man lost in the jungle of prohibition Chicago. In order to protect his bourgeois values against the demonic Al Capone, he must get in touch with his darker qualities and learn "the Chicago way" of violence and treachery, in which he is tutored by the ethnic intermediary Malone (Sean Connery)—an Irishman apparently being midway between a WASP and an Italian. It's male bonding of an intense order—Malone virtually replaces Ness' wife—and in the end the triumphant Fed can say: "I have violated every law I have sworn to uphold; I have become what I beheld; and I believe I have done right."

The doubling in the more operatic *Scarface* is more complex. The initial couple consists of Cuban emigré gangsters Tony Montana (Al Pacino) and his buddy Manny Ray (Steven Bauer). The two bond and prevail, rising in the underworld ranks. But Tony is enticed by the gelid Elvira (Michelle Pfeiffer), the near inert embodiment of woman as beautiful object. And Manny takes a shine to Tony's sister Gina (Mary Elizabeth Mastrantonio), with whom Tony too is incestuously infatuated. Unable to reconcile his contempt for Elvira, his unacknowledged desire for Gina, and his jealousy of Manny, Tony breaks down and everyone dies in a catharsis of violence.

The theme of the double is expressed most profoundly and provocatively, however, in those films that dwell on the ambiguities of gender and identity. *Sisters, Phantom of the Paradise, Obsession, The Fury, Dressed to Kill* and *Body Double* literally embody the dualities of male and female, of good and evil, and of ego and id in twins, split personalities and false identities. An even more important duality for the filmmaker is that between subjectivity and alienated experience, the subject of another film alluded to in *Raising Cain, Peeping Tom*. "It ended Powell's career, too, I might add," De Palma notes archly. "*Peeping Tom* had to do with a psychologist who is traumatizing his child and taping movies of it. Ultimately the child grows up and is obsessed by fear and proceeds to kill people and record their responses. In *Raising Cain*, the psychologist has all kinds of theories about multiple personality and creates a multiple-personality child with his own son."

In *Peeping Tom*, the mad psychologist father forces his son to observe his own fear, making his experience both the object and subject of his voyeurism. It is an extreme representation of the film-maker's—and film audience's—plight: complete detachment, but complete involvement in what happens on screen.

The situation is dramatized in *Blow Out*, which De Palma sees as his most personal film. John Travolta plays a sound engineer who electronically eavesdrops on the planning of a political assassination. He falls in love with a prostitute who is entangled in the conspiracy, and the more involved he becomes, the less control he has over what happens. "I feel very political about what I observe and the world around me," explains De Palma, "but I also feel I'm very much on the fringe and have very little effect on it. Directing is standing behind the camera and watching what other people do. You are a person with an active, provocative role and then you're a person that has to have a very quiet, sensory presence. So there is much of the split personality there. You have to make things happen and then you have to sit back and see what you have created and in order to make it effective, you've got to be detached. So it's a schizophrenic profession."

Perhaps it's this "schizophrenia," and not misogyny or even De Palma's self-confessed exploitativeness, that accounts for his depiction of women. As he has observed, women serve well as victims because the audience identifies more easily with their vulnerability. Consequently they are objects of empathy as much as of voyeurism—like the killer in *Peeping Tom*, we experience the victim's terror even as we observe it. The endangered woman resolves the duality of the director's, and the viewer's, experience. And so in films such as *Sisters*, *Carrie*, *The Fury*, *Dressed to Kill*, *Blow Out* and *Body Double*, women are not just the victims, but the heroes, and sometimes the villains.

De Palma's obsession with duality is also reflected in his films' narrative structure. In *Raising Cain*, we are barely introduced to Carter Nix and his nefarious father and twin when the film is blindsided by another story—that of his wife's guilty affair with vacant hunk Steven Bauer. The two stories bounce off one another in a wacky fugue, baroquely ornamented by De Palma's melodramatic excesses. "That has always been my structure," says De Palma. "From *Greetings* and *Hi, Mom!* I have one story colliding into another in the most absurdist way, completely turning the other one around. That's what's happening in *Raising Cain*. Even though those people are married, they are involved in completely different psychological storylines. One is fantasizing about multiples and twins and dead or perhaps not dead fathers, while the other is off on a fantasy about a lost love. They just happen to stumble across each other, which causes all the impending tragedy of the movie."

Despite the artifice of their style, De Palma is convinced that his movies reflect the psychological reality of experience much more accurately than the conventional pabulum that passes for film today. "Things happen because absurdities interact upon each other, by chance rather than as a result of man's endless philosophizing and rationalization. But audiences are very much used to being told what they're going to see and feel, so they're very comfortable with that. Any movie that makes you a little uncomfortable is good news to me, because it means you're experiencing things that you are not familiar with. But when you make a film that plays with form it throws a lot of people off. They're not used to playing with form the way we did in the 60s and 70s with Godard or Antonioni.

"I don't know what the solution is. With *Bonfire*, we tried to please too many people and pleased none of them. But movies cost huge sums of money; if you deviate too far from the mainstream you're going to have no audience."

De Palma is currently working on *Carlito's Way*, a gangster film starring Al Pacino. It seems likely to have less of the operatic excess of the disastrous *Scarface* and more of the slick commerciality of the money-making *The Untouchables*. "It's very conventional," admits De Palma. "otherwise you find you get reviews like: 'it doesn't make any sense,' 'it's ridiculous,' or 'it's laughable.'"

Emotion Pictures: Quentin Tarantino Talks to Brian De Palma

QUENTIN TARANTINO/1994

THE DATE IS 10 AUGUST 1994. The place is a room in the Four Seasons Hotel in Los Angeles, much beloved by the studios and PR companies as a venue for their marathon press junkets. On this occasion a film crew were taping a discussion between Quentin Tarantino and Brian De Palma, for inclusion in a BBC *Omnibus* profile of Tarantino which I was directing.

I'd had the opportunity to meet the young director of *Reservoir Dogs* and *Pulp Fiction* at the "Shots in the Dark" Festival in Nottingham a few months earlier. Our conversation ranged over many topics, but one unfamiliar to me from my preliminary research was his admiration for Brian De Palma, whom he viewed as the best living American director. In his developing years as a cinephile, Tarantino had kept a scrapbook of interviews and articles about De Palma, and would anxiously await every new film from the master. After counting down the days, and dreaming about what the film might be like, he would go to the very first public show alone, then return for the midnight screening with friends. He told me that when he finally met De Palma, it was as if they already knew each other. My suggestion of arranging another encounter met with an enthusiastic response. Fortunately, Brian De Palma also proved a willing participant.

Only a fragment of their discussion could be included in the final *Omnibus,* so here it is at greater length. For the record, *Pulp Fiction* had yet to open

From *Projections 5*. Edited by John Boorman and Walter Donohue. London: Faber and Faber, Ltd., 1996, 25–38. Reprinted by permission of Faber and Faber, Ltd.

and De Palma had not seen it; *Prince and the City* was finally made by Sidney Lumet with Treat Williams in the lead role; and Pauline Kael did briefly give her verdict on *Reservoir Dogs* in a special issue of the *New Yorker* devoted to the cinema. My thanks go to Ned Rosen for helping to organize the event, and to both participants for approving the transcript for publication.

David Thompson

QUENTIN TARANTINO: *Before we first met, I spoke to someone who knew you and who told me you were going to see* Reservoir Dogs. *And I said, "Whoa, he won't like it at all," and they go, "Well, how come?" I said, "Well, he doesn't like pictures of people talking to each other, and that's all my movie is, people just talking to each other!" But then you saw it, you liked it, and you wanted to meet me. Actually, you did something very sweet, because you didn't know then if I had a distributor or not, and you were giving me really practical advice; like, you have always to remember that you're in the business of making movies, you want to do the movies you want to do, but once in a while you need a* Carrie, *something to keep your career going.*

BRIAN DE PALMA: Right. You have to make a movie that moves into the mainstream, because you can make strange, idiosyncratic movies, and I made a lot of them—*Greetings, The Phantom of the Paradise,* and so on—but if you do a lot of movies that don't make much money, it gets more and more difficult to raise the finance. So every once in a while, you have to move into the mainstream and use your particular cinematic abilities and work in a kind of genre, and the first one where I did that and it was really successful was *Carrie.* I read the book and said, "I know how to make this," and then sought out the people who owned it and basically begged for the job.

QT: *One of the things I've started to notice, by looking at different directorial careers, is that what you're talking about is not even just a commercial consideration, it can even be an artistic consideration. Some directors, they just go straight to Hollywood . . .*

BDP: . . . and they become more and more successful and their work becomes progressively less and less interesting.

QT: *Exactly. Then you have directors who go down another route, and make their special kind of film for their special kind of audience, and they can say, "I don't care what you think, I'm going to do what I want to do"—and that's a perfectly valid argument. However, I think in the long run that when you look at these two paths, they equally can go to unrewarding places, because if you're making the kind of film that you do for your audience, I think you have a tendency to climb up your own ass . . .*

BDP: And duplicate your best successes.

QT: *Then there's the middle road, that you took, and Scorsese and Demme . . .*

BDP: Right.

QT: *. . . where with each one of your films, it's definitely you guys who made them, no doubt about it. But to me, what's interesting is that, as films, they're all individualistic. It's not just working towards some major oeuvre; each of the films has a vitality of its own. When you make a new movie, I go to see the new Brian De Palma movie, not the next Brian De Palma movie.*

BDP: Well, you always have to try to find something that you can bring your particular sensibility to, like the shoot-out on the stairs in *The Untouchables,* when you're working in a genre piece. I have nothing against people talking to each other, if the talking's good—say, if it's written by David Mamet and it has bite and real character. I'm not against emotion in movies. I think movies are essentially an emotional art form, and I don't believe in these very cold, removed, aesthetic experiences. I want the audience to be moved by my characters, so there's nothing wrong with delving into big close-ups and having people feel things about each other by using really good dialogue and dramatic situations. A movie can be all those things, then it can break into something spectacular. It's when the whole movie is two people talking to each other that I nod out.

QT: *If people say they like* Reservoir Dogs, *I always ask the question, "What's your favourite scene?" And when I met you and you said you liked it, I asked you that, and you said, "Oh, I don't know, just the way you structured the story." Then two or three months later,* Raising Cain *opened and when I saw the structural gymnastics you did, I thought, "I see why he said that, it all makes sense."*

BDP: The structure of your movie is amazing. I mean, it's so audacious to tell a story that way. *Raising Cain* was an idea I had for a long time, to tell a story using flashbacks where you defy all kinds of dramatic story telling. I was watching *The Killing* the other day on television, and the idea that you're setting up the heist at the race track, and then just as they're about to take the money they stop and say, "Well, why don't we go back five hours . . ."

QT: *Right.*
BDP: . . . When some guy's waking up and having coffee with his wife. I thought, boy, is this audacious!

QT: *In an interview I read, you said when an audience is watching one of your films, what you don't want is a situation where the images are just glazing over you. Audiences today are very sophisticated and can follow a lot of different types of story, because they're used to watching shows like* LA Law *where the stories are constantly cutting back and forth between different characters. But they're not used to being given the opportunity in the cinema, because in most movies you see today, I think you can pretty well figure out what the movie's going to be in the first ten minutes. The audience knows everything, but in a subconscious way.*
BDP: I think you're right. They're sophisticated with story forms because television has done every sort of story form you can think up, and when they're running out of ideas they shake them all up and try any kind of juxtaposition possible. But I still think audiences are very unsophisticated or untrained in the way of looking at movies as a visual experience. And this leads to the same kind of criticism that Hitchcock got and I get: that you're a clever technician, you know how to make things that move and jump and dance, but where's the substance, where are the characters? Hitchcock always used to say, "Well, what is the content of a still life?" I mean, the content is just exactly what it is, we're visual artists, and if you can't see what we're doing, then why are you here, why don't you go home and watch television?

QT: *In my first two movies I've broken up the structure, and that's not* just *my thing, because if I had a film that worked dramatically better from the beginning, middle and end perspective, then I would tell it that way. But one thing that's cool is that, by breaking up the linear structure, when I watch the films with an audience, it does break that alpha state.*
BDP: You try to make them work.

QT: *Yeah, it's like, all of a sudden I gotta watch this . . .*
BDP: . . . I gotta listen . . .

QT: . . . *I gotta pay attention. And you can almost feel everybody moving in their seats. It's actually fun to watch an audience in some ways chase after a movie, because I know for me, when I'm an audience member, if I'm confused, emotionally I check out, because 90 percent of the time if I'm confused, I wasn't meant to be confused. But if I'm not sure exactly what's going on but I feel I'm in good hands, that's a whole different experience.*

BDP: But again, how do you think an audience today would deal with something like *2001*, where the time sense is knocked into outer space, and the story sense is very unusual? They would have to get into this different rhythm of story-telling.

QT: *Well, the opening twenty minutes was non-narrative . . .*

BDP: And all the stuff with the bones, they'd be lost.

QT: *Part of the fun of that movie is that you go through the first twenty minutes and then all of a sudden, boom! a narrative comes out of nowhere.*

BDP: Exactly. And I find that audiences have lost the real tradition of these very bizarre story structures, and when I try to throw something like *Raising Cain* at them, they can't figure out what the hell I'm doing. Now, I didn't think that it was *Remembrance of Things Past!*

QT: *When I saw* Raising Cain, *what was really interesting to me—and feel completely free to disagree with me on this—was that you were doing a thriller, but I got the impression that doing a thriller wasn't interesting to you any more.*

BDP: Yeah, you're right.

QT: *The audience I saw it with were with the movie 110 percent: they laughed in all the right places, they were scared, and in the final sequence they were going, "Oh my God, what's going to happen?" But just because you didn't give them the little pats that they wanted, some people walked out saying, "That movie sucked!" And I was there in the theatre, and they did not feel that way, they enjoyed the movie.*

BDP: Well, that's funny, because you see that at previews all the time. You're watching an audience and trying to gauge how they're reacting to a movie emotionally, and they seem to be laughing at the right places and jumping at the right places, and then you read the cards: "This is the worst movie I've ever seen," "This guy should be taken out and shot," "What does

De Palma think he's doing?" That's one of the great mysteries I don't quite understand, because I sit there and watch the audience to see how they're reacting, and you know when you've got the audience in the palm of your hand.

QT: *To me, the whole idea of preview cards is ludicrous. Any director in the world can watch a movie with a bunch of strangers and basically know everything that they're feeling, when they didn't get a plot point and when they did catch up with it.*

BDP: That's right, absolutely. All you discover in a preview is: my God, this isn't like *Die Hard,* give it an up ending, get these scores up 10 or 20 points and take out all that stuff that bothers them: all those kind of intense, original, crazy scenes that make our movies the kind of experiences they are!

QT: *And if you killed off a character at the end, like you did in* Blow Out, *the question is asked, "Did you want them to die?" Of course you didn't* want *them to die. If you had a choice to make them live or die, you'd want them to live, but that doesn't mean the audience has a bad time.*

BDP: Exactly, exactly, and I think that's had a terrible effect on contemporary cinema. I mean, if *Scarface* had gone through all that! Actually, we had one preview with *Scarface* and I wouldn't even look at the cards, and in those days you had the kind of directorial power where you could say, "Guys, I'm not going to do this, this is the movie, just release it!"

QT: *So what is your situation now? Are previews an issue in the contract?*

BDP: These days you have to just deal with it, it's part of contemporary movie-making. If the scores aren't high, or if you're making an unconventional movie, you have to battle with them.

QT: *But does it change the movie that much at the end of the day?*

BDP: Well, fortunately with *Carlito's Way* I refused to have any cards at the first preview, which made the studio extremely unhappy! But I said, "All you do is you come to the previews and you see that the audience likes it, then you read the scores and you get depressed, and decide how to save money by cutting down on the advertising." I forced them to watch the movie without any preview cards, which had them pissed off going in, but then the audience reaction was so strong that they felt good. Of course they insisted on having another preview anyway and fortunately the scores were good, so that was the end of it. The other great thing was that I was locked into an extremely quick post-production schedule with dates already booked, so there was no way out, the movie was two hours and twenty minutes long. Of course they asked, "Is there any way to make it shorter, to get in those extra shows?" So I said, "Hey, guys, do you want to have the movie open November 8th, or do you want me to figure out how to take twenty minutes out of it?" And they went, "No, let's go for November 8th." But it has a lot to do with luck.

Q T : *It's funny you bring up that example, because in both the movies I've made, I've had an extremely short post-production schedule. With* Dogs, *we were rushing to get to Sundance in time, so we were literally delivering a wet print to them: with* Pulp, *it was the same thing for Cannes—I saw the print of the movie for the first time three days before I got on the plane! Actually, I kind of like working like that, you know, making the decision, let's go, let's do it, making the hard decisions all the way down the line.*

B D P : Well, that way you make your most audacious decisions, and then you don't get all this feedback which makes you have second thoughts about the audacious decisions you make. You might say to yourself, "Well, maybe this is a little too reckless, maybe I'd better rethink this," but usually your first instincts are the best.

Q T : *That's totally how I feel. Of course, in either case, if I thought I wasn't there yet I would say, "Well, the hell with Sundance and the hell with Cannes, we're going to make the movie better."*

B D P : Your scene with the cop in *Reservoir Dogs* would never have survived a preview. They would have said, "Ah, are you kidding? Cut it out!" Don't you think?

Q T : *Well, Sundance was the first time a real audience saw the movie, so they were our preview audience in a way. And people were freaking out about the ear scene, yeah.*

B D P : I had a particularly difficult fight with the ratings board over *Scarface*, in which I cut the picture back some four times and they still gave me an "X," so ultimately I had to appeal in front of the whole board. Now, that's a really difficult fight, because nobody wants to be on your side. The studios just say, "Get an "R" and leave us alone." Fortunately we had a very influential narcotics cop who got up and said, "Everybody should see this movie, because cocaine is killing everybody and this movie will tell you what really happens when you get involved in this insane cocaine world." So after the battles, which had started with *Dressed to Kill,* I said, "OK, you want to see violence? You want to see sex? Then I'll show it to you," and I went out and made *Body Double!* And that ultimately gave me the worst kind of press experience. I remember when the press had seen the movie, one of the heads of the studio called me up and said, "They're going to kill you tomorrow!" Because, as you know, I was also the producer of the movie, so I had to get out there and go on all the shows, and deal with all those violence questions, because this was a way to sell the movie. But the reaction against it was so intense, it really didn't help much.

QT: *I was going through the scrapbook that I used to keep of interviews you did around that time—I hadn't looked at it in maybe six years—and I'm seeing all the pull-quotes on violence, and the Hitchcock influence. I never thought about it back then, but now it's like, "Oh my God, what I've been going through having to talk about violence, and what I think about it, well, Brian's been going through this for the last fifteen years."*
BDP: Well, the think about that, especially on television, is that when we talk about *violence,* everyone suddenly tunes in. And while we're discussing *violence,* they'll show a sequence from one of our most *violent* pictures, and they're going to sell a lot of products!

QT: *I also collected on tape TV segments about* Body Double, *and looking at them again, they were hammering in on the violence all the time.*
BDP: Look at the O. J. Simpson case. They can run all this stuff, it's cheap to begin with, and in the same way they can have us talking, they can show all the violent sequences from our movies, and of course say, "They're morally reprehensible, we're embarrassed to have them on air, but please keep watching!" And at the same time, we're just used as a product. I learned this a long time ago when I was making movies like *Greetings* and *Hi, Mom!* I'd be out there saying, "We've got to blow everything up, we've got to change everything, the revolution is coming," and then there'd be an aspirin commercial coming on after me.

QT: *Right.*

BDP: So you become part of the product, part of the process, because violence becomes a great product, especially for the media because we make those violent sequences look so good through the camera.

QT: *One of the things that you said, which I've used in different interviews because it was so right on the money, was that as a film-maker, when you deal with violence, you're actually penalized for doing a good job.*

BDP: Absolutely, because you want to make these sequences as effective and moving as possible, and you use all the things that you've learned from other directors and those that you've invented yourself. You and I are interested in a form of visual language and story-telling that nobody understands basically because they're blown away by it, and then they say, "Well, my God, somebody was being knifed or somebody was being shot. This is horrible and reprehensible, I denounce it and feel bad about enjoying it!" But, as we've said a thousand times, cinema is a visual medium, and we're interested in terrific visual sequences, and many of them happen to be [*whispers*] violent.

QT: *Well, one of the analogies I've always used is that I have no more problem with violence in movies than I do with musical sequences in Vincente Minnelli movies; it's simply one of the things that you can do in cinema that's interesting to watch. And I feel totally great and fine in saying that in real life I have a major problem with violence, that I do think our society is too violent, but I have no problem going to a film and seeing violence on the screen.*

BDP: I've never thought that the argument which is constantly used, that people imitate the violence they see in our movies, makes any sense. Basically, we go to movies to have this violence acted out, we participate in them and maybe cheer them like we do at football games, and that's it. We don't pick up a baseball bat and go hit somebody over the head.

QT: *What you said once before was also really interesting, that if you see a movie that's only a bunch of violent sequences, that's boring, and it can be why people don't go to see it.*

BDP: Absolutely.

QT: *In fact, it's funny when people ask me, "Did you put violence in your movies to make them more commercial?" Because the violence that I do in fact takes it out of the mainstream and puts it in a kind of specialized area. In our films there's a tremendous amount of humour. As far as I'm concerned, you're one of the greatest satirists that we have, and Pauline Kael understood that. But most of the people on the street, they'll just talk about the two murder sequences that are in your movie, and forget about everything else.*

BDP: Right.

QT: *I know people who could have seen* Reservoir Dogs *and would have been fine with it, but when they heard violence, violence, they began talking about it as if it was the most violent movie ever made. Now some day I may make the most violent movie ever made, and I wouldn't mind people saying that then, but* Dogs *wasn't. The humour was lost in any kind of discussion of the film, and even in the good reviews I got, they all carried a Surgeon-General's-type warning, a little paragraph telling you how violent this movie is, and that you might not be able to take it.*

BDP: That happened with *Scarface* too, in that because of the discussion about violence a lot of people didn't go to see it in the theatres, they were scared by the chainsaws—you know, "Get me out of here!"

QT: *That chainsaw scene is a good comparison, because apart from that, personally I can't remember a single movie which had something like the ear scene in* Dogs *that was talked about so much in any review or discussion of the film. By the same token, I'm not crying, because we all know what we're getting into, it's the price of doing business.*

BDP: But in fact we don't realize that it's going to dominate what everybody thinks about the movie.

QT: *Exactly.*

BDP: And it's always the first question you get in an interview, and it's like, "Wait a minute, what about all the other stuff!"

QT: *I mean, imagine I'm the husband of some young couple, and we're just sitting there and I say, "Well, what do you want to see tonight, honey? You want to see* Forrest Gump?" "That's the movie in which Tom Hanks plays the retarded guy and meets John F. Kennedy?" "OK. Well, what else do you want to see?* Clear and Present Danger? "*What's that?*" "*Well, that's the new Harrison Ford movie. Or* *do you want to see* Reservoir Dogs?" "What's that?" "Well, that's the movie *where the guy gets his ear cut off!"*

B D P : Yeah, I want to see a good scene like that!

Q T : *As anybody who's read anything about me knows, my three favourite movies of all time are, not in any order,* Rio Bravo, Taxi Driver *and* Blow Out.

B D P : Wow, what a list.

Q T : *Three great movies.*

B D P : And I'm on it!

Q T : *Now. I've always been a big fan of John Travolta, but his performance in* Blow Out *has to be one of my favourite performances of all time, I think he's just absolutely shattering in that movie. And to me, you have one of the most heart-breaking closing shots in the history of cinema, when he's listening to the scream . . .*

B D P : It's a good scream.

Q T : *. . . and you see that he's broken and everything. When I saw the movie for the first time, it affected me so much that for two weeks, not a single day went by when I didn't reflect on that shot. And no director's really used John to that effect since you did in* Blow Out, *and before I worked with him, I felt he was like the secret weapon that nobody's using!*

B D P : Well, I think it had a lot to do with the fact that he was considered to be an adolescent star, with *Saturday Night Fever* and *Grease* coming out back to back, and everybody thought of him as a sassy street guy from Brooklyn. But there's a tremendous amount of sensitivity and vulnerability in John, and that never seemed to translate into him being an adult star. Then he was in a couple of movies that weren't very successful and, of course, in this town that means you fall off the preferred "A" list and you're in limbo until some-one rediscovers you. Then everybody says, "My God, where's that guy been?" Another great actor that springs to mind is Jon Voight . . .

Q T : *Yeah, exactly.*

B D P : . . . who sort of vanished and you wonder what happened to him.

Q T : *He's become like Mr Comeback! He'll do a comeback, everyone'll say this guy is the best there is, he'll disappear for another five years, then come back again. He did that twice with* Coming Home *and* Runaway Train.

BDP: That's right. Basically John [Travolta], like all great actors, needs a great role and a great director to bring out his particular qualities. Now *Blow Out* was always thought of as a very small movie, probably much on the level of the movies you're making, not particularly expensive because it was such a bizarre kind of idea. I remember I called up John as he'd heard about my script, and he said, "Why don't you let me read it?" Of course, he'd been in *Carrie* and we'd talked about other projects, but he read the script and said, "I want to do it." Well, suddenly it became a big production with John Travolta, it went from an $8 million movie to an $18 million movie, and after the success of *Dressed to Kill* it was: "Whatever De Palma wants to do, we'll let him loose!" So I went for it, and I'll never forget the first time the distribution companies saw the movie with that ending, which is completely devastating . . .

QT: *Right!*
BDP: . . . because he doesn't save the girl, he gets there too late. And there were no pollsters running previews in those days!

QT: *It's funny that you talk about John's sensitive quality, because in* Pulp Fiction *he plays a hit man, and at the beginning he's this cool dude blowing people away, but then later on you see he's really this sweet guy who everybody likes! Now in* Blow Out, *and you're the one director to use him this way, the sensitivities only peeped through, because that character, Jack Terry, is actually a sarcastic jerk, a cold fish.*
BDP: Right.

QT: *And John's natural sensitivity comes through and makes this jerk, who makes no apologies for the way he is, actually likeable, without trying to make him likeable.*
BDP: He plays the kind of cynical guy who's making silly effects for really grim "B" exploitation films, and he's become cynical for a very good reason. And I basically got that material from a lot of work I did on *Prince of the City,* where you're dealing with a narcotics cop wearing a wire and setting up his brother cops so they go down supposedly for the greater good. So that was a very important flashback in *Blow Out,* to set up the reason why he was so

cynical. And what does he ultimately do but put the girl in exactly the same position and get her killed, just as he got the first guy killed.

QT: *I've always thought of* Prince of the City *directed by you and starring John Travolta as one of the tragic movies that were never made.*
BDP: It was a great tragedy, because he would have been great for the part, and what I thought was completely missed when they made *Prince of the City* was the overpowering charm of this guy. The real guy who was this character could talk to you about setting somebody up, a best buddy who would get killed, and you would be empathetic towards him! He was unbelievable— you looked into his eyes and said, "God, you poor guy, you had to do that, you got the guy killed," and you had tears in your eyes because of his tragedy. That's how good he was, and that's the kind of thing John would have brought to it.

QT: *When we were shooting* Pulp Fiction, Carlito's Way *came out in the theatres and I had the weekend off, so I saw it on Saturday, on the second to opening night. I was blown away by the movie, and in particular the last twenty minutes. I think that final chase is the best action scene you've ever done. I've seen the film four times, and every time you cut to the exterior of that disco, until the end credits roll, you know you're going to be washed away!*
BDP: What's amazing about Al Pacino in that scene is that he has a tremendous ability to take directions—like, look left, look right, duck. Al has a lot of physical grace, and he could do all the moves like he'd done them a hundred times, rehearsed it and rehearsed it and rehearsed it, while in reality he was improvising everything! He had never done a complicated Steadicam shot like that in his life.

QT: *Really? And he just took to it?*
BDP: He just took to it. Al is very unaware of the camera when we're shooting. On *Scarface,* when he was watching rushes, he began to realize that I was doing interesting things with the camera movement, and suddenly said, "Wow, something's going on here!"

QT: *It's funny because I had told John I was going to see Brian's new movie, and when I showed up at work on Monday, I walked in the door of his trailer and the first thing he said was, "How'd you like it?" And I went, "Oh man, it's great," and*

I started telling him about it and said, "Wait till you get to the last twenty min-utes!" And as I was describing it to him, John was sitting there getting excited that I was excited.

BDP: It's very interesting seeing movies when you're making movies. When I was making *Blow Out* in Philadelphia, *Raging Bull* came out. And when I saw that first shot in black and white, with the opera music, I said [*holding hands to eyes*], "Scorsese, he's done it again!"

QT: *Oh yeah!*

BDP: Every time you think you have an original or great idea, there's always Marty Scorsese! It's like that Western where he's always looking back and these guys are always chasing him . . .

QT: *As in* Butch Cassidy and the Sundance Kid—*who are those guys?!*

BDP: . . . and there's Scorsese! He had that great Steadicam shot when they bring the guy into the ring . . .

QT: *Yeah.*

BDP: . . . and it was the first time I'd seen a Steadicam shot like that. I thought I was pretty good at doing those kinds of shots, but when I saw that I said, "Whoa!" And that's when I started using very complicated shots with the Steadicam.

QT: *I loved Pauline Kael's review of* Blow Out, *which is actually one of the best reviews she's ever written, and that's saying a hell of a lot!*

BDP: It's an unfortunate thing for your generation of film-makers, but we had Pauline Kael, and whatever you say about her, whether you liked her opinions or not, she wrote with such passion . . .

QT: *Oh, I know.*

BDP: . . . and such excitement about movies. And for the life of me, I cannot find a writer today who I can read with as much interest and excitement.

QT: *Actually, I've a lot of respect for the critical profession. Not for all the people who practise it, but for the profession itself, because I could easily see myself being a film critic if I hadn't been a film-maker. When I meet critics, I know their reviews, and I know if I agree with them or if I don't, or if I like their style or if I don't. But when I talk to other film-makers about different critics, they don't seem to have any respect for them at all. They just regard critics as people who take pot shots at them.*

BDP: Four stars, three stars, thumbs up, thumbs down.

QT: *I'm not really talking about those TV guys. I mean, I'm friends with Terry Gilliam, and when I brought up the subject of Pauline Kael with him he said, "Oh, she hated* Brazil!*" And I said, "But I read that review, and she didn't hate* Brazil. *She had problems with it, but she didn't slam you." And he said, "Well, I couldn't help but look at it that way." That's what I find with other film-makers, that we read things differently.*

BDP: I always read reviews, and I've had some really great ones and some really horrendous ones. But Pauline Kael was a great reviewer who wrote with such passion about cinema in her era. When a movie comes out today, I don't know who to read, because you know from the first paragraph whether they liked it or not. Also, they write in such a lacklustre, shovelling-dirt kind of way, and their perceptions, whether they're off or on, are not written about interestingly.

QT: *In some ways Pauline Kael was as influential to me as any film-maker. She helped me at a young age to develop my aesthetic, which doesn't mean I didn't disagree with her, but that she was like a teacher to me.*

BDP: Exactly.

QT: *She quit the business when I was in pre-production on* Dogs, *and I feel weird about it. Maybe because she was so important to me, I don't want to know what she thought of it! But when I was younger, I always used to fantasize about her picking my movie to review, because she didn't review everything, and that Pauline Kael would refer to me by my last name—"When Tarantino does da, da, da, da"— and how cool that would be!*

Brian De Palma

WADE MAJOR/1998

HAVING DIRECTED SOME OF THE most memorable and controversial films of the past 30 years, Brian De Palma can afford to relax a little. So why doesn't he? Because he loves what he does, that's why. As he begins his fourth decade as one of Hollywood's most in-demand directors, the maker of *Scarface, Carrie, Blow Out, Body Double, Dressed to Kill, Carlito's Way,* and *The Untouchables* is enjoying his status as an entertainment industry institution, a visionary stylist whose past films continue to inspire and provoke new generations of filmmakers as well as his own contemporaries.

Having only recently scored his biggest career success to date with *Mission: Impossible,* De Palma is enjoying more creative freedom than he has had in years. It comes as little surprise, then, that he should seize the chance to once again return to the genre for which he is best known, the psychological thriller. Starring Oscar-winner Nicolas Cage and Oscar-nominee Gary Sinise, *Snake Eyes* is a highly-stylized, claustrophobic, real-time thriller set during and after an Atlantic City boxing match where the United States Secretary of Defense is assassinated. Sinise plays Navy Commander Kevin Dunne, the head of the security detail charged with protecting the Secretary. Cage is Dunne's childhood buddy, a tainted Atlantic City police detective forced to rise to the occasion when the murder literally falls in his lap. Together they must race with fate and an impending hurricane to unravel a labyrinthine

From www.MrShowbiz.com, posted August 1998. Reprinted by permission of the author and www.MrShowbiz.com.

puzzle meticulously designed by De Palma and his preferred screenwriter of late, David Koepp (*Mission: Impossible* and *Carlito's Way*).

Still, all due labors on the script notwithstanding, it wouldn't be a true De Palma film without the director's trademark visual fireworks. And on that count, De Palma makes it clear that, if nothing else, *Snake Eyes* is a way of celebrating his own personal independence day.

WM: *Just when you finally appeared to have left the Hitchcock comparisons behind, what drew you back to doing a thriller?*

BDP: The thing you can determine from me and my career is that I never gave a damn what anybody thought. I always did what I thought was best for myself, and if anyone else thought it was like Hitchcock, too bad! I was there, basically, to learn something, or else I was interested in a piece of material. And if I wanted to make that kind of movie and everybody else thought it wasn't the right thing for me to be doing, or if they had some kind of comment about it, it never made any difference to me. As long as I thought I could get the movie made, I didn't care.

WM: *Could you talk about designing the visual map of the film, specifically conceiving the complex visual and flashback structure?*

BDP: Hopefully, because we thought of it from the ground up, we came up with a strong visual idea for the film. David [Koepp] wanted to write a movie from multiple points of view. Well, when you do multiple points of view, how do you do that? Also, the big problem of going back and forth over a crime is that you're at the same place all the time and you just keep going back and forth. So you ask yourself, "Does it feel repetitive?" and "Are our flashbacks going to stop the story from going forward?" So I had to come up with a visual way in order to do that.

The whole trick of it was to get the characters back to where they started and make it look different and let them find out information they hadn't had before. That was a big physical challenge. Plus there was the whole challenge of whether I could make a movie where we're basically indoors the whole time, working in these very limited spaces. Could I get away with that? It's that *Rope* concept of trying to box yourself in aesthetically. It's like *Rear Window* where you can't move the camera outside the room. How do you make that work? It forces you to come up with all kinds of ingenious solutions and pushes you into a visual area that would have never even occurred to you before.

WM: *How hard was it to execute that elaborate opening tracking shot?*
BDP: Basically you have to find the spaces to do it in. You start on the boardwalk with the television interview which is on the monitors. And from the monitors you have to follow Nic upstairs and then he's got to see Luis and chase him down the escalator and sort of beat him up. And then you've got to start this voyage of the bloody hundred-dollar bill. I think we did that in three sections. Then you've got to find a place to wipe the frame so that you can go from one section to another so it'll look seamless. And then once you get them downstairs, there's the stuff in the arena. We actually go around the arena twice—once he walks around the arena and then he goes once around with Gary. And then you've got to sit them down and you have to have them look at all the places around them and try to make that work as a shot, make it visually and aurally exciting so the audience is listening to stuff so that later on it's going to drive them crazy when they're hearing the fight but not seeing it. Nobody's been to a fight where you never saw the fight. Then they're going to really want to know what happens when the fighter tells his story. Are we going to see the fight now we just heard? And after you do the fight, then that reveals the woman in red, and who the hell is she? But I'm taking you all the way through the movie now.

WM: *Did you conceive that the first shot was going to be continuous or did that evolve from the script?*
BDP: As we laid out all this exposition in the beginning, and I was wrestling with the idea of how to make it visually different from the different flash-backs. It occurred to me to do it like one steadicam shot, make it all on Nic, his world, his life, and make it move as fast as you physically can, make him talk a mile-a-minute, just get the energy pumped up to the max and make it look like a freight train going by so fast the audience can't take everything in. I find movies so redundant in the way that they're photographed. I mean, you're like, "Oh, please. Get me out of here." The ideas are redundant. The visual ideas are hopelessly redundant. So you want to give them just a taste, and then you're going to force them to go back.

One of the big problems with detective movies is it's basically going from place to place and getting information. Well, that may work great in a novel but it's kind of boring in a movie.

W M : *But not in this movie.*

B D P : Because we made it so that it's not that place you've seen before. It looks a little different because you're in an entirely different place in the arena. And the other reason is you've got some clues from the first time you went through and now you're starting to put the puzzle together yourself.

W M : *How hard was it to work out the flashbacks and the splitscreens so that the simultaneous threads all intersected just perfectly?*

B D P : I'd say the trickiest part was the splitscreen because there's so much information that it's hard to follow both sides of the screen simultaneously. [The film] was a lot longer in earlier cuts, and there was a lot more of the splitscreen stuff. But you can't absorb it all. There's too much going on. So it's like, "Whoa! Wait a minute." I worked on that for a very long time. I couldn't even follow it there was so much going on. It is very tricky and, again, like with the end of the movie, we kept pulling stuff out, pulling stuff out, because it becomes too much to take in. You get confused. And once you get confused, you're dead in a movie like this.

W M : *As long as you brought it up, why was the tidal wave sequence cut from the end of the film?*

B D P : When we did the water sequence, we had a big wave and it just took people out of the movie. It was too big for the story, dealing with this confrontation and then suddenly they were looking at this big wave. This isn't a meteor picture. It was my mistake, basically, because I thought we needed the storm to be "The Storm," and it got a little out of hand. So we cut it all out.

W M : *Wasn't that hard to do?*

B D P : We can make mistakes. It's possible.

W M : *That almost seems antithetical to present Hollywood thinking, where the end always has to be beefed up with bigger and bigger set pieces.*

B D P : It's quite ironic. The trouble is you begin to find the shape of the movie and when you start putting it in front of audiences they react to certain things and not to others. And it sort of tells you what works and what doesn't. So you change it. It's just like previewing a show. Of course with the press and everyone else watching everything we do, they think, "Oh, my God! They're in trouble! They're changing the ending!" But this happens all the time. When you read 400 preview response cards and 399 of them say, "What's up with that wave? That didn't look right!," then you start to realize that maybe something is wrong with your wave.

WM: *Would you agree that your work falls into two categories: the uniquely obsessive and very personal Brian De Palma stuff*—Sisters, Blow Out, Obsession, Dressed to kill—*and everything else like* Scarface, Mission: Impossible, Carlito's Way *and* The Untouchables?
BDP: I kind of think it's like a writer that writes under two names. I get tired of making these Brian De Palma movies. You get tired of your own obsessions, the betrayals, the voyeurism, the twisted sexuality. I've made a lot of movies like this, so you're glad to get out there with those Cuban or Puerto Rican gangsters. It gives you a little relief. That's not to say you won't be drawn back to your particular world, but I look upon them as a welcome relief from what's going on in my brain.

WM: *Does it restore you creatively to switch off between the two?*
BDP: Yes, it does. When I'm thinking about Puerto Rican gangsters, I'm not thinking about long tracking shots down corridors.

WM: *Have you ever found yourself at a loss for new visual devices or new ways to keep the style of a film fresh?*
BDP: No, I've never had that. You are up against your limitations to some extent. So there are certain things I try to keep away from. I try to keep away from comedies.

WM: *Why no comedies?*
BDP: Because I just feel that I have a kind of 60s sense of humor and you cannot compete with the kind of comedy that you see on television. It's a mastery of comedic form. You've got all those great writers and those great comedians. And making comedies in movies is almost, I think, one of the most difficult things to do. They're all stand-ups and they train in front of live audiences. That's invaluable for comedy. It's really hard to be directing

a comedy on a sound stage and have a sense that this is really funny. So I try to avoid that.

But, quite to the contrary, I'm feeling quite invigorated as I come to the end of my fiftieth year because I've made the most successful movie of my career, *Mission: Impossible*. It's better to make them at the end rather than at the beginning. And I'm full of ideas, more ideas than I can ever make. My head is just bouncing. I was up until 3:30 this morning working on the Howard Hughes movie that David and I are writing for Nic. And I've got a couple of other ones that are rummaging around in my brain. So I feel like I don't have enough time now. That's why I have so little patience with everything. Plus I have a couple of children. So my life is basically divided between making movies and my children.

W M : *Since you are going to go on and work with Nic again on the Howard Hughes biography, is it fair to say that your pairing on this film worked out well?*
B D P : We're very similar in many ways. Nic is an accomplished performer and he's a dedicated artist. And he loves to work, which is how I would describe myself, basically. Plus, he has no ego. It's all about the work. Which is exactly how I feel. How do we make it better? And he's a real gentleman. That always sounds like something from the nineteenth century, but it's true. He has incredible manners, he's very sensitive to how other people are feeling about things, and he feels real lucky, I guess, that he has all this opportunity, just like I do. How did we get here? This is great. We're going to get a chance to make a movie about Howard Hughes? Wow. And we're both Italian-Americans—maybe that has something to do with it. He's got brothers, I've got brothers. I don't know. Maybe there's a whole bunch of stuff there.

W M : *Considering all the changes you've seen in the industry, from the escalating budgets to the role of special effects, have these things made your job easier or more difficult?*
B D P : I think that something new is coming. I really think that the conventional moviemaking world is over and the greatest world is over and the greatest work is behind us. I really do. The industry sort of peaked in the forties, fifties and sixties. Mainly because of the turmoil, the wars, all that stuff. The European influx into Hollywood. That was the beginning of the movies, and it's over. it's never going to be again. I think the next thing

that's going to happen is going to happen on the Internet and with interactive media. Now you can have all this video technology, your own little video camera and edit stuff at home. You can make movies like novels now, you really can. You can make them very inexpensively and get your friends together. You can do the whole thing yourself, post it on the Internet for everybody to look at and have an immediate audience of billions of people. I think you're going to see some incredible things.

WM: *Does this mean that the art of filmmaking is a thing of the past?*
BDP: This form, I think, is over. I really do. I mean, everybody complains about how they're not as good as they used to be. Well, they're not.

WM: *What would you say has been the downfall of the art form?*
BDP: Well, again, I feel it has a lot to do with what's happening in history. What's happening now? Nothing. Can you remember the eighties? Do you remember anything? I was talking to one journalist and she said, "Well, I remember the sixties." And I said, "I remember the sixties. Things were happening in the sixties. But the seventies? Disco? What is there to remember? What is there to remember in the eighties? And the nineties? Greed is good. That's what we remember. That's the signature for the end of this century.

WM: *So if we're moving into a new phase, what is it that keeps you motivated?*
BDP: Because I'm a guy that used to build computers. I'm right at the cutting edge of what's going on in this whole new revolution. I watch this stuff all the time and I'm fascinated every time some new development happens—and it happens every other month in this industry. Every time something new happens, every time some new technology comes in, you see whole new story forms developing and you go, "Wow. This is exciting."

The Filmmaker Series: Brian De Palma

ANNE THOMPSON/1998

NEVER THE TYPE OF FILMMAKER you'd call mainstream, Brian De Palma is one of those masters of cinema whose movies have tended to polarize the critics. While he's had his ardent advocates (notably former *New Yorker* critic Pauline Kael), he has never achieved the level of acclaim enjoyed by his peers. This is probably because De Palma movies are generally more violent, dark, paranoid, and controversial than movies by other members of the filmmaking circle he came of age with in the '70s, which included Steven Spielberg, Francis Ford Coppola, Martin Scorsese, and George Lucas. After such stylistic experiments as *Phantom of the Paradise* and *Obsession*, De Palma broke through with 1976's *Carrie*, a spine-tingling exercise in terror, thus beginning his long tug-of-war both with audiences and with the Hollywood establishment.

Cross-dressing murderers (*Dressed to Kill*), paranoid conspiracies (*Blow Out*), coke-snorting gangsters (*Scarface*), voyeuristic obsessives (*Body Double*), and Vietnam soldiers on a rampage (*Casualties of War*) may not seem like extreme subjects for movies today, but they were back in the '70s and '80s. The fact is, De Palma has delighted in pushing viewers to the edge of revulsion and terror, and he has often been taken to task for it. At the same time, he has done well by actors: He cast Robert De Niro in several films in the late '60s, and gave significant career boosts to John Travolta (*Blow Out* was one reason Quentin Tarantino cast him in *Pulp Fiction*), Melanie Griffith, and Kevin Costner. As he's matured as a director, De Palma has learned to balance

From *Premiere*, September 1998: 49–53. Reprinted by permission of the author.

directing other people's more accessible material (*The Untouchables, Carlito's Way, Mission: Impossible*) with his own, darker work (*Raising Cain*). His latest paranoid thriller, *Snake Eyes,* stars Nicolas Cage as a corrupt Atlantic City cop who is trying to unravel an assassination conspiracy.

At 57, De Palma is tall and stoop-shouldered, with gray-streaked hair and beard; he has abandoned his trademark khaki safari jacket. His initial manner is abrupt. But once he starts talking, over tea at a Santa Monica beach hotel, he is articulate, passionate, and amusing. He makes reference to Dostoyevsky and Tolstoy; to the lost European influence in Hollywood cinema; and to his idols Billy Wilder, Alfred Hitchcock, and David Lean. He admits that he surfs the Internet from the same lower-Fifth Avenue, New York, apartment he has lived in for many years, ordering books from amazon.com and checking out educational software for his two little girls, Lolita, six, and Piper, nineteen months. Finally, De Palma is lighter and more charming in person than his notoriously provocative film oeuvre would indicate.

PREMIERE: *What would you say was your last personal film, a real Brian De Palma film?*

BRIAN DE PALMA: I think *Snake Eyes* is a very Brian De Palma film. I wrote the story with David Koepp [*Carlito's Way*], he wrote the screenplay, and we sold the script for $4 million. It has a very inventive visual style. I'm always trying to come up with interesting, concise visual ways to tell stories. And I'm interested in movies that are intelligent, that challenge the viewer. This is basically a murder mystery around an assassination.

PREMIERE: *There's a government conspiracy, and when the Nicolas Cage character does the right thing, he gets punished for it. It's a pretty bleak worldview.*

DE PALMA: There's a line he will not cross. No good deed goes unpunished. [*Laughs*] I don't know why that is. It keeps on happening a lot [in my movies]. Maybe God works in very odd ways.

PREMIERE: *Are you, as film critic David Thomson has suggested, a misanthrope and a cynic?*

DE PALMA: No. I basically believe in a moral order, which is sort of reflected in *Snake Eyes*. It may be one that we can't quite comprehend, but it's there. And no matter what man does, there's some kind of morality that supersedes whatever greedy plight he happens to be in.

PREMIERE: *Your leading men often seem ineffectual, dwarfed by insurmountable obstacles.*

DE PALMA: The establishment kind of overwhelms the protagonists in my movies. And it's like the tar baby—it's very difficult to beat. You keep socking it, but you just keep on getting another limb sucked in.

PREMIERE: *I understand that you computerize your storyboards.*

DE PALMA: I've been doing that for years. I used to draw them, then I used computer programs to draw them, then I used the slide programs in order to look at them one after another. Basically it's making little architecture drawings and moving things around within the spaces. I don't think anybody else does it.

PREMIERE: *Do you use a laptop during filming?*

DE PALMA: No, no. By the time you've been wandering around that space on a computer for months, it's like you've memorized a symphony.

PREMIERE: *You started off* The Bonfire of the Vanities *with one long, elaborate take, and you do it again in* Snake Eyes. *How long is this one?*

DE PALMA: The movie starts out on the boardwalk; you're outside the [Atlantic City] casino world and then you go into it. The shot establishes Nic Cage's character as he wanders through the environment of the boxing arena, the casino floor, casino hotel, and it takes Nic right up until the assassination. You see his whole life within this world; he's sort of king of this contained universe. It's a Steadicam shot that goes on for about twelve minutes. One continuous shot can really be the length of a 35mm magazine, a 400-foot load. In *Bonfire* that was one [five-minute] shot—we just went as far as we could go. Of course you can make it look a lot longer, like [Hitchcock's] *Rope,* have somebody pass in front of the camera and keep going. You need artful staging and very good actors.

PREMIERE: *Like Nic Cage?*

DE PALMA: He's extremely experienced, because he's made a lot of movies. And he's an incredible gentleman—something that has gone out of a lot of the stars of our era. I mean, he's, "Thank God we have the job. And isn't it exciting to be working on this material with these people?" And very open about collaborating. Whatever happened to manners in moviemaking? I know it sounds like an anachronism.

PREMIERE: *Well, you've been described as being aloof during the moviemaking process.*

DE PALMA: Only to the people who don't know me. Because basically I'm very focused. When I walk onto a movie set, I don't have any time for manners, to say, "Hello, how are you this morning?" I have to focus on what is in front of me because I'm about to photograph it, and it's going to be with me the rest of my life. When I'm sitting in a rocking chair, my grandchildren around, and I have a shelf up there—I guess they'll be DVDs—I'm going to remember that I wasn't paying attention back in 1998, and there it is, up on the screen, for me to watch for the rest of my life.

PREMIERE: Mission: Impossible *was a mammoth, technologically advanced undertaking—*

DE PALMA: I followed it perfectly! [But] I became sort of the poster boy for incoherent storytelling. When [Tom Cruise and Jon Voight] are lying to each other and you're laying out all this exposition of what really happened, that was very tricky, but, I thought, interesting. Not according to 99 percent of the reviews. [*Laughs*]

PREMIERE: *Your producer-star, Tom Cruise, must have gone through that script with a fine-tooth comb, considering that he's a demon for details.*

DE PALMA: Absolutely. Yes, he is. But when you're so close to a movie and you're seeing it over and over again, you're the ones who are going to miss the big pink elephant standing right in the middle of the living room. When we previewed it, we did not have any kind of confusion in terms of the way the story played.

PREMIERE: *Is it true that you and Cruise didn't always agree?*

DE PALMA: Not necessarily. Tom is a very smart guy, and he had very strong opinions about things. We would argue, but he always said, "Whatever you want to do, Brian." I made all the final decisions. We were deciding whether we needed the helicopter chase at the end. Tom thought about resolving the scene in the boxcar; I was pushing for the helicopter chase. I said, "We're making Mission: Impossible here; we better have some wham-bang ending." I argued strongly about why I thought this would work, and he ultimately, I think, made the correct decision.

PREMIERE: *You did not have a dispute with Cruise in the editing room over the final cut of the film?*
DE PALMA: Absolutely not.

PREMIERE: *When you didn't show up for the junket interviews, it was interpreted as a protest.*
DE PALMA: I'm telling you, after I finished that movie, I hadn't been home in a long time, I just went back to New York. . . . I mean, I know everybody thought there was a rift between Tom and me, but not really. I was at my exhaustion point with *Mission: Impossible.* I'll never forget when they came to do the electronic press kit: I sat down in front of the camera and the guy said, "Why did you make *Mission: Impossible?*" And I froze. [*Laughs*] My mind went blank. Probably after about ten, fifteen seconds, he said, "Cut, cut." It told me how exhausted I was.

PREMIERE: *Are you pleased with the final results?*
DE PALMA: You know, there was so much effort and so many hours put into it. For me it's almost difficult to even look at now. In a couple of years, I'm sure I'll warm up to it, but I just can't even . . . Five months in ILM [Industrial Light and Magic] Land, I mean, I applaud the people who go through that. It is agonizingly detailed. Up there on the farm [George Lucas's ranch in Marin, California], staring out at the deer staring back at me and wondering when I was gonna get outta there. "That sparkle when the cable hits the side of the tunnel looks a little artificial; we need more shading." Looking at that stuff every day, on a loop, over and over again.

PREMIERE: *You got a boost up to the A-list after* The Untouchables. *Does it bother you that many people gave credit for* Mission: Impossible *to Cruise?*
DE PALMA: I proceeded to make *Snake Eyes,* for which we got paid a lot of money. The fact is, you can always evaluate what the community thinks about you by how much they're willing to pay you. You can go out there with a spec script, and when everybody wants to make a development deal, you realize that your stock is low. Which happened to me when I went out with *Ambrose Chapel,* a thriller that I wrote after *Carlito's Way.* I can't make a

gangster picture any better than *Carlito's Way*. But it was not commercially successful, and I couldn't get $20 million to make [*Ambrose Chapel*]. That tells you that you need a hit. I hadn't had a really big hit since *The Untouchables*.

PREMIERE: *You've said that you're afraid of becoming like Orson Welles, a filmmaking genius who couldn't get any movies made in Hollywood after* Touch of Evil, *released in 1958. Does that mean you have to compromise to make hits?*
DE PALMA: No, it doesn't have to do with compromise. Compromising what? *Mission: Impossible* may be the best movie we'll ever make, the one we'll be remembered for. Who knows? Did I say, "Boy, I can't wait to make *Mission: Impossible,* what a great deal!" Not really. It's not what kept me up at night in my creative life. I said, "That's a very good idea. I think I'll do that."

PREMIERE: *Don't you think that talented directors of a certain stature, such as you or Oliver Stone, should be given carte blanche to do whatever they think is interesting?*
DE PALMA: No, I don't agree with that. You are working in a popular art form, and if your audience doesn't show up, you'd better find out why. Because they're going to stop giving you money. And if you say, "Well, I'm a genius, and nobody understands me"—fine, go be a genius at home.

You get into the big game and you gotta deal with the big players. But you can also have a successful career at the low-budget end of the industry. Certainly never slowed down Woody Allen.

PREMIERE: *Is that a model to emulate?*
DE PALMA: Absolutely. But that's not what I do. I need that big train set that Orson Welles talked about. Because I know how to use the technology, I know how to do the big set pieces, so consequently I've gotta go back and forth sometimes from lower-budget movies to the higher-budget movies. I've never made an astronomically expensive movie.

PREMIERE: *What do you think of* Titanic?
DE PALMA: It's great, basically because Jim [Cameron] is fearless; he believes in what he feels and thinks, and he's willing to take a tremendous amount of criticism in order to accomplish what he wants. More power to him. But I think, on the other hand, you get the incredibly expensive, mind-

less—sorry to use *Godzilla* as an example—movies built to exploit anything you can think of, from toys to Happy Meals. That's okay. I mean, *Stars Wars* was the beginning of this. But when you make such a not-so-good movie, it's very unfortunate, and hopefully these guys [Roland Emmerich and Dean Devlin] will learn a lesson from it.

PREMIERE: *It seems that after you have a big hit like* Independence Day, *you start to think you're invincible.*
DE PALMA: I never had that problem. [*Laughs*] I never had one of those runaway successful hits and thought I was God.

PREMIERE: *What about* The Untouchables?
DE PALMA: Just remember my group. Steven Spielberg, George Lucas, Francis Coppola, and Marty Scorsese.

PREMIERE: *They always seemed more successful?*
DE PALMA: They *were* more successful. So I never had the terrible ego problem.

PREMIERE: *But you're Brian De Palma. Your taste is darker . . .*
DE PALMA: Absolutely.

PREMIERE: *More violent . . .*
DE PALMA: Absolutely.

PREMIERE: *More sexual . . .*
De PALMA: Absolutely. And I'm a bit of a '60s iconoclast. I have a very skeptical eye about the establishment. I view the whole media world as what's for sale this week.

PREMIERE: *Do you think that you were ahead of the curve with the dark, violent, sexual material that you dealt with in such films as* Body Double, Dressed to Kill, *and* Scarface, *much of which seems more commonplace now?*
DE PALMA: Well, when a movie's released, you're always measured against the fashion of the times. And the work goes on. I mean, I read in one book that reviews video-cassettes that now *Blow Out* is considered a more inventive picture than *Blow-Up*. That's shocking to me—that somehow *Blow-Up*

has aged badly. But in retrospect, all you want is your work to be around, maybe a couple of decades, maybe into the next century if it's *really* good. And you have to pay less attention to what's being said about you when the movie comes out. I mean, there was nobody more lacerated than me when *Body Double* came out. I can't tell you how I was grilled and attacked in the press. But now, somehow, this is a movie of mine that is remembered. *Scarface* is another example. Believe me, you didn't want to be around for the preview of *Scarface*. Or the opening. People were outraged—you saw people running up the aisle. I remember the opening-night party, I thought they were going to skin me alive. It did very well when it came out, but it was not popularly reviewed in the press. I've been used to this my whole career.

PREMIERE: *In Peter Biskind's book* Easy Riders, Raging Bulls, *you and your generation of directors—Scorsese, Coppola, Lucas, Spielberg—are portrayed as not having supported one another.*
DE PALMA: If I hear about that screening of *Star Wars* one more time, about how everybody was trying to attack George. . . . We were rooting for George a hundred percent, you know. I've always had a, shall we say, cutting wit, but everybody who knows me knows I only have their best interest at heart. And George Lucas is my friend to this day, as are Martin Scorsese and Steven Spielberg. George was very helpful when I showed him *Mission: Impossible*. He looked at it, and he said, "You know, this is missing, that's missing"; he was as tough with it as I was with *Star Wars*. You go to the best critics you can get, who are basically directors of your stature.

PREMIERE: *Is Spielberg showing you his movies?*
DE PALMA: Not anymore. Steven has gotten, you know, *Steven,* but basically that has a lot more to do with proximity. I am sorry that this kind of interaction is not as fluid as it used to be, but in terms of material and actors, we're always in communication with each other.

PREMIERE: *Did you finally read your friend Julie Salamon's book* The Devil's Candy, *which details your directing* The Bonfire of the Vanities?
DE PALMA: Oh, sure. I didn't read it when it came out, but I read it years later. I thought it was extremely accurate reporting, painful though it may be. It's so revealing, you know? My intention was always to let her see everything.

PREMIERE: *It was brave of you.*

DE PALMA: Extremely brave. And extremely stupid.

PREMIERE: *What was the most painful thing she revealed about you?*

DE PALMA: Oh, I would say the David Lean [American Film Institute Tribute] dinner. It was basically that I was motivated by a failed love affair.

PREMIERE: *The moment when you wanted [production executive] Kathy Lingg to be impressed by where you were sitting?*

DE PALMA: Yeah. See there, everybody knows the Kathy Lingg thing. Talk about revealing.

PREMIERE: *What have you learned from your three wives?*

DE PALMA: Caring, loving . . . I'd say I've learned more from my children than [from] my wives. I haven't been too successful with my wives.

PREMIERE: *Why is that?*

DE PALMA: I'm too focused on what I'm doing, basically. And I work best by myself. When I get attached emotionally, it doesn't free me the way I have to be freed. 'Cause a lot of being a growing artist is going through everything—whether it's success or failure—by yourself.

PREMIERE: *Next, you're going to film another bank heist, in* Nazi Gold. *Will it be better than* Mission: Impossible?

DE PALMA: You bet. It's something I've been thinking about for years, since the '60s. When I was shooting documentaries in the early days of the Treasury Department [*laughs*], we used to wander around with a bank examiner, and he would walk up to a bank and knock on the door, and that was the day of the bank examination. We just followed him in. They opened up the vault while the film crew shot it. What a great way to rob a bank! My cowriter, Jay Cocks, and I sold *Nazi Gold* to MGM for $5 million. Besides the moral outrage of the Swiss Bank's not giving the poor people back their money, I just thought, What a great idea, to have that kind of a *Mission: Impossible* group go in and rob it. That's the only way they're ever going to get it. 'Cause you know it's going to disappear.

PREMIERE: *Is it true that you and Scorsese were once ready to throw in the towel and walk away from Hollywood?*

DE PALMA: We began to sound like a bunch of old warriors complaining. But the fact that we've been making movies since the '60s is, in itself, a miracle. We have great jobs, too. We didn't get this off the ground or that off the ground, but, boy, we have the ability to think up an idea, put it together, sell it, and go off to some foreign place to make it. I mean, come on.

De Palma on *Mission to Mars*

BILL FENTUM/2000

WHEN *DIRECTED BY BRIAN DE PALMA* went online in October of last year, one of the hopes I had for its future was that I would eventually have the opportunity to interview the director himself, possibly in connection with the release of one of his films. However, knowing it would be quite a while before the site was anywhere near "completion," I hadn't given much thought to that in recent weeks, as we all prepared for the March 10 U.S. release of *Mission to Mars.*

Well, from now on, I'll know to be more prepared! On March 9, Mr. De Palma contacted me, saying that because current U.S. press junkets are only exploitative publicity events, he would like to offer this site the first—and possibly only—American interview for the film. When the interview took place three days later, we discussed not just the making of *Mission to Mars,* but issues involving critical perception of his work, plans for the future, and, at the start, another science fiction project he had planned some twenty-two years ago.

BILL FENTUM: *Until* Mission to Mars, *the only other science fiction project you've come close to making was an adaptation of Alfred Bester's* The Demolished Man, *in 1978. But is this a genre you've always been interested in?*
BRIAN DE PALMA: Well no, the only real "science fiction" material that I ever liked was *The Demolished Man.* And I always thought you could remake *Forbidden Planet.* I thought that was a marvelous story. But besides that, noth-

From www.briandepalma.net, posted March 2000. Reprinted by permission of the author.

ing else. Kurt Vonnegut's *The Sirens of Titan* is another great science fiction book they had made a few scripts of, but never quite solved. And they're still writing scripts on *The Demolished Man*. In fact, there's a new draft that they recently called me about. It's been going on for many decades now.

B F : *Is there a chance that you'd ever return to that project?*
B D P : I'd have to read the script. But because this movie was so exhausting, I basically said I don't want to look at anything for a while.

B F : *The intense shooting schedule on* Mission to Mars *couldn't have been the way you preferred to work.*
B D P : Well, I thought it was a little insane, the date. I thought we should try to beat out the other Mars movie, but during the year that we were making the film, the other one automatically fell way behind us. But the studio locked into this March 10 date and just never moved off it. And my attitude was, "Guys, you want it March 10, you're gonna get it March 10!"

B F : *Having longtime collaborators on the film—Paul Hirsch, Stephen H. Burum, Eric Schwab—how much easier did that make this schedule?*
B D P : Oh, we never could have done it without these people. It just makes the work so much easier because they know exactly what you want. You give them certain directions and they do exactly as you would have done. So consequently, it makes all that very easy. And my assistant director, Chris Soldo, who I've worked with on many films, just makes the whole process move as efficiently as possible. Also, we were two weeks ahead of schedule, which took a lot of the financial pressure off. I'm still amazed, when I see the movie, that we were able to accomplish so much within a year's time.

I also never realized exactly what I was getting into until I was in the midst of it, because we had so many shots that went out to a lot of different digital effects houses, which compounded the problem. Because some of them are quite good at what they do, and others are not as good. Everything you do takes ten times as long, because you have to keep sending the shot back when it's not exactly right. The communication between you and the digital effects supervisor is crucial. And though I was very fortunate to work with John Knoll at ILM, the rest of the digital effects houses—and there were about five other ones—were hardly at his level.

B F : *I remember you once said that* Mission: Impossible *was the most exhausting film you had ever made. How did this compare?*

B D P : Well, *Mission: Impossible* was sort of open-ended. We had a lot more time to refine things and try things, and then if they didn't work, try something else. With this one, I more or less had to focus in on the essence of the sequences, and just immediately storyboard them and move them into animatics and edit the animatics and then lock into the whole cinematic montage right from the get-go.

B F : *Was it more difficult on* Mission to Mars, *with those elaborate sets, to get the fluid camera movements we've come to expect from your work?*

B D P : Well, I had to come up with a whole different way of doing things because of the weightlessness. And the whole thing about outer space is that there's no up and down. So I had to think of ways to convey that to the audience.

B F : *I loved your use of the disorienting camera angles, the rotating shots . . .*

B D P : Yeah, shots like that helped the audience to understand what the particular problem is. And the other thing is that we were always attempting to be as scientifically realistic as possible. We had all kinds of NASA advisors so that everything was as real as could be. And right from the beginning, I scaled the script down so that there was just a finite number of catastrophes, very specific. Because the way it was before, we would have been two years making this movie.

B F : *It's interesting how technology has helped you evolve your storyboarding techniques.*

B D P : Well, "animatics" is a process that I used here for the first time. I did it in kind of a half-assed way with my own little storyboards before, but these that were actually moving were primitive, *Toy Story*-style animatics that are three dimensional representations of the characters, the space and what the shot does. So when they start creating the shot, they have very strong guidelines about what it is. And the more specific you are with the animatic, the more it becomes a literal blueprint for the shot that ultimately gets rendered. The process of rendering a shot from beginning to end took about a year, and there were close to 600 of them.

BF: *Did you plan the entire film that way?*

BDP: No, I didn't have time to do that. I basically storyboarded the catastrophe with the hole in the ship, the losing of Woody—that whole sequence from when the micrometeoroid hits until Woody dies. I also storyboarded the whole end of the movie, from when they walk into the planetarium, and the vortex sequence.

BF: *How flexible are you in changing these angles once you're on the set?*

BDP: You can't do much, once you've locked into this. Because once you sign off on the storyboard, you can always add shots that don't affect what the digital people are doing, like close-ups. But when you're using anything that's digitally painted in, you're kind of locked into those shots.

BF: *By focusing in a hopeful way on our exploration of space,* Mission to Mars *is one of your most optimistic films.*

BDP: Yes.

BF: *That's very different for you.*

BDP: Well, it's part of the genre, and it's one of the few things we can be optimistic about. If you talk to these astronauts, and we spent a lot of time with them—I mean, it's "the last frontier." And it's completely devoid of the usual hellish corruption that I represent in a lot of my movies. So it's kind of a beautiful thing and a departure for me. It gets wearing to be so cynical all the time. And this is one area where you don't find cynicism.

BF: *As in many of your films, we see a longing for family here . . . within marriages, between parents and children, even the bonding of the crew members. It seems to be a recurring theme for you.*

BDP: Yeah, I would say that. But these are things you only discover when thinking about what your work says, years after you've done it. Because a lot of decisions you make are things that have to be done "in the moment," and a lot of those choices are intuitive. But there's certainly a road map to your unconscious, and you start seeing these particular themes appearing again and again. As somebody pointed out to me from *Cahiers du Cinema* the other day, there's the fact that with *Mission to Mars* I've let another character die, who is greatly loved, but nobody can do anything about it.

B F : *You're often referred to as a cold or calculating director, but I've never found that to be true. I think a lot of your films show a strong empathy for their characters. In fact, we see that from the earliest moments in this film.*

B D P : Well, I certainly feel that. But that could hardly be what the critical establishment feels. They have an almost preprogrammed idea of "what De Palma is," and then they just walk into a screening and measure it against that immediately, without ever opening their eyes and watching what's on the screen.

B F : *That must become tiresome.*

B D P : It is tiresome, and it's upsetting. Because you say, "Wait a minute. Didn't you see what was there?" I go through critical attacks like this, sometimes very abrasive—like in the days of *Dressed to Kill . . . Body Double . . . Scarface,* certainly. And then they sort of go all out, as with this film or *Bonfire of the Vanities,* and there's no end to it!

B F : *Well, I'm hoping that the forums on this site can turn some of that around. Even if we attract a few people who dislike your work, at least they're talking.*

B D P : Yes. And fortunately, in France, that's not the problem. They don't quite understand how the American critics react the way they do. I've given up wondering why, and the fact that I can go on making movies is all that really matters.

B F : *Is filmmaking still as rewarding as it's been in the past?*

B D P : Well, when you've made as many movies as I have, you really have to try to find things that are going to stir your imagination, because you've traveled a lot of ground already. And you want to avoid being repetitive . . . even though you don't realize you ARE being repetitive. Which happens to all directors, I would say, in the late period in their lives—they somehow keep on making the same movie over and over again.

So I often force myself into different genres, to try to see what happens, and get inspired by a whole different set of aesthetic problems, different characters and different storylines from other writers. And then I'll go back and do something that I've been thinking about myself for a while. It's a continuing process with me. It's never easy to get a movie made—any movie. So you try to pick what you do pretty carefully, though you're seldom in a situation where anything you want to make, gets made.

BF: *Is there a chance of* Mr. Hughes *coming together again?*

BDP: Hopefully. It's one of those things that depends on when Nic Cage can work it into his schedule. He's committed to about four pictures in a row, and until he sort of clears his mind, I don't know if he can really make a decision in relationship to this material. But that's what moviemaking is like all the time, you know. Certain things happen, and then certain things don't happen. And it's not something that you can completely control. The fact that you're healthy and can keep working is more than anybody can ask for at my age.

BF: *I think* The Demolished Man *was my first lesson in preparing for disappointment, even when a film seems certain to be made.*

BDP: Yeah, I remember I worked on a version of *The Demolished Man*, I believe in the . . . oh, it's got to be in the late fifties. All by myself, not owning anything, just having the book and making a script out of it. So it's been coming back and forth at me for decades. It's the whole problem of trying to figure out a way of doing the telepathy in a purely visual way, which is an ominous task, let me tell you!

BF: *Well, if anyone could solve it, you could.*

BDP: I surely hope so. But the problem, also, of having so much experience is that you know what the pitfalls are, and you know what doesn't work. As in all movies, one is continually surprised by what the reaction is. It always amazes me. It's never exactly what you think. I mean, certainly with *Mission to Mars,* you've got to look at it with an uncynical eye. Like when I went to see *Destination Moon.* You've got to look at it with an uncynical eye! You start laughing at this stuff, and it's over. I never realized that they would start laughing at *Mission to Mars* so universally.

BF: *I think it's one of those films where it's best to go in viewing it in the same way that the children in the audience are able to see it.*

BDP: Absolutely, absolutely. And the thing about it is—that's what these guys are like. I mean, I know it's hard to imagine a world with men like astronauts, who have this purity about them, but that's what I experienced in the times I spent with them. And also, they have that kind of starry-eyed look, because they've seen things that we will never see. They've been out there, hanging off the shuttle somewhere, fixing something on one of the satellites, and they've been looking around the universe. They come back with this look in their eyes! There's something magical about it. And that was what I was attempting to show, with Gary Sinise's journey through the material. These guys have been somewhere and done things that no man has ever done before. But it's amazing how they just schlock it in with "it's sort of *The Abyss*, it's sort of *Close Encounters* . . ."

BF: *Well, your fans certainly don't feel that way.*
BDP: Thank God for my fans! And I truly believe that our lives will continue on the Web. And not only in the fan websites. You know, they're not "fan" in the sense of some crazy guy running around trying to get you to sign a photograph. I mean, these are intelligent people. And that's what you get when you go on to these sites, and you see that they're not a bunch of goof-balls, kibbitzing around. Some of the essays they write in terms of these forums, are like. . . . Wow. I mean these guys are really thinking about it!

That's also what you find with the French critics. I mean, those guys . . . that's why it's interesting to talk to them. Because they really have studied you. Their insights into what you're doing make you think. And that's something you will never find in a press junket in the United States.

Interview with Brian De Palma

GEOFF BERAN/2002

ON THE WAY TO INTERVIEW Brian De Palma at his apartment in Paris, his assistant Sophie alerted me to the fact that Mr. De Palma had already moved past thinking of *Femme Fatale,* which had yet to be released, as "the new film." She said to be careful if you say "the new movie" to him and expect to be talking about *Femme Fatale,* because he will start talking in terms of the new project that is already in his head. That new project, I had heard before, involved a paranormal thriller that De Palma was thinking about filming in Paris and Italy. I had been told that with this one, De Palma really wanted to scare people.

Meanwhile, there was a retrospective of the director's work continuing at Paris's Pompidou museum, where every one of De Palma's films was being screened to packed audiences. At a press conference on opening night, De Palma was asked why he chose *Blow Out* to open the retrospective with. He replied that he had seen on the Internet where *Blow Out* was chosen by his own fans as being his best film. De Palma was referring to a semi-annual poll of his fans taken by Canadian Carl Rodrigue and American Tony Suppa, co-Webmasters of "Le Paradis de Brian De Palma," in which *Blow Out* consistently ranks at the top of the list. Finding the fans for the poll is easy: Rodrigue and Suppa simply log on to the "De Palma Forum," located at Bill Fentum's website, "Directed by Brian De Palma," and ask fans to rank their top fifteen or so favorite De Palma films. The two of them add up the tallies,

Interview conducted February 26, 2002, in Paris, France. Copyright © 2002 Geoff Beran, "De Palma à la Mod," www.angelfire.com/de/palma. Reprinted by permission of the author.

and voila! The press conference itself was transcribed, with pictures, for De Palma's fans around the globe by Romain Desbiens, at his site "Brian De Palma: Le Virtuose du 7ème Art." De Palma may have exiled himself in France, but the network created and maintained by his fans around the globe made him seem more universal than ever.

De Palma had come to Paris in March 2000, the same week his *Mission to Mars* opened in America. Even before he attended his first ever Cannes Film Festival that May, where *Mission to Mars* screened out of competition, he had written a screenplay called *Femme Fatale*. It wasn't long before he had adapted the screenplay to a Paris setting and put the wheels in motion to shoot his next film in France, where he found himself living. By the time of the next Cannes Film Festival, in May 2001, he had further tailored the script to suit his new star, Rebecca Romijn-Stamos, assembled a mostly-French film crew, and was shooting the opening scenes of *Femme Fatale* on the famous steps of the Festival Palais. As the retrospective opened in February of 2002, rumors persisted that *Femme Fatale* would make its debut at that year's Cannes Festival. When asked about this, De Palma replied that he was "not allowed" to reply.

I had come to Paris initially for the retrospective. More than five years earlier, when I started my own De Palma website, I titled it "De Palma à la Mod" in homage to *Murder à la Mod,* a film so rare it had been rumored that De Palma himself owned the only existing print. Of course, I had never seen it, but I had really wanted to. I needed to. I had developed a theory about De Palma's work which insisted that his earlier films were key to understanding the complex layers of his later ones. *Murder à la Mod,* along with several other rarities, were part of the retrospective, and I could not resist. I knew it would be the rarest of opportunities to view these early films, and within the context of a such a complete program in a city where the director's work was truly appreciated . . . well, I knew it was a situation that may only happen once in a lifetime. And as long as I was in Paris, I figured I might as well ask De Palma himself for an interview.

A few nights prior to our conversation, De Palma had joined Laurent Vachaud, coauthor of *Brian De Palma: Entretiens avec Samuel Blumenfeld et Laurent Vachaud,* for a question-and-answer session following a screening of his *Dionysus in '69.* Vachaud would participate in the discussion, and also act as translator between the mostly French-speaking audience and the filmmaker. Sophie hinted to me that De Palma was getting tired of the same old questions, so before beginning with him, I told him that I had tried to come up with some new ones. That made him laugh.

GEOFF BERAN: *In the earlier days of your career, you seemed a little more open toward talking with people, when there was a more responsive atmosphere to your films. And now, that seems to have come full circle here in Paris, where people here are really appreciating your work. Do you think this frees you up as an artist? Do you feel freer now than you did before to make the kinds of films that you want to make?*

BRIAN DE PALMA: Well, I just think through your career you go through different phases, and I just got uninspired by the whole studio process of making and releasing films. There's not much joy in it, even if it's a success or a failure. And there's all this pressure to get it done on a certain day, even though it has nothing to do with the realities of the movie you're making. You're making a movie for a budget and a release date. And then you go and have these press junkets where you're thrown into a hotel suite and doing three-minute television interviews, and they get it all over in maybe two days. Nobody's really interested in asking you anything interesting. It's just stuff to put on television. And in my case, I just don't think they're much interested in directors anymore. It's all a celebrity business. They're interested in the movie stars, so what's the point of going? I have tried to avoid a couple of these press junkets. I managed to avoid the *Mission to Mars* junket. I did some stuff in New York on *Snake Eyes,* but I missed the *Mission: Impossible* one completely. I don't mind promoting a movie or talking to the press if it's going to be *used* in some way. But if they shoot television stuff, which is a *bore* to do, and they don't use it—because like I said before, they're just interested in the movie stars—and it's just this little 30-second blurb on television, then it's like, come on.

I came to Paris to do a lot of promotion for *Mission to Mars* when it opened in Europe. And then I said, "Well, why don't I make movies here?" It's beautiful, I've always wanted to work in Europe again, and that's why I stayed. I mean, I don't think there's any sort of grand design to it.

GB: *Just kind of where it led you?*
BDP: Yeah, I mean, it's great working here. It wouldn't have occurred to me unless I came here and just started to live here.

GB: *I understand that you already have plans for a new movie. Laurent Vachaud said you want to make a really scary movie this time.*

BDP: Yes, I had an idea to make a very scary movie, based on a kind of serial murderer who preys on tourists. So I came up with a very good idea, and that's what I've been working on. But I've written a couple of scripts, and at this stage now, I'm sort of deciding. . . . You go through a process of reading a lot of material—books, scripts, writing—until you get something that's going to get you interested enough to make the movie. And as you get older, it just gets harder. You say to yourself, "Do I want to spend all this time making something I'm not a hundred percent sure will be moving me another step forward? What am I saying with this movie? Am I involving some kind of cinematic idea I'm working on?" I ponder these things all the time.

GB: *You say "moving another step"—do you see the whole cinematic process for you as an almost scientific one, a heuristic process building on not only what you've done, but also the work that others have done?*

BDP: Yeah, you're trying to push the envelope a little bit all the time. And I think in terms of pure visual storytelling, nobody else is doing this besides me. You see it in some other directors occasionally, but I've been obsessed with this kind of visual storytelling for quite a while, and I try to create material that allows me to explore it. I did quite a lot of it in *Femme Fatale*. And it put me on a course of, "How can I find visual ideas and work them into stories I want to tell?" That's something that haunts me all the time.

GB: *At the recent Pompidou screening of* Dionysus in '69, *you talked about the energy of the play, and the effect it had on you which inspired you to film it. Did you feel that you and your fellow cameramen were a part of that energy while you were filming? Or did you feel separated from it?*

BDP: Well, anytime you're shooting documentary stuff, you have to be in the moment and be able to be in control enough to capture what's happening. I saw some footage once where a bunch of guys were shooting a rock band touring across the country, and they were as stoned as the rock band. Consequently, what they shot wasn't very good. So you have to sort of be there, you have to feel it, and you have to be detached enough to record it and get it on film and get the camera in the right position when these things are happening.

GB: *You seem to satirize that energy in* Hi, Mom! *and* Phantom of the Paradise, *almost to the point where up to* Casualties of War, *there seems to be that same sort of energy in that whole sense of freedom they feel out in the fields. And it seems like there, it becomes almost a moral issue. It could just be my interpretation, but it seems like you did progress to a point where you took a stand . . .*

BDP: You mean with that speech of Eriksson's in *Casualties of War,* where he says, "We've gotta be careful about what we're doing, because we may be dead the next moment?"

GB: *Yes.*

BDP: (long sigh) Well, there was a kind of spontaneity there, and a kind of adventurous generation that . . . I don't know, you're part of the new generation. I don't know how much we see it anymore. And that's what's so inspirational about something like *Dionysus in '69.* It actually records the moment that it happened. It's a document of the period. And it catches the kind of feel of the '60s, which is very elusive when you're trying to tell about this period. There's a kind of idealistic, revolutionary, anti-establishment, almost absurdist energy. You know, "We want it and we want it now." The establishment has just sucked it all up and made a product out of it, and that kind of destroyed it.

GB: *With* Femme Fatale, *you seemed very inspired by Rebecca Romijn-Stamos. What struck you most about her?*

BDP: Well, I think I've really discovered somebody. It's always great when you discover someone. I think she's just stunning, and embodies this part. And I'll be very excited to see if she's launched by this film. It's always great to discover a new star of tomorrow.

GB: *I want to talk a little bit about the songs in your films. I haven't seen* Murder à la Mod *yet, but I understand William Finley has a song at the beginning.*

BDP: Yes.

GB: *And then there's* Greetings . . .

BDP: Yes.

GB: *All the way up to* Snake Eyes, *with Meredith Brooks, who wrote the song at the end . . .*

BDP: "Sin City."

G B :   *Yes. The songs seem to use a lot of lines from the actual films.*
B D P :   Yes.

G B :   *Is that something, for instance, when you met with Meredith Brooks, did you go through that with her? Or did you show her the script and ask her to write a song?*
B D P :   I spent some time with her because I saw one of her videos from her "Bitch" album. And I thought she was remarkable on film. And then I sort of just ran her down in Los Angeles. And I liked her. We got along extremely well. And then I went out on tour with her. I don't know when I got the idea for her to write a song. I was thinking of doing something—I've always had a fascination with watching these kids on MTV videos. I'm always looking for a new musical entity to move into a motion picture venue. And I thought her videos were extremely good, and I really liked her music. Now, I think I showed the movie to her, and that's how she picked up some of the lyrics. And then she sang the song to me, and I made some suggestions, some of which she took, some of which she didn't. And that's how the song evolved.

G B :   *It's interesting, because it seems similar to the older songs from your '60s movies where the title is prominent.*
B D P :   We have two really interesting French songs in *Femme Fatale*. One, because we couldn't get the rights to use the song that Rebecca worked with, which was an old classic rock and roll song that was just too expensive. We had to decide whether to use it or not. So we looked around, and the choreographer found a whole bunch of alternate ideas, and came up with a sensational French song by a group called Saez called "Sex," which is one of the sexiest songs I've ever heard and works very well with this strip tease sequence. And then we use a very little bit of an Elli Medeiros song when they're in the bathroom listening to their MP3 players as they're making out. I don't know if there's much rhyme or reason to this. You know, I listen to contemporary music all the time.

G B :   *On the soundtrack for* Carlito's Way, *Patrick Doyle has a music cue for the love scene, but you wound up using the Joe Cocker song, which of course is reprised at the end of the film.*
B D P :   Right.

G B :   *Where did the idea come about to use that song?*

BDP: Well, you know, there's always something on the temp track, and I thought the temp track with Joe Cocker's song worked better than what Patrick had written. Composers hate when you do this. Ryuichi Sakamoto was not very happy about me putting the Meredith Brooks song at the end of *Snake Eyes.* I used just a very little bit of an Elli Medeiros song in *Femme Fatale,* and she's a very good friend of mine. But I always have to make these tough decisions, whether people are friends or not. I just look at it and think, this is the best music for this section of the movie. Sakamoto had composed a whole long section for the end of *Snake Eyes.* I just felt we needed a shift of mood—you know, when Nicolas Cage says, "What the hell, at least I got to be on television"—that had to shift the mood up. There has to be an irony there, and I felt the song reflected it better.

GB: *Was Morricone's score for* The Untouchables *a conscious reworking of his score for* The Battle of Algiers, *as one writer has claimed?*
BDP: That I can't comment on, because I'm not that familiar with that score. I know a lot of Morricone's scores, and I may have heard it on one of the compilation records that I have, but I can't hum a little *The Battle of Algiers* for you. It's not something that immediately comes to mind, such as, say, *Once upon a Time in the West.* Morricone wrote a tremendous number of scores. You know, I was listening to his score for *Bugsy* the other day, and it's very similar to *The Untouchables.*

GB: *There's this book called* Afterimage, *written by Richard A. Blake, a Jesuit priest. He has separate chapters on Scorsese, Capra, Coppola, Hitchcock, Ford, and you, at the end. His idea of the "afterimage" is how the Catholic upbringing of these directors is still there in the imagery of their movies. And he uses you as kind of a test case, because he says that you're probably the least Catholic among the bunch. Do you think your Catholic background has affected your movies in such a way?*
BDP: Well, both my parents are Catholic, and my grandparents are all Italian-speaking Catholics on both sides. However, ironically, I was baptized Presbyterian, and went to a Quaker school for 12 years. So that's why I have all of this Catholic imagery, because it was always around me from my grandparents. You know, the funerals, the church services we'd go to occasionally, and the family gatherings—just filled with all kinds of Catholic images. However, I spent most of my time in a Quaker school. So you get this whole other

sort of very restrained, religious framework that you're brought up in. And that's why I think you have this sort of strange mix with me.

G B : *Oliver Stone said that as he was writing* Scarface, *he thought of it as a kind of comic* Richard III. *And in Pauline Kael's review of the film, she goes so far as to call it slapstick. Were you thinking in terms of comedy at all when you were direct-ing the film?*
B D P : No. If anyone's been around some very long cocaine evenings, there's nothing that's in *Scarface* that we all haven't seen before. Of course, I have a very operatic style, but people on cocaine tend to be a little operatic. When you see that crazy sequence in *GoodFellas,* when Ray Liotta's running around, he's cooking, and he's gotta get the stuff, I mean, it's so perfect. And I just took it in another direction with *Scarface.*

G B : *The marketing of* Scarface *seemed to bring to mind* The Godfather, *which Pacino was well known for. Do you think that by making it a lengthy film along those lines, you were going for that kind of vibe? A* Godfather *type of feel?*
B D P : Well, when they have Al Pacino as a gangster, to the advertising department it's another *Godfather* because of the success of those films. But I remember specifically looking at the ad campaign, and they had Al in a black suit, holding a gun. And I said, "This is not a black suit Mafia guy. This is a white suit Cuban gangster." So they reversed the suit so it was a white suit, and that was the little effect I had on the merchandising, or the selling of the movie.

G B : *A month after* Scarface *was released, in Michigan somewhere it was reported that some teenager got up in front of the screen before the movie started and tried to rally the crowd, saying something like, "This is a great film. It shows how to get ahead in America, they shoot people good in this film. . . ." That sort of thing. If that happened at a screening where you were present, would you feel compelled to comment to such a person in any way?*
B D P : Well, *Scarface* was always in a swirl of controversy. The battle I had with the MPAA to not have an X rating . . . you know, some people loved the movie, and it made a lot of people incredibly angry . . . so, please, nothing would have surprised me in that period.

G B : *I'm sure I could go on and keep asking you questions all day, I have so many . . .*

BDP: Well, let's keep going. Let me ask you a few questions. When did you start your website?

GB: *That would have been right before* Snake Eyes, *in 1996 or 1997.*
BDP: And what inspires someone to do a website?

GB: *Actually, I was staying at my mom's in Colorado. I was bored one night, and I had never been on the Web before, and I had access to the Internet. I just got on, and I was looking for information about your films. I found a site, Angelfire, where you can make a free website. And I just decided to gather up all the information I'd found, and just started it like that.*
BDP: Wow. And what drives you on?

GB: *Well, Bill Fentum would e-mail me . . .*
BDP: Have you met Bill?

GB: *Just once or twice on the phone, and we've mailed each other things. But he did an article, and we put it up on my site. And there were people, like this other guy, Brett, who would e-mail me wanting to discuss* Snake Eyes. *I guess it was really the first site about you, although there was a Canadian site that was never really kept up at the time. And it was just a place where people who liked your work could go. And of course, Bill, who is much more technically inclined than I am, developed "Directed by Brian De Palma" . . .*
BDP: Right.

GB: *And so he and Carl Rodrigue started the "De Palma Forum," which was very helpful . . .*
BDP: Right, right. Yes, it's quite incredible. That's why I think it's important for directors to support their forums, or their websites. Because, like I said to Bill, this is where we will live and exist, on the Web. All this stuff will ultimately go on the Web. When people want to get any research information, it will all exist on these websites. Don't you think?

GB: *Yeah, I agree. I mean, there's already so much information that someone like me can get at the push of a button.*
BDP: Yeah, when I write all the time, the advantage of using the Web to find out information is just unbelievable. And I especially like working here

in Paris, just because I can get a very fast modem line. It's all cable modem lines here.

G B : *And of course, there is misinformation . . .*
B D P : Oh, all the time.

G B : *Like when my site started out, I listed* Crocodile Tears *as one of the films you were working on [the title was eventually changed to* Falling Sky*] . . .*
B D P : Yeah, what *is Crocodile Tears?*

G B : *I actually found out more about it recently, because I had e-mail contact with a guy who worked on it. It was made by a guy whose name is similar to yours ["Brian J. De Palma"]. And I actually have a copy of it from Hong Kong. It stars Brittany Murphy and Karen Allen, her alcoholic mother. They live in Las Vegas, and the daughter just keeps trying to get the mom to straighten up and work. It's a teenage coming-of-age movie.*
B D P : . . . that went right to video and nobody saw.

G B : *Yeah, not even in America. I had to buy it on eBay from Hong Kong.*
B D P : (laughs) So you just came to Paris for a little vacation?

G B : *Well, I've always wanted to see* Murder à la Mod, *which is why I titled the site after that movie, and when I saw it was going to be here, along with* The Responsive Eye *and* Wotan's Wake . . .
B D P : Right, *Wotan's Wake.* . . . You've seen everything else?

G B : *Yes, except for your other shorts and documentaries.*
B D P : Yep.

G B : *Who knows, maybe you'll release them on DVD sometime, in 50 years . . .*
B D P : If I can find them. You know, finding those negatives . . .

G B : *Speaking of the old films, there was one called* Mod . . .
B D P : It was never finished. The whole thing was financed with some friends, and I think they ran out of money. But I shot a lot of stuff, needless to say. I shot a lot of the rock and roll groups in London. I shot The Who at the Marquee Club, I shot the Rolling Stones at Fourteenth Street. I shot Peter

Gordon. And then I think Bob Fiore went over and shot a lot of the Manchester groups. But I think the producers ran out of money. And that was the end of it.

GB: *All that stuff is just kind of sitting around somewhere?*
BDP: I have no idea where it is. I think Bill Finley's got it in his attic somewhere.

GB: *Among your early influences, you've mentioned Godard and Truffaut, of course. Was Chabrol ever an influence, either earlier or later on?*
BDP: Chabrol did *The Cousins?* Was that Chabrol?

GB: *Yes.*
BDP: *Le Beau Serge . . .*

GB: *Yes.*
DBP: No, I think the basic influence was Godard, mainly because the Godardian manner had a lot of influence on *Greetings* and *Hi, Mom!,* going out in the street, improvising. Except we didn't do so much improvising ultimately because we rehearsed everything so much, and we just didn't have enough film to improvise. When you figure it all out, the most expensive thing in *Greetings* was the stock and getting it processed. But that spontaneity, telling stories that are happening to you politically at the time, the people who are your friends that you went to college with, stuff like that, I'd say Godard was the most influential. Plus he had this very stunning visual style and was full of ideas. Godard is incredibly brilliant, the things he says. Apparently here in France, the most interesting thing when a new film of his is going to come out are his press conferences, because he's so brilliant.

GB: *He seems to be very anti-Spielberg lately.*
BDP: Yes. Yes. I've noticed that.

GB: *I have a copy of the script for* Mission: Impossible, *and in the big revelation scene between Tom Cruise and Jon Voight, the final product is very different from the script. Is that something that was that worked out in the editing room?*
BDP: Where they're lying to each other?

GB: *Yes.*

BDP: I think the scene was always written with them lying to each other, and then I. . . . It's an idea I've used before, all the way back to *Murder à la Mod,* really, where you actually have one character completely lie in a retelling of the story, which is something you also see in *Snake Eyes.* So that, you know, this whole idea that film is truth 24 times a second is, of course, nonsense. You can make it seem true, but you can lie with it just as effectively. And when people see things on the screen they assume that's what happened. It's like when you watch television and the news, you think that's what happened. But of course, you can control it and make it say anything you want it to say.

GB: *In your films, as we were discussing before, you strive to go a step beyond every time, to advance the cinema. And yet, especially in the earlier days, your films have a sort of immediacy about them. And it seems that throughout your career, you've kept a certain sort of tension between being visionary, and at the same time, creating something of the moment.*

BDP: You know it's always amazed me—I think the most startling thing that's happened in the last couple of decades is that there is no sort of objective reporting anymore. And it's kind of amazing when you think of how light and portable video equipment is. We were always stunned by the documentaries made in the beginning of the 1960s, with the lightweight 16-millimeter equipment. The Drew Associates and the Maysles brothers were following people around, recording what was happening, and we were seeing things we had never seen before. I would assume now that would be infinitely easier. Yet we see nothing like that, ever. Which is kind of perplexing to me.

You know, do you think they could ever get somebody to follow Donald Rumsfeld around with a video camera today? Or see how the inside of the White House works? It'll never happen, even though it's the easiest thing in the world to do now. It's amazing, that with this new technology, we're not able to expose the sort of machinations of what's ever going on with the powers that be. Which means that, of course, it's all controlled now with all of these infomercials of whatever they want us to believe. Which is the death of truth, in a way. Because, you know, the reporter was always that struggling guy who works for nothing, who fought to get the story. Now they all have talk shows and multimillion dollar publishing contracts. So the purity of a guy trying to find out "what happened" is kind of lost.

And we've become very doubtful of our information sources, because they're all controlled by these huge multilateral corporations. And of course, when we see something on television, it's there because they want us to see it. They're selling us something. You know, if we're seeing starving kids in North Africa *this* week—they've always been there. Suddenly, why are we seeing it *this* week? And that's always bothered me a lot about what's happened in American journalism. The last sort of "ray of light" was during the Vietnam war, when journalists were actually out there, seeing stuff and recording it, shooting it. Not anymore.

GB: *I did see a story on the Internet a couple of weeks ago where somebody was trying to release a video or film they shot of President Bush on a plane, in some kind of party atmosphere. But the administration was trying to block the release of it.*

BDP: That's fantastic. I think that's great. That's the hope of the Internet, you know, if the government won't clamp down on it. But absolutely—why aren't we able to see what goes on in the corridors of power anymore? You know, we're all surrounded by spin doctors and public relations people, *telling* us what happened.

Why do you think that my fans are so young? What is it about your generation? I saw Romain, the French website guy. I mean, he looks like he's 15! Why are my films speaking to this generation?

GB: *Well, I know some are drawn in through the cult of* Scarface, *but it seems as if somebody like Romain is really attracted to your more personal films. I don't know. That's a good question. Of course, there are very interesting visuals going on in your films . . .*

BDP: But, well, who are the favorite directors of the younger generation?

GB: *I like Tarantino . . . um . . .*
BDP: Paul Anderson?

GB: *Paul Anderson . . . yeah, I really like* Magnolia *a lot . . .*
BDP: Coen Brothers?

GB: *I love the Coen Brothers . . .*
BDP: Chris Nolan?

GB: *Chris Nolan—*Memento, *yes, definitely.*

BDP: (laughs) Sounds like we've got the right group.

GB: *Around the time that* Mission to Mars *came out, someone on the forum had a question about cybernetics, which you had studied early in your life. Was there any connection between cybernetics and your interest in that film?*

BDP: Only in the fact that I was kind of a science wonk in the 1950s. You know, won a lot of science fairs, built computers. And I always try and get people to understand my attitude about *Mission to Mars.* I tried to bring the sensibility of the kid I was when I went to see *Destination Moon.* It's kind of a magical thing. And my experience working with people from NASA is, they have that kind of magical glow. I know people think it's a very unusual movie for me to make, but one gets tired of this grim cynicism all the time. There are areas where there's a scientific purity and an idealism, and all those kinds of things that we believed in growing up in the 1950s.

GB: *I understand that part of* Femme Fatale *takes place in the near future. Did you get the idea for that because your previous film,* Mission to Mars, *took place in the near future?*

BDP: Um . . . no. It takes place in the present, and then we go forward seven years into the future. But it has nothing to do with *Mission to Mars.*

GB: *I see. You know, just trying to figure out where some of your ideas come from . . .*

BDP: From my subconscious.

INDEX

Tri-Star Pictures, 114
Truffaut, François, xi, 72, 114, 184
20th Century-Fox, 20, 21, 44
2001: A Space Odyssey, xi, 22, 34, 139

United Artists, 38, 73
Universal Pictures, 17, 23, 89, 128
Urban Cowboy, 77
Us magazine, 47

Vachaud, Laurent, 175, 177
Variety, 13, 41
Verhoeven, Paul, xiv
Vertigo, xi, xvii, 4, 16, 33, 40, 50, 86, 131
Voight, Jon, 145; *Mission: Impossible*, 160, 184
Vonnegut, Kurt, 168

Wadleigh, Michael, 26
Warden, Jonathan, 25
Warner Bros., vii, x, xvii, 29–30, 35, 84, 110
Watergate, 73–74, 78
Weine, Robert, xi
Welch, Raquel, 33, 73

Welcome Back Kotter, 39, 78
Welles, Orson, 20, 131, 162; *Get to Know Your Rabbit*, 29–30
What Lies Beneath, xii
Who, The, 183
Wild in the Streets, 19
Wilder, Billy, 158
Williams, Paul, 17–18
Williams, Treat, 136
Williams, Vanessa, 102–03
Willis, Bruce, 127
Wolfe, Tom, 110, 121
Women Against Pornography (WAP), 93
Women Against Violence in Pornography and Media (WAVPM), 93
Woodstock, 9, 21, 26
Woodward, Bob, 74

Yablans, Frank, 47, 49–51, 72–73
Yablonski, Jock, 74, 77, 89, 123

Zabriske Point, 28
Zardoz, 34
Zemeckis, Robert, xii

CONVERSATIONS WITH FILMMAKERS SERIES

PETER BRUNETTE, GENERAL EDITOR

The collected interviews with notable modern directors, including

Robert Altman • Theo Angelopolous • Bernardo Bertolucci • Jane Campion • George Cukor • Clint Eastwood • John Ford • Jean-Luc Godard • Peter Greenaway • John Huston • Jim Jarmusch • Elia Kazan • Stanley Kubrick • Spike Lee • Mike Leigh • George Lucas • Martin Ritt • Carlos Saura • John Sayles • Martin Scorsese • Steven Soderbergh • Steven Spielberg • Oliver Stone • Quentin Tarantino • Orson Welles • Billy Wilder • Zhang Yimou